Building the Agile Enterprise
with SOA, BPM and MBM

Morgan Kaufmann OMG Press

Morgan Kaufmann Publishers and the Object Management Group™ (OMG) have joined forces to publish a line of books addressing business and technical topics related to OMG's large suite of software standards.

OMG is an international, open membership, not-for-profit computer industry consortium that was founded in 1989. The OMG creates standards for software used in government and corporate environments to enable interoperability and to forge common development environments that encourage the adoption and evolution of new technology. OMG members and its board of directors consist of representatives from a majority of the organizations that shape enterprise and Internet computing today.

OMG's modeling standards, including the Unified Modeling Language™ (UML®) and Model Driven Architecture® (MDA), enable powerful visual design, execution and maintenance of software, and other processes—for example, IT Systems Modeling and Business Process Management. The middleware standards and profiles of the Object Management Group are based on the Common Object Request Broker Architecture® (CORBA) and support a wide variety of industries.

More information about OMG can be found at *http://www.omg.org/*.

Morgan Kaufmann OMG Press Titles

Database Archiving: How to Keep Lots of Data for a Very Long Time
Jack Olson

Master Data Management
David Loshin

Building the Agile Enterprise: With SOA, BPM and MBM
Fred Cummins

Business Modeling: A Practical Guide to Realizing Business Value
Dave Bridgeland and Ron Zahavi

A Practical Guide SysML: The Systems Model Language
Sanford Friedenthal, Alan Moore, Rick Steiner

Systems Engineering with SysML/UML: Modeling, Analysis, Design
Tim Weilkiens

UML 2 Certification Guide: Fundamental and Intermediate Exams
Tim Weilkiens and Bernd Oestereich

Real-Life MDA: Solving Business Problems with Model Driven Architecture
Michael Guttman and John Parodi

Building the Agile Enterprise
with SOA, BPM and MBM

Fred A. Cummins

ELSEVIER

AMSTERDAM • BOSTON • HEIDELBERG • LONDON
NEW YORK • OXFORD • PARIS • SAN DIEGO
SAN FRANCISCO • SINGAPORE • SYDNEY • TOKYO

Morgan Kaufmann Publishers is an imprint of Elsevier

Morgan Kaufmann Publishers is an imprint of Elsevier.
30 Corporate Drive, Suite 400, Burlington, MA 01803, USA

This book is printed on acid-free paper.

Library of Congress Cataloging-in-Publication Data
Application Submitted

ISBN: 978-0-12-374445-6

For information on all Morgan Kaufmann publications,
visit our Web site at www.mkp.com or www.elsevierdirect.com

Printed in the United States of America
Transferred to Digital Printing, 2010

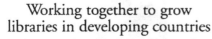

Contents

Acknowledgments

I want to thank my wife, Hope, for her encouragement and for tolerating all the time I spent working on this book, and Tom Hill, EDS Fellow, for his encouragement and support on this effort. I owe many co-workers at EDS and collaborators at OMG for insights I have gained over the years—in particular, at EDS, Jef Meerts, Wafa Khorsheed, Carleen Christner, Ivan Lomelli, and the EDS Fellows community; and at OMG, Cory Casanave, Antoine Lonjon, Conrad Bock, Donald Chapin, John Hall, Manfred Koethe, Karl Frank, Henk de Man, and many others. Finally, I want to thank Richard Soley for his support and for writing the Foreword to this book and John Parodi for his thoughtful editorial comments.

Foreword

Like every young industry, the information technology (IT) business is rife with confusing, competitive, and cockamamie terms and acronyms. I have often wondered at the industrywide propensity to invent and promulgate TLAs (three-letter acronyms, of course!). It seems almost refreshing when a new acronym sports four or five letters, or better yet, eschews compressed forms altogether. But no, the favored approach to technology innovation remains confusing acronyms.

This is not an invention of the 21st or even the 20th century. Electric lamps and the internal-combustion powered automobile, both introduced in the late 19th century, were young technology industries that thrived on spurious differentiation. And youth lasts a long time in a technical industry: The battle royal fought between the Edison group of companies and the Westinghouse company over the electrical standard for the United States was at its peak when Nikola Tesla plied his trade in Westinghouse's workshops (after leaving Edison's employ) in the late 1880s; it had already been a decade since the invention of the light bulb and would be some two decades more before the war was over and Westinghouse's embrace of Tesla's polyphase alternating current had succeeded.

It is unlikely, however, that more than a few consumers of electric lamp technology had any idea what the direct current vs. alternating current debate was about. The level of complexity was obviously far too high for the average buyer; the same can be said about the technical choices in the automobile purchases by the vast majority of car buyers, prompting automotive marketing departments to simply train us that fuel injectors are good and carburetors are bad.

Unfortunately, the same technology complexity and resulting market simplification continue to plague our young IT industry. The resulting apparent "speed of innovation" that worries chief information officers might or might not reference true technical innovation, but it certainly pertains to the innovation in new terminology! Certainly there is constantly changing technology in corners of the IT industry, but much of it is simply new wine in old bottles.

The good news is that old bottles form a strong, solid container for that new wine, and the smart consumer of "new technology" can see through the terminology, the acronyms and the labels, to the real business problems and the ways technology can have a positive effect on operations along the only axes that really count: better, cheaper, and faster. That's where the "agile enterprise" comes in—an "agile" organization reacts quickly to change, recognizes both internal and external (customer and supplier change) quickly, perceives the need for change in the future, and accepts that need as a cost of doing business.

The next step is the hard one and in fact the reason for the book you are holding (and the nexus of the TLAs on the cover). The hard part of IT integration isn't the technology per se; the reason we can see further is that we stand on the shoulders of giants. The complex chemistry and optics used to create our integrated circuits are far below our level of detail; we can depend on others to solve those problems. No, the hard part of IT has always been, and remains today, the enormous gap between management of operations and technology that supports those operations.

How can this be? After more than 50 years of computing, well over 30 years of computing in large organizations, and some 20 years into the pervasive (personal) computing revolution, why should it still be difficult to recognize business challenges in a way that technical solutions clearly address those challenges? The answer is simple: Like other young technology fields, from the marine architecture field a half a millennium ago to the century-old technologies just mentioned, shared languages are just coming into use.

By "shared languages" I do not mean the languages of management (natural languages such as English or abstract but unstructured languages such as spreadsheets and presentations); nor do I mean the languages of computer technologists (such as Java, LISP, and C++). I mean languages that are readable from both sides of that divide: modeling languages. This isn't a new idea, of course; in marine and building architecture we use blueprints. Blueprints speak to the buyer, the seller, the builder, even the makers of parts and the builders that use those parts. Blueprints can be turned, relatively directly, into three-dimensional models for the home buyer as well as parts lists for the electrician. Blueprints are standardized, structured, and well accepted. What we need to do is take that broad step in the IT industry.

Though this book starts off with three TLAs on the cover, you'll find that the real coverage is both more and less. "More" in the sense that you will find more acronyms and ideas inside, but connected together in a way that makes sense; and "less" in the sense that all these ideas sum to one basic idea: If modeling works in other engineering fields, it will work in the IT field. Agility in the enterprise—better, faster, cheaper—comes from being able to structure organizations to take advantage of reusable business capabilities; from the ability to recognize, precisely capture, store, and retrieve the definitions of those capabilities; and from the ability to capture all that information in a shared, widely understandable model of the enterprise.

Those are, respectively, service-oriented architecture (SOA), business process management (BPM), and model-based management (MBM)—thus the title and contents of this book.

You will find herein a wealth of knowledge about how models change the way a business can, should, and will operate. Though there are technology underpinnings to these ideas, don't miss the fact that these innovations are about organizational management more than about IT. Some of the ideas surely are new wine in old bottles; have a sip, though, because those old bottles definitely add flavor!

—Richard Mark Soley, Ph.D.
Chairman and CEO
Object Management Group, Inc. Lexington, Massachusetts
8 June 2008

Preface

Enterprise management is at the dawn of a new era. Information technology has created global markets; changed enterprise relationships with employees, customers, and business partners; and accelerated the pace of change. These forces, along with service-oriented architecture (SOA), business process management (BPM), and model-based management (MBM), change the way enterprises will be organized and managed in the future.

We in the IT industry are focused on applying the technology. We can reduce the costs of development and maintenance, we can improve the performance and quality of systems, and we can provide better information about the operation of the enterprise. We can make it easier to change the information systems to meet new business requirements. However, these improvements have only a fraction of the potential value that can be realized by changing the design of the enterprise to exploit the full potential of information technology.

The need for change is driving widespread interest in SOA, BPM, and MBM. SOA provides a flexible business structure; BPM streamlines and adapts how work is done, and MBM provides models to support the management of complexity and optimize enterprise operations and agility. The business benefits of these disciplines can far exceed IT benefits from the associated technologies. Realization of these benefits requires transformation of the enterprise. Enterprises that fully exploit this paradigm shift are identified as *agile*. They continually improve the speed, cost, and quality of operations, and they rapidly respond to new business opportunities.

TARGET AUDIENCE

Within the enterprise, the chief information officer (CIO) is positioned to lead the transformation. The CIO has a broad view of enterprise operations, responsibility for the enabling technology, a supporting role in the implementation of business improvements, and a staff with skills in systems analysis and design as well as knowledge of current information systems.

This book provides a vision of the future for IT leaders—CIOs, chief technology officers (CTOs), enterprise architects, and management consultants. They must bring to top management the insights, skills, and resources to accomplish enterprise transformation. The next wave of changes cannot simply be driven by incremental automation and integration of computer applications; it requires redesign and reorganization of business functions, driven from the top down. Supporting technology exists and can be improved with an understanding of the requirements. The challenge is to gain top management commitment and support, to establish the necessary governance and infrastructure, and to define a roadmap for achieving a strategic transformation.

BOOK ORGANIZATION

These concepts and more are developed throughout the rest of this book. Each chapter describes a major aspect of the agile enterprise from a business perspective. The goal is to equip IT leaders to understand and communicate the business impact of the agile enterprise as well as the business requirements that must be supported with information technology. The chapters are summarized in the following subsections.

The Agile Enterprise (Chapter 1)

Chapter 1 outlines basic concepts along with the challenges and objectives addressed by the agile enterprise. The SOA Maturity Model provides the foundation for development of an enterprise transformation roadmap.

Service-Oriented Architecture (Chapter 2)

SOA defines discrete capabilities as sharable *service units* and establishes an enterprise as a composition of sharable business capabilities that can be rapidly rearranged and adapted to meet changing business needs. This architecture supports optimization of resource utilization, economies of scale, and improved accountability, control, and agility.

Business Process Management (Chapter 3)

BPM is a management discipline for the design, management, automation, and continuous improvement of business processes. In an agile enterprise, business processes define how services are performed—including the organization of activities to meet a service objective, the integration of supporting services, and the choreography of relationships and operations among organizations.

Business Rules (Chapter 4)

Business rules support concise expression of management intent, independent of the implementation technology. Mechanisms for integration of business rules enable the enterprise to rapidly adapt to changes in regulations, enterprise improvements, and technological capabilities. A number of types of business rules affect the operation of the enterprise in different ways.

Enterprise Information Management (Chapter 5)

The enterprise must operate on the basis of a common Enterprise Logical Data Model (ELDM) to support meaningful communication and interaction of people and systems. This model must be complemented by appropriate data access and analytical tools so that business decision making and planning can be optimized from an enterprise perspective.

SOA Security (Chapter 6)

The electronic integration of disparate organizations and the sharing of data across the enterprise and with business partners and customers greatly increase the potential for harmful exposure of operations and information. Access must be controlled to ensure that it is appropriately authorized, that enterprise facilities are not vulnerable to attack, and that data communications are appropriately protected. In addition, exchange of electronic business documents affecting enterprise assets and government regulations requires electronic signatures to ensure that participants are authenticated, authorized, and accountable.

The Agile Organization Structure (Chapter 7)

The enterprise will evolve to a network of interacting service units that manage enterprise capabilities to deliver business value. The organization structure must define how people participate in the operation and management of service units. Service units must be aligned to an organization hierarchy that manages the service unit capabilities for optimal performance. Additional relationships must support collaboration, coordination, innovation, and control, all of which allow the enterprise to optimize and adapt to deliver customer value.

Event-Driven Agility (Chapter 8)

Though services are most often performed in response to a request, some services are initiated by disruptive events that indicate a need to respond outside the bounds of normal operating processes. Processing of disruptive events is the starting point for automation of processes for adapting the enterprise to changing requirements. Various techniques must be used to identify and capture relevant events. Some individual events may be of little interest, but in combination with other events, the "complex events" may be significant.

Agile Governance (Chapter 9)

Initial efforts to implement SOA may be bottom-up transformations based on business opportunities. However, in the long term, the agile enterprise requires a top-down design that defines the enterprise structure and the context in which local improvements can be developed. This requires a management commitment and governance structure to design, transform, and continuously improve and adapt the enterprise from an overall perspective, with IT support. The recommended governance structure provides support for continuous strategic planning, top-down leadership of enterprise design and transformation, and improved visibility and accountability to executive management and the board of directors to ensure appropriate leadership and control.

Model-Based Management (MBM) (Chapter 10)

Today's enterprises and the ecosystems in which they operate are very complex. Managers need models connected to the business operations and the business environment in order to gain a better awareness of problems and a greater understanding of the factors involved in solutions. Such models enable more timely and appropriate responses to threats and opportunities. Management of the agile enterprise is supported by an Enterprise Business Model (EBM) that is the integration of a number of different viewpoint models.

THE VISION

This book presents a vision of the agile enterprise based on current industry trends and standards. There are no current examples of such an agile enterprise as described here. The fundamental business concepts have existed for many years, and supporting technology exists but must be appropriately applied. Executive leaders must adopt a new approach to business design and management in order to realize the vision.

Key to this vision is an understanding of the role played by service-oriented architecture (SOA), business process management (BPM), and model-based management (MBM) on an enterprise level rather than on an IT level. SOA, BPM, and MBM are supported by technologies that emphasize reuse of software functions, systems integration standards, automation of business processes, and use of interactive, computer-based business models, thus improving technical consistency and efficiency as well as achieving economies of scale.

This book uses the terms *SOA technology*, *BPM technology*, and *MBM technology* to distinguish supporting applications, tools, and standards from the broader business disciplines used to create and manage the agile enterprise; these terms are used when the context is the supporting IT technology. When the context is enterprise agility, the terms *SOA*, *BPM*, and *MBM* are used without qualification.

Though this book covers many of the most important issues that need to be addressed in applying SOA, BPM, and MBM technologies, its primary intent is to describe how these technologies enable more effective design, optimization, and adaptation of the enterprise as a whole.

Thus the book describes the transformation of an enterprise's existing business architecture to an agile enterprise architecture. This requires the application of SOA principles in creating a service-oriented organization, the application of BPM principles in the definition and control of all business activities, and the use of MBM to increase visibility into, and understanding of, all business-related operations.

This book draws on many years of experiences with EDS and General Motors, along with insights gained from work on the development of industry standards, to pull together a consistent view of the agile enterprise. It is hoped that this provides insights for both transformation of enterprises and the further development of industry standards to complete the MBM picture developed in Chapter 10.

The Agile Enterprise

Agility is an essential quality of the enterprise of the future. An agile enterprise rapidly adapts to changing business challenges and opportunities. It continuously improves to optimize cost, quality, and speed of delivery. It enables top management to quickly implement new strategies and control key business parameters to gain competitive advantage. Agility resolves some common business challenges faced by many enterprises. But the agile enterprise does not fit current business models. It requires a new business paradigm—a new way of thinking about the business and new ways of planning, organizing, operating, and controlling the business.

SOA, BPM, and MBM are important aspects of this new agile enterprise business paradigm that is enabled by the supporting technologies. The change in thinking applies existing concepts and develops new concepts and relationships developed in considerable detail in the remainder of this book. This chapter introduces basic concepts.

These concepts and relationships are applicable across many industries. Manufacturing provides a rich diversity of business functions and challenges, and it touches on most other industries. In financial services, much of the ability to develop and deliver new products depends on information technology. Telecommunications and financial services typically have great opportunities to exploit SOA, since these companies tend to experience many unresolved mergers and acquisitions. The telecommunications business is just starting to undergo major transformation with wireless technology and convergence with cable, the Internet, and entertainment.

The telecommunication industry has also developed eTOM, the best practices process framework that provides a good starting point for definition of services, as described in Chapter 2 and elsewhere.

The nature of telecommunications has caused that industry to be more receptive to development of standards and to be less secretive about its practices.

Regardless of the industry, top management must understand the necessity of agility, assess the current state of the enterprise, and commit to a transformation that may take a number of years. This chapter provides a foundation for later chapters by identifying major business opportunities to be realized by the agile enterprise, positioning its emergence in the evolution of information technology, and outlining the new way of thinking that is the basis of the agile enterprise. Later in this chapter we introduce the SOA Maturity Model, which provides a basis for assessment and planning phases of improvement leading to enterprise agility. Finally, several critical success factors (CSFs) are suggested to drive the transformation.

Readers are probably familiar with the information technology notions of service-oriented architecture (SOA), business process management (BPM), and model-driven architecture (MDA) because so many IT organizations are investigating these technologies, if they haven't already begun adopting them. SOA technology has enabled rapid and flexible integration of systems across organizational boundaries. BPM technology is improving flexibility and optimization of business processes. MDA technology is an enabling technology for MBM. MDA introduced standards for generating applications from models and more recently supports business modeling languages.

The current awareness of and experience with these technologies is a good thing, for two reasons. First, it means that most readers are familiar with the basic concepts as well as the reasons behind applying them (reuse, consistency, economies of scale) for IT cost reductions and systems flexibility.

The second reason is that in applying these technologies, IT organizations are beginning to understand that realization of the full business value of these technologies requires changes in the operation of the business. The traditional delivery of information technology is bottom-up, opportunistically introducing automation and integration but leaving the design of the business fundamentally the same. The new economies of scale and flexibility are not just in the use of shared code and component software architecture but in consolidation of business functions and an adaptive business architecture. Applying SOA, BPM, and model-based management (MBM) to create the agile enterprise requires a transition to a "top-down," business-driven approach that puts bottom-up automation, integration, and optimization in a proper business context.

Thus readers can benefit from this book no matter where an enterprise is on the adoption curve for SOA, BPM, and MDA technologies. Whether an organization is at the investigation, design, or implementation stage, it is never too late or too early to use these IT approaches as a springboard to creating an agile enterprise. And though many enterprises will achieve significant benefits from implementing these IT technologies, the most successful enterprises will be those that exploit these technologies to achieve enterprise agility.

WHEN AGILITY PAYS OFF

The following discussion outlines several major challenges faced by many enterprises today. An agile enterprise is prepared to face these challenges, mitigating the risks and realizing the opportunities.

Consolidations

A major source of business benefit in early adoption of SOA, BPM, and MBM is through consolidation of redundant business operations. Opportunities for consolidation are particularly prevalent as a result of mergers and acquisitions. Typically, the combined enterprise organization reflects aggregation without consolidation. This is common in financial services companies, telecommunications companies, and information technology companies. But the synergy and economies of scale that might have been envisioned are typically not achieved, because each organization continues to operate in its own silo, each with its own computer applications. Large corporations with decentralized divisions or product-line organizations often have similar opportunities for consolidations.

With considerable effort, some consolidation of operations may occur over a period of years. But because mergers and acquisitions occur frequently, especially in the industries noted, it is difficult for operational consolidation efforts to keep up.

In contrast to the norm, an agile enterprise is able to define a plan for consolidation and consolidate key redundant operations very quickly—perhaps even before the merger or acquisition is finalized. The agile enterprise achieves this at a fraction of the time, cost, and risk experienced by a conventional enterprise. If each of the original companies has an agile architecture, this consolidation can be faster.

Consolidation is the primary source of benefits in the early stages of SOA adoption. Table 1.1 outlines benefits of consolidation that were captured by the SOA Consortium. These examples highlight actual projects in various industries.

Table 1.1 Examples of SOA Benefits Through Consolidation by Industry

Industry	Realized Benefits
Automobile	Improved customer satisfaction Reduced duplication of customer data and near-real-time access to vehicle information Increased agility through a governance focus Easier integration with partners
Energy	Flexibility and speed in changing business processes Business optimization and risk mitigation: accurate real-time commercial, financial, and profitability data across the value chain System reliability: simplification of interfaces by duplicate master data reduction
Pharmaceutical	Improved visibility into product line Increased agility in taking pharmaceutical products to market Cost savings and reduced headcount Better use of core architecture, providing improved data integration, management, and reusability Achieving 99.999% uptime on a stable platform
Telecommunications	Elimination of network outages Stronger focus on strategic initiatives while reducing cost of IT operations to 30% of previous level More transparency by masking systems complexity from users $80 million in value over two years from improved efficiency, responsiveness, and adaptability of the organization 67% reduction in mobile phone provisioning costs 50% reduction in cost of third-party development bids, and faster development times (hours vs. weeks) due to SOA environment and automated tools Faster time-to-market for new services Seamless migration to a convergent system of prepaid and post-paid customers Lower maintenance costs Improved scalability
Transportation	Flexibility and speed in providing new services to customers Ability to grow higher-margin businesses in the United States and overseas Reduced cost of supporting infrastructure for internal/external customers Easier integration of acquisitions though a common core set of services Rapid transformation and reuse of processes and services Elimination of errors and shortening of response cycle through automated processes Significantly scaled-up usage of self services and end-to-end process integration
Entertainment	Consolidation of multiple content rights systems into one 50% decrease in time needed for year-end accounting closure

In the short term, as an enterprise is moving toward agility, consolidation of redundant capabilities is a major source of value, even when the enterprise is still in the early stages of transformation. These consolidations will often have an IT focus, but they necessarily involve the consolidation of the associated organizations. This will demonstrate the business value of shared business capabilities and is representative of the current level of transformation of most early adopters. Other benefits of SOA, discussed in the following sections, are not as apparent in the early stages.

New Product or Line of Business

Top management may recognize an opportunity to introduce a new product or enter a new line of business in an emerging marketplace in a way that builds on some of the key strengths of the current enterprise. Though some weaknesses will need to be addressed, rapid entry into a new market will be critical to long-term success.

A traditional enterprise might address this opportunity by forming a separate division or acquiring an existing company to avoid the burden and risks of adapting existing operations to the new market, because existing processes and computer applications are designed to optimize those current lines of business. However, at the same time, smart management understands that a new business silo cannot utilize the strengths and potential economies of scale of the parent enterprise.

The agile enterprise is able to engage existing capabilities of the enterprise in the new line of business without penalizing the existing business. Top management is able to quickly assess the impact of the new business, determine realistic operating costs and competitive pricing, assess the required investment, and implement the new product-line capability.

The benefits of agility in introducing a new product line or business have been realized in a number of industries, including telecommunications, pharmaceuticals, and transportation. The benefits include (1) increased visibility and control into the product line, (2) the ability to utilize a core architecture to improve data integration and consistency of implementations, (3) significant improvements in development schedules and time to market, and (4) higher customer satisfaction, in part due to reduced cost of using services.

Outsourcing

Much of the cost of doing business goes into necessary operating activities that are not part the enterprise's core business and do not provide competitive value. Business operations such as finance and accounting, human resource management, and information technology require special skills and are increasingly complex, particularly for multinational enterprises. At the same time, these activities require considerable management attention and are challenged to achieve industry best practices for regulatory compliance, efficiency, and effectiveness.

Large enterprises have adopted outsourcing as a long-term strategy to mitigate these problems. IT outsourcing has been adopted in all industries. Outsourcing of financial and human resource management services is gaining in popularity. The agility benefits for outsourcing include (1) scalability—the ability to quickly accommodate increased or reduced workload, (2) expertise—outsourcing providers can maintain skilled people to deal with change such as regulatory requirements, and (3) internationalization—a outsourcing provider should be prepared to support the client in expansion into new countries. It should be noted that small enterprises and startups in all industries can benefit immediately from agile outsourcing thus reducing the barriers to entry of new competitors.

Outsourcing offers the opportunity to exploit the expertise and economies of scale of a service provider while reducing the management burden associated with these operations. However, these supporting services are often intertwined throughout the enterprise, and the division of responsibilities may be inconsistent across the enterprise. The disruptive effect of a transition to an outsource service provider could have a major impact on the rest of the business.

The agile enterprise is able to quickly identify the business activities to be outsourced and their relationships to other business activities. The business units are components of the enterprise, just as an engine is a component of an automobile. A more powerful engine might require some changes in other automobile components, but the relationships to the controls and other components should be relatively easy to identify, evaluate, and resolve.

Thus outsourcing is another source of substantial business value that can be realized in the early stages of enterprise transformation, as long as the integration is compatible with a strategic information technology infrastructure.

Government Regulation

Government regulation is an increasing concern. Managers are being held responsible for the integrity of their operations and protection of stockholder interests. Multinational enterprises must comply with business regulations of countries in which they operate as well as regulations for products or services in countries in which they sell. Not only are regulations constantly changing, but changes to the business organization itself can create risks of violations. Regulatory compliance affects all industries.

Implementation of compliance is a challenge in conventional organizations because the affected processes may be undocumented and may be performed in multiple organizations in different ways.

The agile enterprise is able to quickly and reliably assess the implications of regulations to the business and plan appropriate changes and controls to ensure compliance. The consistent business architecture, along with consolidation of sharable business capabilities, clarifies responsibility and accountability for compliance. Formally defined business processes and business process automation support the implementation and enforcement of regulations.

An important aspect of regulatory compliance is reliable recordkeeping. Formal definition and automation of business processes support the capture of appropriate records. Electronic identity and signatures ensure proper authorization and accountability for record content.

Outsourcing regulated activities such as accounting, human resource management, and IT reduces an enterprise's burden and provides greater assurance that appropriate expertise is applied to implementation of regulations and related changes.

Governance

To optimize enterprise operation and ensure appropriate accountability, control, and agility, enterprise design requires a disciplined approach and consistent architecture.

The conventional enterprise reflects adaptations from enterprise design that, in many cases, predates the use of computers. Responsibility for continued design has been delegated to large departments or lines of business that focus on optimization within their local spheres of influence. Large departments or product lines tend to be geographically isolated or located in separate buildings so that their internal capabilities are easily coordinated. In many cases, capabilities are developed rather than shared because it is easier to develop and adapt a capability if you own it yourself.

Electronic technology has substantially reduced the barriers to coordinating and sharing capabilities, but many opportunities for improvement, particularly from an enterprise perspective, have not been realized. Organizations will resist shared capabilities because they represent a loss of control. Furthermore, this evolved organizational design has made the enterprise increasingly complex, making it difficult to maintain accountability and control and difficult to adapt to changing business needs.

For example, a large information technology company entered the IT services business and incurred substantial losses. The board of directors was not aware of the extent of the losses because the losses were obscured by profits from its successful hardware business. In contrast, an agile enterprise has a clear picture of product costs so there is recognition of successes and accountability for failures. The agile enterprise is also better equipped to assess the challenges and risks of a new product or line of business because applicable existing capabilities and new capability requirements can be defined as elements of a rigorous product value chain.

The agile enterprise has a consistent architecture and is composed of service units with well-defined interfaces and performance objectives. This provides a consistent basis for evaluation of performance and accountability. In addition, the performance of service units can be evaluated in the context of contributions of value to customer products and successful operation of the enterprise. Consequently, top management has a clear view of the operation of the enterprise and its strengths and weaknesses, and the board of directors can better assess whether the enterprise is doing the right thing and doing it well.

Technology Modernization

Technology modernization may encompass any technology upgrade or improvement to a business capability. Many enterprises are captive to information systems developed long ago, many of which have locked the enterprise into ways of doing business that were optimal at the time but have since become outdated. The design of the systems as well as the technology used to implement them may be obsolete and difficult to support or change.

Obsolete technology is a challenge in enterprises in every industry. The challenges are particularly pronounced in industries such as financial services and telecommunications, where there have been multiple mergers and acquisitions, with systems implemented in different technologies and tightly coupled to particular product lines or markets.

The challenge becomes not only the upgrade of technology but consolidation of the business logic and processes and integration of consolidated solutions with the remaining legacy systems that support different lines of business.

Duplication of functionality also occurs where the legacy systems cannot easily be adapted to support new lines of business, so the legacy functions are duplicated in new systems. Replacement of legacy systems almost always requires major investments and entails substantial risk. But replacements of legacy systems without also providing enterprise-wide shared services only leads to more inefficiency and inflexibility.

The agile enterprise makes business processes visible and adaptable and relies on more focused and finer-grained applications that can be individually upgraded or replaced without major upheavals. Here, application modernization tools can help in the transformation of legacy systems, making business processes more visible and supporting more finely grained shared services.

Agility in technology modernization, like governance, tends to provide more benefit to SOA-mature organizations because fewer business processes are embedded in applications and because applications (and other technology) will be more fine-grained and therefore replacement can be more limited in scope. This makes it possible to replace a capability's implementation with less impact to related services.

HOW WE GOT HERE

It is useful to consider the evolution of the business use of information technology to understand how the current "hairball" of systems and communications developed over time and why the time for the agile enterprise has come. This mish-mash is the legacy that we must transform to realize the agile enterprise.

Task Automation

Early, widespread applications of the computer were for task automation. The computer could do monotonous, repetitive tasks faster, cheaper, and more reliably than people could. Computers were kept in controlled environments, and people brought the work to the computer and picked it up when it was done.

As more tasks were automated, they were bundled together into increasingly large applications. People interacted with the applications online, so the data stayed with the applications and was eventually stored in departmental databases. Some workflow management systems emerged to direct the flow of records between tasks performed by people. But most of the flow of work between the tasks was built into the systems, sometimes through the transfer of magnetic tapes and sometimes embedded in program code.

Large applications grew within departments to streamline their operations, and files were transferred between departments, initially on magnetic tapes and later through electronic transfer of files. The movement of files between applications was automated for efficiency and control. Within large applications, embedded business processes could move transactions between tasks as they occurred, but records were still batched for transfer to the applications of other organizations.

The transfer of files between applications extended outside the enterprise, to suppliers, large customers, health care insurers, and financial institutions. Industry standards were developed for electronic data interchange (EDI). File transfers were typically a daily occurrence—batches of records from the day's business activity. This movement of files between applications was generally point-to-point communications, as depicted in Figure 1.1a. For remote applications, the communications occurred over dedicated telephone lines.

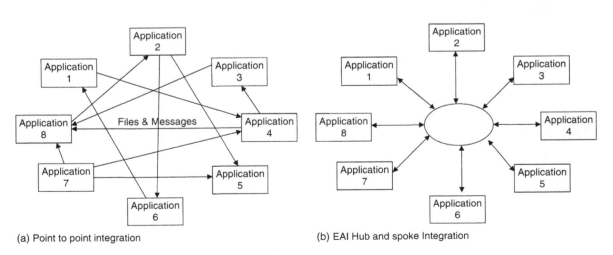

(a) Point to point integration

(b) EAI Hub and spoke Integration

■ **FIGURE 1.1** Transition from Ad Hoc Integration to EAI Middleware Integration.

Enterprise Application Integration

Enterprise application integration (EAI) middleware emerged in the marketplace. It brought the hub-and-spoke communication model depicted in Figure 1.1b. Within an enterprise, the middleware could route messages from many sources to many destinations, reducing the number of communication links and improving control. In addition, there was no longer the need to send records in batches, but individual records could be sent as messages as they became available.

EAI middleware enabled a transition from batch-oriented enterprise integration to transaction-driven integration. The EAI middleware provides a buffer so that a message can be sent when a receiver is not yet ready to receive. It can also provide a buffer between legacy batch processing systems and those systems that process and send transactions as they occur. EAI middleware products provide adapter software to integrate systems implemented with diverse technologies and message transformation services, to make the data structures compatible between applications. Transaction-driven systems accelerate the delivery of results; for example, a customer order for stock items might be processed and the order shipped the same day.

Of course, the hub-and-spoke configuration relies on the use of shared middleware. Unfortunately, this is a barrier to integration between enterprises and sometimes within a large enterprise, particularly in the absence of interoperability standards for message exchange.

The Internet

As EAI was gaining widespread adoption, the Internet and the World Wide Web were gaining momentum. The Internet opened the door to many-to-many communications in a different way: The public Internet was the global hub through which messages could be directed from any Internet subscriber to any other Internet subscriber. Dedicated telephone lines were no longer needed between business partners.

There is no industry standard for message exchange using EAI middleware, so a standard format was required for communicating between diverse systems over the Internet. Web pages were already being communicated between diverse systems, so this technology was adapted to communication of messages between business systems.

Hyper Text Transport Protocol (HTTP) from the Internet Engineering Task Force (IETF) and the World Wide Web Consortium (W3C) became the accepted messaging protocol, and HyperText Markup Language

(HTML) from W3C became a basis for exchange of content; it was already allowed to pass through corporate firewalls for Web access. Since the messages were not intended for graphical display, HTML per se was not appropriate for application integration, but eXtensible Markup Language (XML), also from W3C, shares the underlying technology of HTML that enables interpretation by diverse computer systems, but it also provides greater flexibility for content specification and transformation. XML is discussed further in Chapter 5.

The Internet became the medium of exchange for business-to-business communications. IT industry leaders recognized a potential for ad hoc relationships between businesses to be established automatically, at a moment's notice, if only there were industry standards by which these relationships could be specified and discovered.

Web Services and SOA

The concept of "Web services" emerged. Figure 1.2 illustrates the vision. The arrows depict request-response relationships. In concept, an enterprise posts a service offering on a public registry. Another enterprise in need of a service queries the registry to obtain information on available services. The registry includes information about the service and the protocol for using the service. The service user then sends a message to the service provider, initiating the exchange. All this is expected to be performed automatically by applications of the participating enterprises. Within the enterprises, the exchanges are mediated by automated business processes.

Standards for Web services have been developed, but the ad hoc, automated selection of services has not caught on. Business leaders are not ready to trust computer systems to establish and manage business relationships, not least because the current abilities to express the actual semantics of a given service offering leaves a lot to be

■ **FIGURE 1.2** Web Services Vision.

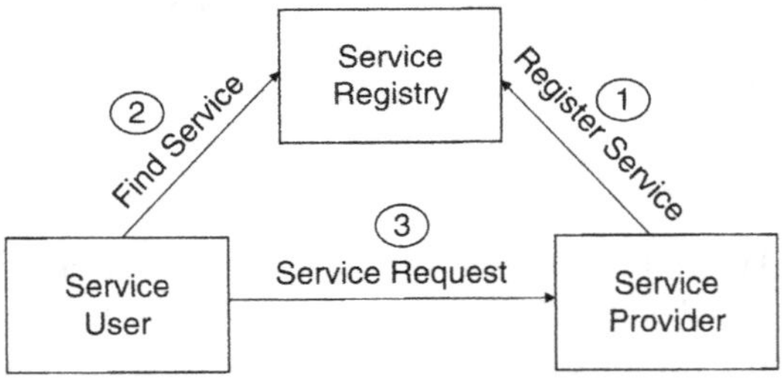

desired. However, much of the technology has been adopted, and relationships established by humans can quickly be automated for exchange of business transactions over the Internet.

The concept of accessing services over the Internet and the development of standards for communications with services led to a new kind of service-oriented architecture (SOA) in which Internet-based technologies support an integration of systems offering services and using services. Not only can the technology be used over the public Internet, it can be used within enterprises to integrate systems. This greatly expanded the market for a new breed of middleware to perform Internet-based communications and drive interactions with automated business processes.

Within the enterprise, SOA has been viewed as a way to implement shared application components. Functionality used in different areas of the business could be implemented as shared services and invoked by other applications. Web services technology was promoted as an alternative to EAI middleware. Rather than route all messages through a central hub, Web services technology would enable direct communications between applications over the enterprise intranet (an internal network using Internet technology). The concept of the enterprise service bus (ESB) emerged as middleware that enabled applications to be connected over the intranet using Web services technology. Essentially, an ESB is decentralized EAI middleware with standards-based communications.

However, the major impact of SOA will be realized as a business architecture rather than an IT architecture. For the business community, SOA is an approach to the design of an enterprise in which distinct business capabilities are offered through well-defined mechanisms and media of exchange so that the capabilities can be used in multiple business endeavors now and in the future. This enables the capabilities to be managed for consistency and economies of scale, allowing the enterprise to more easily adapt to new endeavors by making these capabilities shareable.

The idea of SOA as a business architecture is beginning to emerge in the industry. Unfortunately, though the potential benefits are great, the challenges are also great. The principal challenge is to change the way both business people and IT people think about the way the enterprise is organized and managed and the way it is supported by IT. We return to these concepts in the discussion of SOA infrastructure in the next chapter.

A NEW WAY OF THINKING

Intense competition, a changing world, complexity, and increased risks demand a new approach to enterprise management to optimize enterprise performance and agility. SOA, BPM, and MBM, with support from related information technology, enable and *require* a management paradigm shift—a change in the way of thinking about the operation and management of the enterprise.

SOA brings a fundamental change to the structure of the enterprise. Traditionally, an enterprise operates as a number of distinct departments or divisions, each with its own systems and business operations in its own silo, as depicted in Figure 1.3. In the diagram, A and B might be different divisions or product-line organizations. Each division has its own specialized business units, contributing capabilities to the divisional efforts. Some of these are duplicated between the divisions as indicated by the boxed letters, which represent business capabilities. Each division has its own applications used by people within the division. Interactions between divisions and with outside customers and suppliers are through well-defined channels. Access to the internal capabilities is restricted by locked doors and passwords.

Initially, these silos were connected through transfers of files; later, EAI improved the speed and flexibility of communications. But those communications, for the most part, are in controlled environments between known and trusted systems. Typically, the transfer of business transaction data from one department to another also transfers

■ **FIGURE 1.3** Conventional Business Unit Silos.

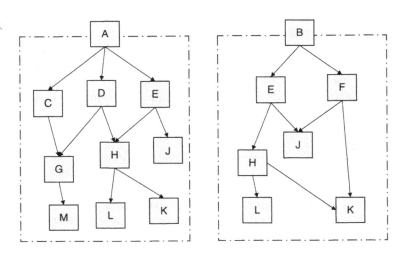

responsibility and control for the transaction. The sending system is trusted to send valid records and the receiving system accepts responsibility for subsequent action. The sources and destinations of these data transfers are well known and stable. Changes to business processes are restricted by the flow between systems and the hardcoded processes that integrate capabilities within the systems.

SOA (with the help of SOA technology) opens up these silos and makes capabilities within them available for use as sharable services. Similar capabilities can be consolidated for economies of scale and to achieve consistency across the enterprise.

As a result, a SOA has interorganizational interactions and sharing of capabilities at a lower level of granularity, as depicted in Figure 1.4, that represents a transformation from Figure 1.3. Each of these boxes represents an organizational *service unit* providing and/or using a service. The arrows represent request-response relationships.

Each of these service units can contribute their capabilities to address similar needs in different contexts. The divisions or product lines, A and B, still exist from a product management and marketing perspective, but they share common capabilities.

A service unit (further defined in a moment) participates as a service provider to support a requester's objective. The same service provider may participate as a requester to incorporate the capabilities of other services. Consequently, a request for one service may propagate to many other services. The smaller granularity of service units enables the capabilities to be more stable and usable in different contexts, both as the enterprise currently operates and in future business

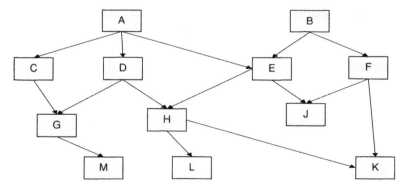

■ **FIGURE 1.4** SOA Network of Services.

endeavors. The service units can be used selectively, instead of the larger, more complex "department" being adapted for the specific requirements of each new undertaking.

This sharing of capabilities across the enterprise has been enabled by information technology. Information technology has become an integral part of the fabric of doing business. It's no longer just about automation of tasks and faster communications. Information technology has changed the business equilibrium.

Traditional organization structures, work environments, access to information, international trade, and customer expectations have changed. They are still changing, and technology has accelerated the pace of change. Optimization of enterprise operations not only involves more variables, but the enterprise must continuously change to adapt to new challenges and opportunities. Agility has become a competitive necessity, and the bar is rising.

SOA, BPM, and MBM are important components of enterprise agility. Though SOA is being driven by information technology, it reflects a change in organizational responsibilities and relationships as a result of IT. BPM is primarily a business process management discipline, but it reflects technological support for monitoring, modeling, and automating business processes.

Though managers have financial models, MBM brings computer-based tools to manage complexity and to plan and validate rapid changes to business operations and relationships. Together these disciplines and the supporting technologies enable the more effective governance, leadership, planning, and decision making needed for the agile enterprise.

The new paradigm changes the design and management of the business. The following sections highlight some of the key concepts.

Service

A *service* is an application of a business capability to provide business value needed by a community of service users. A service is requested to fill a need. It is important to distinguish the service—the value provided—from the request for a service and the capability used to deliver the service, since we often call all of these services. Examples of potential services are when a customer receives a product, a machine is repaired, a product is designed, a package is shipped, an account is credited, benefits options are selected, or a purchase is completed.

The corresponding requests are a customer order, a machine repair order, a product design request, a shipping order, an account credit transaction, a benefits selection request, and a purchase order. We define a *service unit* as providing the capability. In fact, every enterprise capability that contributes value in response to a defined business need can be designed to provide a service or a related set of services. Applying business capabilities through services allows the capabilities to be shared, enabling economies of scale and improved consistency, accountability, and control of operations.

Service Units

A *service unit* is a business unit responsible for management of a business capability to provide services—the processes, resources, facilities, intellectual property, computer applications, and operations that perform the service. The service unit is not expected to do everything itself but delegates some responsibilities to other service units for specialized capabilities and for support services, such as human resources, accounting, and information systems services, that support its capability. A service unit is a focal point of responsibility and control for the service delivery capability it offers. Offering capabilities as distinct building blocks that provide stable, sharable services enables the enterprise to adapt more quickly to changing business needs.

Service-Oriented Enterprises

An entire enterprise can be configured as a network of interworking service units to become a *service-oriented enterprise*. In a service-oriented enterprise, each service unit provides a well-defined mechanism by which services are requested, and it assesses costs for each service it performs. Economies of scale are achieved in the development, integration, and support of services, and the consistent architecture provides enterprise transparency, accountability, and control for more effective governance and agility. The consolidation and sharing of capabilities across the enterprise requires a top-down, enterprise perspective to properly select and scope service units, to avoid local suboptimization, and to overcome resistance to loss of ownership and control.

Agile Enterprise

An *agile enterprise* incorporates an SOA along with BPM techniques for process design and optimization and an effective governance structure. In addition, the agile enterprise uses MBM tools to manage complexity, support optimization of enterprise operations, and enable rapid reconfiguration of service units to respond to changing business threats and opportunities. Aspects of an agile enterprise are more fully developed throughout this book.

Process-Driven Services

A *business process* defines the orderly performance of activities that achieve a desired business result. Business processes drive the operation of each service unit and its use of other services. Each business process operates within the scope of an associated business unit (a service unit) that is responsible for the management and optimization of that business process. When another service is invoked, the action should be viewed as invoking a business process within the other service unit to access the capability of the target service unit for a particular purpose. Consequently, service units define a framework for the definition and integration of business processes.

Model-Based Management

MBM is the use of computer-based models of the enterprise to enable managers to understand, analyze, plan, and make decisions regarding the operation of the enterprise and to respond quickly and effectively to threats and opportunities. Models are linked to the business operations to reflect the current and evolving state of the enterprise, and models are used to plan, evaluate, and manage transformations of the enterprise.

Value Chain

A *value chain* is a dependency network of activities that contribute to the value delivered to a customer. A customer may be an internal business activity, so an enterprise has multiple value chains. A *primary value chain* defines the direct contributions to the value of a unit of production delivered to an end customer. In an agile enterprise, the value chain identifies the contributions of cost, quality, and timeliness of each of the participating service units. The value chain supports product costing and becomes the focus of analysis for pricing and competitive improvement.

There are different points of view on modeling the creation of value. Some of these have been given different names, such as *value network* and *value stream*. We believe the dependency network representation used in this book fits the agile enterprise architecture needs and captures the fundamental concepts to support different analytical viewpoints.

Disruptive Event

A *disruptive event* is an event that suggests the occurrence of an enterprise threat or opportunity. The agile enterprise recognizes, analyzes, and responds to disruptive events that occur in the enterprise ecosystem. Event resolution services must drive adaptive changes or bring the events to an appropriate level of management attention. Events that cannot be resolved by operational or tactical adjustments must be addressed by strategic planning activities that determine the need for more pervasive changes.

Governance

Governance is the set of responsibilities and practices exercised by top management and the board of directors to perform necessary enterprise design, oversight, and control to achieve the desired owner value. In the agile enterprise, governance is not simply the management of budgets, priorities, and sales objectives. Executive staff service units provide enterprise design, metrics, intelligence, modeling, and analysis capabilities as well as mechanisms for accountability and control. These services support effective guidance and leadership by the board of directors and top management. With effective governance, service units have clear responsibilities, visibility, and accountability for (1) management of their capabilities, (2) compliance with policies, laws, and regulations, and (3) delivery of results.

Information Technology Management

Effective utilization of information technology is the responsibility of top management as well as the managers of individual service units. The IT organization, and ultimately the CIO, have responsibility for making appropriate technology available to the service units and optimizing the utilization of IT resources. This availability is provided through supporting infrastructure, operation of data processing and communications services, and development and support of information technology applications that service units require.

The IT organization is itself an aggregation of service units and thereby leverages special skills and resources. The agile enterprise manages the application of technology for enterprise-level optimization of IT investments and economies of scale in the utilization of IT resources.

SOA MATURITY MODEL

Transformation to the agile enterprise is a major, long-term undertaking. Many more books will be written about planning and managing

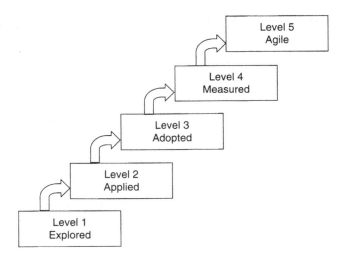

■ **FIGURE 1.5** SOA Maturity Model.

transformation as well as the technology to support the transformation and implement the capabilities. Here we provide insight into the phases of transformation and the dimensions of change.

The SOA Maturity Model developed by EDS and Oracle is depicted in Figure 1.5. The model defines criteria to assess the degree to which an enterprise has realized the potential of SOA and associated disciplines. There are many paths to the future that are well beyond the scope of this book. The SOA Maturity Model provides guidance for planning the enterprise transformation and a basis for objective evaluation of progress.

The SOA Maturity Model is similar in concept to the Capability Maturity Model Integration (CMMI), from the Software Engineering Institute and Carnegie Mellon University. The model provides criteria for assessment of (1) the readiness of an organization to accept and manage the associated discipline and (2) the degree to which the necessary organizational structure, disciplines, and supporting elements are in place.

Some reviews of this maturity model have failed to recognize the significance of the business perspective. It is the business perspective that sets this maturity model apart and provides a foundation for discussion of transformation in this book.

A maturity assessment based on this model identifies the maturity level of an enterprise and the issues that should be addressed to progress to the next level. Each level builds on the capabilities of the levels beneath it. Just as the construction of a building must start with the foundation, progression to SOA maturity and enterprise agility must progress up the levels of the maturity model.

Investments in enterprise capabilities are needed to support future advances. These investments increase some costs in the near term. At the same time, the transformation plan should achieve incremental improvements through projects that each realize business benefits along the way.

Each of these levels is assessed from two perspectives: business with five dimensions and technology with six dimensions. Each of these dimensions has criteria for assessment at each of the five levels.

The details of the intersections of levels and dimensions are not presented here, but we briefly consider each of the levels and each of the dimensions to provide some further insight on the phases of transformation.

Maturity Levels

An enterprise achieves a maturity level when it has substantially achieved the capabilities identified for that level. Though some of the capabilities of higher levels may also be achieved, the overall capability of the enterprise is still limited by those capabilities that have only reached a lower level of maturity. The level of return on investment is lower for transformations undertaken at lower levels of maturity, but the risks are higher if an undertaking is too ambitious for the current level of maturity. Each of the maturity levels is discussed briefly here:

1. *Explored.* An organization is aware of SOA and may be studying the potential impact or doing some proof-of-concept development.

   This is the current "status quo" level of most enterprises. Typically the SOA awareness is in the IT organization (in other words, it is awareness of SOA technology). If other organizations are aware of SOA, they most likely view it as another wave of technology. The business side of the enterprise is more likely to be focused on BPM and process improvement where automation of business processes is viewed as a technique to be considered, but the focus is on the operation of the business.

   A proof-of-concept development should be selected to demonstrate the business potential and organizational capability to consolidate and integrate a capability. In most cases, this will be driven by IT and will focus on consolidation of applications, but the business value and organizational implications of the consolidation should be highlighted. This includes economies of scale, consistency, and accountability as well as delegation to shared services (perceived as loss of control) and commitment to delivery of services in compliance with formal specifications.

2. *Applied.* Top management is committed to SOA, the organization has developed a basic capability to design and implement service units, and selected shared services are being used (bottom-up). The Maturity Model does not distinguish between a service as value delivered and a service as an organization responsible for the supporting capability; in this book we resolve that ambiguity by referring to the organization responsible for the supporting capability as a *service unit*, as discussed earlier.

At this level SOA has become recognized as an important approach to improvement of operating costs, product quality, and agility of the enterprise. It may still be viewed as primarily an adoption of new technology, but there is a realization that it must be driven by top management to achieve strategic value and avoid suboptimal solutions. There is an understanding that SOA and BPM are complementary views of an enterprise architecture, and that service units are shared business capabilities managed by business organizations. There is an initial commitment to an SOA infrastructure and enterprise standards. Development of service units is essentially bottom-up, based on business value, and should be guided by an industry best-practices framework perspective.

3. *Adopted.* The organization has an SOA infrastructure in place and is committed to standards. There is a system of governance to plan and manage transformation of the organization and to manage the definition and implementation of service units (top-down).

At this level, the transformation has shifted from being driven bottom-up to top-down. Definition of service units is driven by top-down analysis and design by a business architecture activity, and transformation is driven from an enterprise level. Priorities and funding for IT budgets and transformation initiatives are managed at an enterprise level. Service costs are captured, and a charge-back mechanism has been defined to support evaluation of the full cost of services. The enterprise is not yet fully service-oriented, but development of new applications is in a service-oriented context.

Data exchange for established services is consistent with an enterprise logical data model.

4. *Measured.* Service units are monitored and measured for cost, timeliness, quality, and availability and refined for enterprise optimization; in other words, Level 4 capabilities are value chain driven. The contributions of services to the value chain can be reported and analyzed.

   The enterprise is sufficiently service oriented that the value chains can be evaluated as compositions of services. The cost, quality, and timeliness of a value chain are reported and can be traced to the individual service units that contribute value. The organization structure reflects alignment of goals, incentives, and economies of scale in the management of service unit resources. Service performance is monitored in real time, and performance is evaluated against formal service unit performance specifications. Disruptive events, both internal and external, are captured and directed to appropriate service units for resoltion.

5. *Agile.* The organization has a continuous change culture and business processes to adapt the enterprise in response to disruptive events. The enterprise senses disruptive events and, when required, responds to them by reconfiguring relationships between existing service units, with minimal need for capability enhancement or development of new services.

   The governance structure ensures that the enterprise is doing the right thing and doing it well. The enterprise accepts change as a way of life. Continuous strategic planning is responsive to change and drives strategic changes to the enterprise. There is rapid response to disruptive events through business processes based on comprehensive risk management and an understanding of the enterprise ecosystem. Service unit managers work to continuously improve their services based on needs of service users and enterprise objectives. Service units are sharable building blocks that enable rapid configuration, evaluation, and implementation of a product life-cycle model to address new business opportunities.

Business Dimensions

Each of the maturity levels is evaluated, from a business perspective, in five dimensions. The following points briefly describe the business dimensions:

- *Processes.* Business processes must first be documented and repeatable. They must then be aligned to service units and measured. The agile enterprise has business processes that determine the operation of the enterprise but also processes that drive change.

- *Organization.* The business organization evolves to an organization of service units that are later organized for effective management of capabilities and incentives for improvement.

- *Governance.* Governance evolves from delegation of optimization and change in business silos to enterprise-level planning, priority setting, accountability, and control, to achieve a consistent enterprise design and responsive, coordinated change.

- *Portfolio.* The portfolio of shared business capabilities goes from a functional organization chart to a well-defined collection of shared service units and, finally, a comprehensive model of a network of service units contributing to value chains.

- *Finance.* Funding of information systems evolves from departmental discretion to investment based on enterprise priorities. The cost of services is determined and supported by a billing mechanism for assessment of the full cost of each service rendered, including other services used.

Technology Dimensions

The six dimensions of the technology perspective are focused on particular concerns of the IT organization and the capabilities needed to provide information technology support to the rest of the business:

1. *Infrastructure.* Infrastructure moves from ad hoc, point-to-point integration of systems to a common messaging and integration infrastructure with single sign-on and role-based access control. Business process automation and, later, event notification and complex event processing are included in the infrastructure.

2. *Architecture.* The architecture evolves from support for integration of applications to design of technical solutions to support and integrate service units and, later, support for detection and resolution of disruptive events. Technical standards and product selections support economies of scale in IT development and operations.

3. *Data.* Data models evolve from project-driven data modeling to development and application of an enterprise logical data model

that defines data exchanged between service units, the content of master data records, and the integration of data to support enterprise intelligence (which includes analysis of events and trends).

4. *Governance.* Technology governance evolves from project-based to program-based (multiple organizations and projects) to enterprise-based management of technology investments, standards, and product selection. Technology governance becomes an aspect of enterprise governance.

5. *Organization.* The IT organization evolves from a departmental/application focus to a capability focus with development of special skills to support the design and implementation of an agile enterprise.

6. *Operations.* The IT operations activities move from management of individual applications to monitoring and management of service unit dependencies and a virtualized computing environment. In the latter, computing devices are no longer dedicated to particular organizations or applications in order to enable operational economies of scale, dynamic performance optimization, and high reliability and security.

CRITICAL SUCCESS FACTORS ON THE JOURNEY TO AGILITY

The transformation to agility is a journey up the levels of the maturity model. The roadmap for the journey differs for each enterprise because each enterprise faces different challenges. However, we can highlight some critical success factors (CSFs) to help top management drive the transformation in the right direction.

Governance for Enterprise Optimization and Control

Top management must ensure that investments, improvements, and economies of scale are considered from a strategic enterprise perspective. In particular, information technology must be managed to control proliferation of diverse technologies and to achieve economies of scale in technical resources. Departmental or line-of-business silos must give up control of duplicated capabilities to realize enterprise-level economies of scale and flexibility of shared services. Service units must be held accountable for compliance with service specifications, business rules, and security requirements.

Enterprise Models

To optimize enterprise operations and respond effectively to challenges and opportunities, top management must have models that provide information about the enterprise ecosystem, current operations, operating cost, quality and performance, and opportunities for improvements as well as new business. These models go well beyond the "executive dashboard," to enable analysis of disruptive events, consideration of what-if scenarios, and exercise of operational controls. Value chain analysis must provide an understanding of the contributions to cost, quality, and performance for each current or planned product or service. Business activity monitoring should identify exceptions and trends in performance. Recognition of events and distribution of notices should keep top management aware of the changing ecosystem.

Technical Infrastructure

A shared technical infrastructure must be established and maintained for economies of scale, integration, flexibility, reliability, security, and support for robust enterprise intelligence. This infrastructure requires initial investment that cannot be justified for individual application development projects; it is intended for use by most or all applications. The technical infrastructure includes services such as messaging, security, naming, business rules repository, logging, and more.

Service-Based Management

Service-based management is fundamental to the paradigm shift. Managers must start to think in terms of providing services either directly to end customers or to other parts of the enterprise. This means formalizing capability offerings and the form of requests, responses, and related information exchanges. It means determining the costs of service units and the unit cost of using individual shared capabilities, including the costs incurred from other services used. It also means accountability for performance measures, security, compliance with policies and regulations, and responsibility for continuous improvement and adaptation to change.

Optimization of service-based management is enabled by an SOA, which is the focus of the next chapter.

Service-Oriented Architecture

A *service-oriented architecture* (SOA) is a new business design paradigm, a fundamental aspect of the design of an agile enterprise that supports improved speed, cost, and quality. Service units are its building blocks. An SOA does not require electronic technology, but automation, integration, and modeling using electronic technologies are essential to an optimal implementation of SOA. The full implementation of SOA transforms the enterprise from top to bottom. This chapter provides a first step in understanding the fundamental nature of this new business design paradigm. As we move through later chapters, we discuss other aspects of the agile enterprise and examine how they complement or support SOA. In Chapter 9, we see how SOA is driven by and supports agile enterprise governance for more effective leadership and accountability.

SOA enables the sharing of business capabilities where those capabilities may be used in a variety of business contexts. SOA provides the transparency that allows a shared capability to be provided by a service unit within the enterprise or as a service of a different enterprise. This offers the following business benefits:

- Economies of scale are realized through sharing resources and optimizing use of those resources.
- Quality and productivity are improved by enabling the development of special skills and capabilities that would not be justified for multiple, smaller operating activities.
- Improved consistency and control are achieved by placing responsibility for management of a capability in a single organization.
- Distributed operations are enabled through loose coupling and Internet-based communication of interactions between service units.

- Process optimization is enhanced by enabling each service unit to optimize the processes of the services it provides, with minimal impact on other service units.
- Greater assurance of regulatory compliance can be achieved through consolidation of regulated processes and related business functions.
- The enterprise gains the ability to utilize the most effective alternative sources of services such as outsourcing or operations in other countries.

In this chapter we begin to establish how these benefits are realized. This starts by developing an understanding of the nature of business services. Next we discuss the supporting infrastructure that is needed for services to be accessed and shared. Then we describe how services needed in an enterprise are identified and specified. We take an initial look at the relationship between SOA and value chain analysis. Finally, we briefly discuss approaches to enterprise transformation to SOA.

BUSINESS SERVICES

Many in the IT industry have viewed services in a SOA as computer applications, components of applications, or technical services that support applications or IT operations. SOA gained popularity as a basis for an enterprise to engage the services of other enterprises over the Internet. The expectation is for a computer application in one enterprise to automatically invoke an automated capability provided by another enterprise through communications over the Internet. This differs from previous systems integration technologies because industry standards now enable the participants to communicate over public facilities, effectively and securely, even though the participants use diverse application technologies and hide their internal operations.

However, this use of services of another organization implies more than just a computer application. It implies the existence of an organization responsible for the application, the existence of a business capability that is offered by a service provider and needed by the service consumer, and a commitment to the exchange of value between the participating organizations. SOA is an architecture for business relationships.

SOA should not be viewed as applicable only to interchanges between enterprises but as an architecture for the composition of an enterprise. The same integration standards that enable integration of services over the Internet also enable organizations within the enterprise to provide and consume services among each other.

In this book we view a service as the delivery of business value through the application of business capabilities. We titled this section "Business Services" to clarify that we are talking about a business perspective and that the services are visible and sharable across organizational boundaries. Throughout this book, when we talk about a *service*, we are referring to the delivery of business value; when we talk about a *service unit*, we are referring to an organization that manages a business capability to deliver services, not just an information technology application or component.

So a "service unit" may offer a repair capability (repair services), and the performance of a specific repair is delivered as a "service." A service unit is not required to use electronic technology, but as a practical matter in most cases it uses electronic communications and computer applications to support the management of its capability and delivery of value.

In this section we explore in greater depth the nature of services and service units as components of the enterprise.

Service Units

A service unit is a sharable capability, as depicted in Figure 2.1. The capability is shared through the exchange of information and value in forms that are understood by the service provider and each service user. We refer to the specification of this interchange as an *interface specification*. A well-defined interface enables different service users

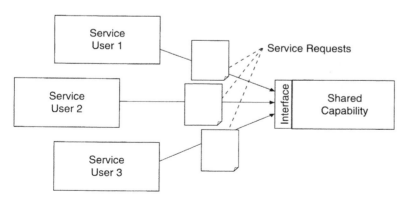

■ **FIGURE 2.1** Service Unit as a Shared Capability.

to incorporate the services into their business activities. It also enables the service provider to change the implementation without requiring implementation of changes by service users.

The interface may involve the exchange of information and assets. The interface specification may include the forms of data exchanged, an exchange protocol, rules regarding restrictions, and levels of performance and quality. For the most part, electronic technology is expected to provide the medium of exchange of information. However, there are still other forms of media, particularly paper forms and voice communications. Whereas electronic media require technical interface specifications, exchanges using paper forms may rely primarily on the specifications embodied in the paper forms and the mechanisms for transport, security, and accountability traditionally accepted for paper-based business transactions. Protocols and content requirements for voice exchanges may be guided by contracts, documents, or spoken instructions. Voice communications are typically captured on paper or entered into an online system. As with other, nonelectronic forms of exchange, mechanisms are required for transformation between paper and electronic forms for integration of services.

The exchange between a service user and the service provider generally begins with a request from the service user. The request defines the requirements that address the specific needs of the user; it establishes the context for the service delivery. In some cases, such as where a service provider solicits business, the exchange may not be initiated by the service user. The common element is that the service user defines the context in which the service is used. So the response to a solicitation may be a specific request that identifies the application of the service to a specific need.

The service is provided by a business entity that takes responsibility for the result. The capability may involve people, raw materials, facilities, and intellectual property.

Some services, such as a tax computation, for example, may be fully automated and on the surface involve only a computer application. However, there is an organization responsible for the computer application and for ensuring its accuracy and reliability. Though people might not be directly involved in the operation, people maintain the tax rates and computations. This may involve other people or other services to identify changes to tax rates and regulations. There may be still other people involved in technical maintenance such as adapting the computation to new information technology. All these capabilities and associated responsibilities are part of delivering a tax computation service. To the user, the tax computation service provides tax computations in response to requests. The implementation of the service obviously involves much more, including the use of other services. These implementation considerations are not a concern of the service user, and the implementation is most likely hidden from the users.

The people, materials, facilities, and intellectual property of the service unit are the responsibility of the service unit manager. A service unit is an organizational component that in some cases may be an independent enterprise but in most cases is a team of people within an enterprise, along with the assets and resources they use to fulfill their responsibilities. So a service unit is a business unit that manages a capability to provide one or more services.

A service unit does not necessarily contain all the capabilities required to deliver its results; some parts of its responsibility may be delegated to other service units. Delegation removes control of the delegated operations and associated resources, but it does not relieve a service unit of the responsibility for delivering its value.

Figure 2.2 illustrates a service unit that uses other service units. A request for a service invokes a business process within service unit A. That business process may engage a person, an application, or other service units (B and C) to fulfill its service objective. Business processes play a key role in the operation and integration of service units, as we will explore in detail in the next chapter. Other supporting service units may be used

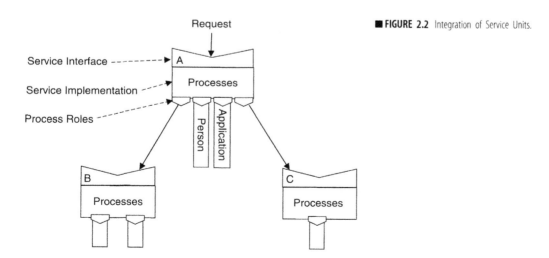

■ **FIGURE 2.2** Integration of Service Units.

by the primary service unit to contribute their special capabilities to the original request or to maintain or improve the primary service capability as support services.

This use of services within an enterprise is not new. Many formerly paper-based services are still evident in today's organizations and are typically embedded in the computer applications that support them. The paper has been replaced by electronic transactions. This is particularly evident with customer order processing, accounting services, human resource management, and purchasing activities. Unfortunately, many internal services that were automated 50 years ago are locked into the processes that are embedded in enterprise applications used to automate them.

SOA for the Enterprise

So an SOA is not simply an approach to designing computer systems; it is an approach to designing the enterprise. Shared capabilities are utilized in different contexts to achieve economies of scale and consistency of operations or control. The computer systems should be designed to align with the design of the business.

In fact, everything an enterprise does can be structured as a composition of service units. These service units are knit together by business processes. If the service units are defined with appropriate granularity, they can be shared and incorporated into new business endeavors as the business continues to change over time. We discuss an approach to identification of appropriate service units later in this chapter.

The organization of a tool and die shop illustrates how SOA supports agility. The shop uses job routings of work to engage a combination of services and to define the sequence of operations needed to deliver custom products. The shop has a number of specialized tools and machines, along with groups of specialized tool and die makers who operate particular machines and apply their skills. The various specialists provide different services. As a job comes into the shop, a dispatcher prepares a job routing (that is, an ad hoc business process) that defines the sequence of services to be performed. The skills, tools, and machines used in each department remain unchanged, but a wide variety of products are produced. The shop is highly adaptive.

Service Unit Template

Figure 2.3 depicts the general characteristics of a service unit. The service unit contains the business processes, applications, rules, resources, and assets to achieve the desired capability. Usually there will be a primary service and ancillary services such as to cancel, change, or request

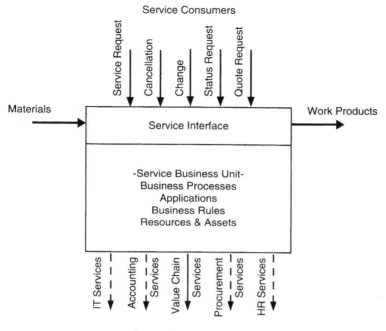

■ **FIGURE** 2.3 A Service Unit Template.

status of a service previously requested. There might also be a request for a quote to establish the charge for a service, given certain parameters, before the actual service request is submitted. The arrows indicate the direction of initiation of an exchange: from the service user to the service provider.

A service unit uses input materials and produces a work product that contributes business value. These materials may be supplied with a request, and the work product may be returned to the requester. However, often the service unit acquires materials in other ways, and the result may be delivered to a consumer other than the service requester. The arrows for materials and work products depict the flow of value consumed and value produced.

For example, in a manufacturing department, a production schedule may direct the manufacturing department to produce batches of certain parts and deliver them to another department. The schedule may also direct source departments to supply batches of materials used to produce the parts. Consequently, the flow of material from source departments and resulting parts to consuming departments is distinct from the flow of control exercised by the scheduling system. This *value flow* is important when discussing value chains and will be visited again later.

A service unit provides a capability, not necessarily just a single service, so a service unit may offer a variety of services to address the different needs of users (usually through different request types defined for the same interface). At the same time, if there are too many different services to access the same capability, the implementation of the service unit may become more complex and less flexible. Multiple services will require multiple processes that will all require consideration if the service implementation changes. It is also likely that specialized services will result in tighter coupling with users, in turn resulting in propagation of effects to users when the service unit makes internal changes. The service unit should be designed to accommodate a variety of service parameters and specifications that enable a generic service to meet a range of user requirements.

Note that billing for services is not explicit in the diagram, but it is an essential aspect of any service. Each service unit must recover its costs, and the cost of each service must include the costs of services it uses. This is essential for effective motivation and governance and will be discussed more extensively in Chapters 7 and 9. The cost of services internal to the enterprise is determined by financial cost analysts, whereas the cost of external services is determined by negotiation of service prices with external providers. Billing is typically incorporated in accounting services, but a statement of charges may be incorporated in the response to a request, particularly if the charges vary depending on the specifics of the request. The behavior of service consumers is influenced by the cost of services, and information on the cost of individual requests may drive cost improvements. Where there is a choice of alternative provider, a quote request may provide the basis for selection.

The service unit may not directly perform all aspects of the service itself. Thus there are requests to other services depicted at the bottom of the diagram. These are other shared capabilities that either do not fit well with the capability of this service unit or are shared by yet another community of users. A requester of this service should not be aware or concerned that other services are invoked to fulfill part of its request.

The Value Chain Services arrow represents the use of services that contribute direct value to the units of production. For example, a product sales service may incorporate an order fulfillment service, and the order fulfillment service may incorporate a stock picking service, a packaging service, and a shipping service. These are all value chain services that contribute directly to the delivery of value to the end customer.

The other services indicated with dashed arrows at the bottom of the diagram are support services that are necessary for the service unit to maintain its capability, but they do not contribute directly to the value of each unit of production. These support services—accounting services, IT services, HR services, and procurement services—have their own value chains that deliver value for the management of the enterprise and the individual services they support. These support services also have value chains that are the focus of analysis in considering the design and performance of support services.

Service Ownership

From an organizational perspective, a service unit, or more specifically, the service unit manager, owns (has financial responsibility for) the service capability. The manager that "owns" the service unit is responsible for the efficiency, reliability, quality, and responsiveness of the services. The service unit employs skilled people and technology to achieve its objectives. It must manage its resources to achieve appropriate business value.

The manager is responsible for maintaining and improving the service capability and for managing the performance of services that meet the specifications of the service unit interface. The manager is responsible for ensuring that delegated services meet the needs of the service unit even though the manager does not have control of the capabilities for the delegated services.

Responsibility also includes the functionality of computer applications used by the service unit, even though technical development, support and execution of the applications generally is delegated to information technology services. The manager may be more directly involved in the specification of automated business processes, depending on the usability of available business process management tools.

The IT organization is one of the service providers that enable other service units to fulfill their responsibilities. From the viewpoint of the requesting service units, the services of the IT organization are business services as well. Managers of IT services have responsibility for effective use of the technology and must manage their services to minimize technical diversity for economies of scale, quality, and responsive support. IT may employ a variety of shared services not visible to the users of IT services.

The interface to a service unit, the specification by which services are requested and delivered, should be well defined and, at the same time, appropriate to utilization of the service in a variety of contexts. Though the service unit owner cannot unilaterally change the interface, it should be possible to change and improve the internal implementation of a service unit with minimal effect on the users of the services or other services it uses. We examine the organizational implications of the service unit in greater detail in Chapter 7, as well as the implications to governance, enterprise optimization, and agility in Chapter 9.

The carving up of the enterprise into well-defined service units assigns responsibility based on the nature of the work. The separation of service use from service implementation enables management to empower service unit managers to take the initiative to improve their operations. It enables management to identify specific service units to resolve problems and to be accountable for results. In Chapters 7 and 9 we will discuss the design of organization structure and governance to drive improvements.

Service Groups

Sometimes services are bundled into a *service group* that is managed by a single organization. The service group represents a composite capability that exposes interfaces to distinct services but may or may not be organized, internally, as a collection of service units. A complex capability that supports a number of interdependent services may be managed in this way for consistency and economies of scale.

The IT organization or the application development and data processing operations segments should be organized as service groups. An outsourcing service provider may be viewed in this way where the provider offers interfaces to various services but does not expose the internal design of its operations. A legacy enterprise application may be "wrapped" (hidden behind a technically compatible interface) to provide services but may not be easily partitioned to support separate service units, so it can be viewed as a service group. A service group may also be used as a phase of transformation where a composite capability is consolidated and later partitioned into separately managed and more independently sharable services.

Services in Electronic Commerce

In general, electronic commerce between enterprises can be viewed as an integration of services in much the same way that services are used within the enterprise. Suppliers in a supply chain are providing the service of delivering products to the production process. Banks provide services for accepting and distributing funds, and transportation carriers provide services for pickup and delivery of packages. The primary difference between internal services and electronic commerce involves concerns about security and trust.

In some cases the information exchanged might not be private and the interaction may be trivial, such as in a request for a stock quote. The service provider may not be particularly concerned about the identity of the service user, but the service user is dependent on the identity of the provider for an accurate and timely stock quote. In other cases, such as the transfer of funds, identities of the service user and service provider are both critical and the information content is highly confidential. Security considerations for SOA are discussed in Chapter 6.

Trust requires a business relationship beyond technical compatibility. Each party must be assured that the other party will fulfill its obligations. Reputation may be a factor in determining the quality and reliability of the service. This assurance still requires human participation in the establishment of business relationships. In some cases this will be established by consortia or other general affiliations that screen members and provide assurance of good faith relationships among them. A discussion of establishing trust is beyond the scope of this book, but electronic signatures that establish legal obligations are addressed in Chapter 6.

Services in a Value Chain

A service delivers value to a service user. If the service unit uses other services to produce its value, we can view the linking of services-using-services as a chain of value contributions—a value chain. Because each service unit contributes in response to a request, the relationships form a tree structure. For a made-to-order product or service, there is a value chain that starts with the service that accepts the customer order and directly or indirectly links to all the services required to produce the customer value.

Figure 2.4 illustrates a service request tree in which the solid-line arrows represent the request-response relationships from services requesting value to services providing value. The dotted line arrows represent value contributions—the value chain. This is a simplified portrayal, since value contributions may not be aligned with the request-response paths, but they can be transfers directly to service units that require them as inputs. Nevertheless, the customer value is a composite of the value contributions of each service unit. If the chain is sequential, the time from

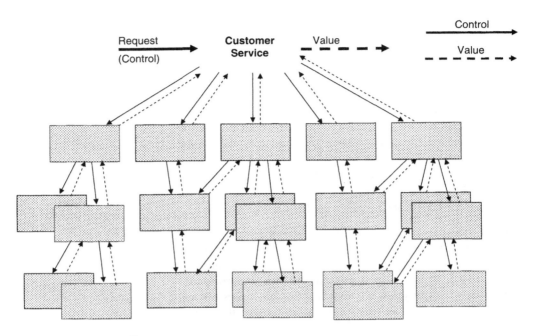

■ **FIGURE 2.4** A Service-Oriented Value Chain.

the request to the delivery of customer value is the sum of the times it takes each service to contribute its value. The quality of the product or service is dependent on the quality of the contributions.

This value chain concept is fundamental to the management of the agile enterprise. Customer value is delivered by management of the production value chain. There are other value chains internal to the enterprise, such as the value delivered to internal customers by accounting or information systems. The cost, quality, and timeliness of future products can be analyzed by consideration of a new product value chain. Analysis of value chains provides insights and priorities for improvement of performance and analysis of feasibility and risk associated with new products.

At the same time, each value chain is a use case of the services it uses. Different lines of business use some of the same service units, with somewhat different requirements, to deliver their value. A goal of the agile enterprise is to define service units that can be incorporated in different value chains with little or no change to the service units.

We will return to further discussion of value chains later in this chapter.

The Organizational Dimension

The service request tree is not an organizational hierarchy. The service unit request tree and the value chain both cross organizational boundaries and engage service units managed by different organizations. Figure 2.5 depicts the relationship between a hypothetical value chain for delivering customer value and the various organizations that contribute value.

The dotted-line boxes represent organizations and the smaller boxes represent service units in those organizations. Though some service units invoke other services within the same organization, the service units are most likely peers within the organization structure. The Process Order service unit manages the customer order from start to end and invokes other services to achieve the desired result.

In contrast, in a traditional enterprise, the left-to-right order of the organization boxes might also be the process flow, starting with the receipt of the order and finishing with the receipt of payment. Each of the departmental systems would complete its responsibility and pass control to the next department. However, such a process flow is very inflexible, and nobody is accountable for the overall result.

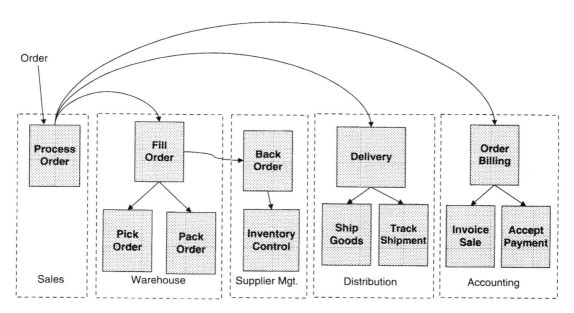

■ **FIGURE 2.5** Service Units in an Organization Structure.

Each department must know where the order goes next. If a different product line is introduced, each department must change its processes to add, modify, or bypass functionality for the new product line and properly direct the result to the next department.

For example, suppose the enterprise decides to sell some products for delivery direct from the manufacturer instead of from a warehouse. There would be no warehouse activities, back orders, or shipment activity for those products. The Process Order service might simply request shipment of the product by the manufacturer and track the shipment once the product was shipped. In the service-oriented value chain, the change would be accomplished by modification of the business process for the Process Order service unit for the new delivery model.

However, it is important to note that material flow does not necessarily follow the service request paths. In Figure 2.5 the products would likely flow from Pick Order to Pack Order and to Ship Goods. The material flow generally aligns with the value chain dependencies that we will explore later. The material flow recipients may be designated with a parameter in the associated service request.

In Chapter 7 we explore in greater detail the relationships between service units and the organization structure.

SERVICE UNIT MANAGEMENT

Service unit management can be viewed from two perspectives: management *controls*, which govern how the service unit participates in enterprise endeavors, and management of the service unit *implementation and operation*, which determines how the service unit produces business value.

Management Controls

Figure 2.6 extends the earlier service unit template with management inputs and outputs. The left side of the diagram depicts inputs that affect the operation of the service as a result of disruptive events, shifts in workloads, changes to requirements from service users, investment for changes, or business rules reflecting changes in policies or regulations. On the right side are outputs required from the service unit to support accountability through cost and performance reporting as well as escalation of opportunities and threats that cannot be addressed effectively by the service unit alone.

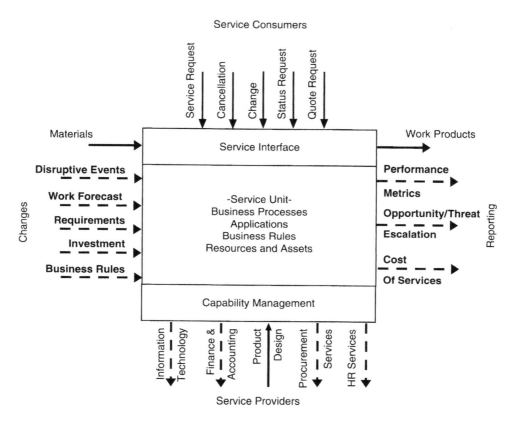

FIGURE 2.6 Addition of Service Management Interfaces.

A service unit is required to comply with its service interface specifications. These specifications are effectively a contract with the rest of the enterprise. They may be changed as a result of new requirements or improvements in the service unit implementation, but they cannot be changed unilaterally. Performance metrics are based on performance against these specifications, and users of the services, as well as potential future users, rely on conformance to the specifications.

Note that the cost of services reported on the right of the diagram includes both the total cost of the service unit and the cost that is billed for individual units of service. The overall service unit cost is a more accurate specification of cost elements and reflects the cost of the service unit during a particular time period with a particular volume and product mix. The cost that is billed is based on a cost analysis that determines the direct costs plus an allocation of overhead costs for each unit of value produced. The requirements of cost accounting are discussed further in Chapter 9. Ideally, for a particular time period, the total computed for production unit costs and the total cost of the service unit are close to the same.

Service Implementation Management

Internally, the manager of a service unit and his or her management chain have responsibility for operational management and change management. Service unit management may have considerable discretion in how the services are performed, as long as they comply with the service interface specification. From a business perspective, the service interface specification includes specifications for the form and content of the request, the specification of interactions, and the level-of-service specifications.

A primary role of the manager and the employees is to optimize operation of the service unit. In a sense, the manager is responsible for an internal enterprise, and the manager and his or her team must work together for the success of their enterprise. In many cases this requires collaboration with related service units to resolve problems and refine interface specifications.

Managers must also respect enterprise rules and standards. Rules include government regulations and constraints that mediate risks. Standards ensure effective integration as well as optimization of other enterprise operations such as consistent use of information technology to achieve IT economies of scale.

A service unit manager is expected to operate the service unit reliably and at minimal cost. At the same time, a service unit manager is expected to continuously improve service unit operations, respond to threats or opportunities within his or her discretion, and adapt to new enterprise requirements that affect how the service unit capability is applied. From an enterprise perspective, service unit performance must be considered in the context of the value chains to which it contributes, and an appropriate balance must be achieved among cost, quality, timeliness, and risk while meeting regulatory and policy requirements. Some changes are strictly within the discretion of the service unit manager, but others, such as investment in new tools or technology changes, may require approval at an enterprise level to ensure enterprise optimization. In Chapter 8 we discuss further the role of the service unit manager in response to disruptive events.

SOA ELECTRONIC INFRASTRUCTURE

SOA for business does not mean that all services are accessed electronically nor that all services use computer applications in their implementation. However, in today's world, the normal case is that integration and implementation are supported by electronic technology. Manually performed services with paper or voice interfaces are the exception. Even those are likely to require some form of integration through the electronic infrastructure.

Therefore, an electronic infrastructure—computing, communications, and associated software and supporting resources—are essential to SOA and the agile enterprise. The infrastructure must support standards and consistent implementation to minimize cost and complexity, to enable sharing and flexibility, and to enhance speed, reliability, and economies of scale.

This infrastructure, along with adaptation of existing systems, requires an up-front investment that increases the costs of early SOA projects but provides significant benefit and lower costs in the long term.

There are several fundamental components that must be part of the enterprise electronic infrastructure to support the integration and operation of service units. Figure 2.7 depicts the key infrastructure components discussed in the following sections.

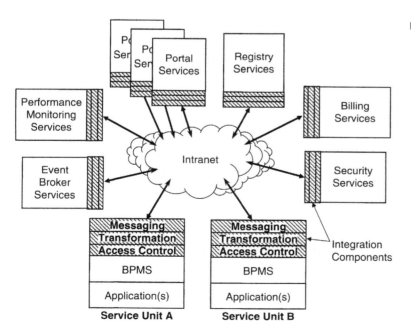

■ **FIGURE 2.7** SOA Electronic Infrastructure.

Reliable Messaging

In an SOA, requests for services and the interactions between requester and provider are communicated as messages. The communications are usually in a *store-and-forward* mode so that a message can be sent by one participant but held until the recipient is ready to receive and process it. A participant may send a message and continue to do other work rather than suspend activities until the recipient responds. This is described as *loose coupling* (more specifically, *temporal loose coupling*) because senders don't need to wait for receivers to be ready or respond, and receivers don't need to take immediate action.

An integration component (including messaging, transformation, and access control) is associated with each of the services in Figure 2.7 (the gray areas). Each service unit is capable of exchanging messages with any other service unit, and these exchanges could extend outside the enterprise.

Generally, messages are communicated with *reliable messaging*. This means that the messaging system ensures that each message is delivered to a recipient once and only once. In a paper-based world, reliable messaging is accomplished with the use of original documents (so there is only one) and transaction numbers such as an order number or invoice number.

In some business environments, it is necessary for service units to be more tightly coupled to meet performance objectives. These environments may use synchronous messaging technology whereby requests are communicated immediately and the requester waits for a response. The disadvantage of such *tight coupling* is that when one of the participants fails, everything stops. There is also less flexibility in the integration of different application technologies, and loose-coupling technology enables easier integration of diverse technologies. Tight coupling is acceptable for applications within the responsibility of a single organization but should be avoided, if possible, when crossing significant organizational boundaries.

Security

The infrastructure must provide appropriate protection for the communications between service users and service providers using encryption as required. It must provide the means for determining the identity of participants (called *authentication*) and for determining whether participants are permitted to make certain requests or receive certain information (called *authorization*). These access control mechanisms must be complemented with logging and audit support, to ensure accountability and expose inappropriate accesses.

Each service unit in Figure 2.7 has an access control component that uses the security service. The security service unit includes identification, authentication, and authorization services.

In an SOA, many users are expected to directly or indirectly access many systems. This is partly because optimization of operations requires cross-enterprise access to data and because shared services may be used in a number of contexts. Users should be able to sign on once and then be able to access a number of systems for which they have authorization; this is called *single sign-on*. In addition, this authentication should be supported with a *Public Key Infrastructure* (PKI) that provides management of identifiers and keys for encryption and electronic signatures. Auditing also becomes more complex because the behavior of many users, potentially in many different locations and organizations, must be assessed to identify security risks and violations. Security issues for SOA and the agile enterprise are discussed in Chapter 6.

Message Transformation

Message transformation is required to convert the format of message content to be consistent with an enterprise logical data model for exchange or to convert the format of a message being sent to meet the requirements of a receiving service or application. Initial service implementations must be integrated with existing systems, so message transformation is required.

Since commercial software products (e.g., enterprise applications) are unlikely to conform to the logical data model of the particular enterprise, transformation is probably required on messages exchanged with these applications. In the long term, there may be less need for transformation, but when there is a change to meet new requirements, message transformation may be required for the transition until all senders or receivers of a message type have been upgraded.

Figure 2.7 depicts a transformation capability at the interface to each of the service units. This anticipates that at various times, as new versions of services are implemented, there will be a need for transformation, if only on a transitional basis.

Registry Services

Registry services maintain current information about available services. At a minimum, a registry should provide links to available services so that users of a service can refer to a logical name of the service and be directed to the appropriate network address that may change over time.

In addition, the registry should identify different versions of service interfaces so that either a compatible version can be located or the interactions can be properly adapted or transformed. The registry should provide criteria for the selection of a service from among similar services. Within an enterprise, there is typically only one appropriate service for a shared capability, but that is not always the case. For example, there could be services based in different time zones or different countries, specialized for different product lines, or located in different physical facilities. The registry might also be extended for identification of approved external services such as supplier services, including, for example, suppliers that might be eligible to bid on a particular class of purchase request.

It may be useful to include additional information on each service for general reference, business management, system configuration, and change control purposes. The registry services should complement or extend the configuration management database (CMDB) of IT operations that supports management of applications and IT infrastructure.

It is necessary for data processing operations people to have access to information about the interoperation of service units, to understand the implications of system failures and to plan for disaster recovery contingencies.

Business Process Management System

Automation of business processes should be an integral part of an SOA implementation. A *business process management system* (BPMS) is a set of applications used to define business processes, execute them as automated processes, and analyze them for process improvement. Though an enterprise may have multiple BPMS software products, a preferred BPMS should be available for automation of business processes anywhere in the enterprise so that it is readily available as new processes are defined and deployed. Use of a single BPMS reduces licensing costs, eliminates incompatibilities, and enables everyone to use the same tools and representation in designing business processes.

In general, the scope of business processes should align to service unit boundaries, and BPMS products should be integrated through exchanges of messages between processes in different service units using the SOA infrastructure.

In Figure 2.7 the BPMS is depicted as a component of the service units. This is to indicate that the business processes executed by the BPMS are components of the service units, but they may, in fact, be executed by one or more shared BPMS products.

Portal Support

Services are not only used by other service units but by humans as well. Even where a service is always invoked by an automated system, there likely is a need for human access to obtain information about the status of a request or associated data. The human users may come from across and outside the enterprise and include employees, investors, business partners, and customers. They need a way to find the appropriate services and to submit requests. This need for visibility of services to human users should be addressed by appropriate portals.

Generally, each portal is designed for use by a particular stakeholder community, and a community portal provides access to a variety of services of potential interest in that community. Community portals should provide Web pages that link users to services of interest. Each portal should be owned by a service unit that manages the interactions with the associated community.

The design of a portal should address the particular needs of the stakeholder community; should have a consistent look and feel, at least for each community; and may include personalization features. Some portals may need to support internationalization and access with mobile devices. In addition, the service unit can address the need to translate the form of expression of requests and responses between the stakeholders' point of view and the internal services that respond to their requests. The infrastructure should support the necessary portal technology.

Service Performance Monitoring

Effective management of the service-oriented enterprise requires that performance data be captured and made available for monitoring and analysis. It should be possible to obtain current performance data on any service unit and aggregate service data to assess performance for a value chain. The nature and implications of value chain analysis are discussed further later in this chapter and in Chapter 9 on governance.

Performance monitoring is depicted as a service unit in Figure 2.7. The service unit may accumulate and report performance data, but the BPMS associated with each service unit being monitored should provide the raw performance data for business activity monitoring (BAM).

Billing for Services

Though costing is primarily a financial responsibility, the IT infrastructure must provide the mechanisms by which service uses are tracked and charges are computed and billed. A billing infrastructure may not be essential in the early stages of transformation to SOA, but it should be part of the strategic infrastructure design.

Each service unit must include in its billing both the costs of its operation and materials and the costs of services it uses, and it must recover its costs from its consumers. Thus a billing represents the full cost of the value delivered by each service, regardless of whether the service unit uses other services to achieve its results or performs all the activities itself. For internal services, these costs do not include any profit margin; for external services the cost is the price charged by the service provider and can be expected to include profit.

As with performance monitoring, the business processes in each service unit must provide billing data to the billing service unit for services rendered.

These charges propagate up the value chains to reflect the current production cost of products and services. This, in turn, supports process improvement planning, pricing, and profitability analysis. Cost accounting is discussed in greater detail in Chapter 9.

DEFINING SERVICE UNITS

How big is a service? From a service user's perspective, services come in all sizes. A tool crib activity is a service. A payroll processing activity is a service. An auto repair shop is a service. A transportation carrier is a service. A Web search engine (such as Google) is a service.

A travel reservation system is a service. Manufacture of a jumbo jet can be viewed as a service. What do these services have in common? They apply business capabilities to deliver value in response to requests from a variety of service users.

The value delivered by these services ranges from application of a specific capability to integration of contributions of multiple capabilities. Whereas a complex service can be delivered by a single service unit, the result may be achieved by engaging other service units that may, in turn, engage still other service units. Delivery of a complex product may engage, directly or indirectly, most of the service units of a large enterprise and potentially some outside the enterprise.

The question is not how big is a service but how big is a service unit. Service units should be relatively small so that they focus on the application of a distinct business capability. The size should represent an appropriate balance between a focused capability and economies of scale. In our examples, the tool crib may be a simple service unit, while a travel reservation system may have a service unit that interacts with the customer but then engages other services to arrange for hotel reservations, rental cars, and airline reservations. The jumbo jet manufacturer may involve multiple service units just to capture and validate an order, and then many services are engaged, directly and indirectly, to build and deliver the jumbo jet.

In this section we describe the process of identifying service units that are the building blocks of an agile enterprise architecture. This is a top-down analysis based on value chains. It identifies service units of a strategic architecture as a basis for understanding business transformation requirements and development of a transformation roadmap. Most enterprises are not ready to undertake such an analysis until they are ready to move to level 3 in the SOA Maturity Model.

Service-Oriented Analysis

This analysis starts with a conventional value chain model. As we have discussed earlier, the enterprise has multiple value chains. Generally, analysis for an enterprise starts with the primary value chain(s) that delivers end-customer value. As the enterprise matures, the scope of analysis expands to include product life-cycle value chains (including product development) and value chains for supporting services.

The ideal approach to identification of services is analysis of the enterprise from the top down. This ensures that the definition of services is driven by the business of the enterprise and avoids repackaging the same old way of doing business. It also provides the greatest opportunity to identify sharable capabilities and to understand how the same capabilities may be used in different contexts. At the same time, it requires a substantial investment in analysis, planning, and design.

Note that the goal of service-oriented analysis is to break out the various business capabilities such that, as much as possible, individual service units experience little or no need for change as the enterprise pursues new business opportunities and goes through substantial transformations. The expectation is that the line-of-business processes may change, and some of the detail of tasks may change, but the service interfaces and their fundamental capabilities persist.

Value Chain Analysis

Figure 2.8 illustrates a conventional value chain model used in strategic planning for a made-to-order product. This value chain depicts broad areas of responsibility and a general transition through those responsibilities to deliver customer value. We refer to each of these responsibilities as a *role*. The figure represents the role of the associated capability in producing value for the end customer. Each of the high-level roles is broken into supporting roles.

We distinguish this conventional value chain from a *robust value chain* (RVC), which is a dependency network defining the contributions of value to the customer result. The conventional value chain represents the common approach used by most enterprises and is sufficient for service-oriented analysis at the lower levels of the SOA Maturity Model. The RVC model is important for achieving the benefits of maturity levels 4 and 5. We will discuss the RVC model in greater detail later in this chapter.

It may be useful to use alternative forms for the value chain decomposition. The conventional value chain model is equivalent to a work breakdown structure, as depicted in Figure 2.8b. Figure 2.8c illustrates the same model in the form of an outline. The outline form is often a more convenient way to capture additional levels of detail, since it is easier to expand multiple levels, but it might not be convenient for capture of the requirements of the specific roles. Regardless of the form, a conventional value chain model is a useful starting point for analysis.

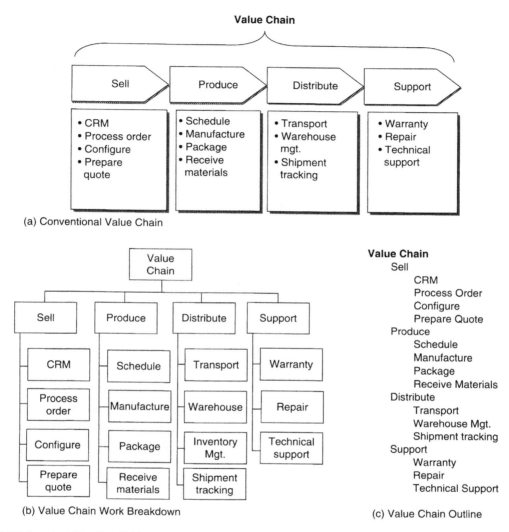

FIGURE 2.8 Conventional Value Chain Models.

The value chain decomposition is sometimes described as a *process model*, but it is at most a high-level abstraction of the processes that actually deliver customer value. A value chain is not intended to be a process model but rather an abstraction of the flow of value contributions. Nevertheless, at times it is helpful to think in terms of a process breakdown to help identify the required capabilities.

We refer to these capability requirements as *roles* because they define the need for a capability to produce a particular result. A role defines a use of a capability. Therefore, the work breakdown structure becomes a hierarchy or tree structure of roles. Using the concept of roles, we focus on what needs to be done rather than who will do it, thus separating the structure of the analysis from the existing organization structure. We'll expand on the concept of *role* in a moment.

The enterprise may have several lines of business with different kinds of products and services. Each of these has a value chain. If they all require generally the same roles, the analysis can proceed with the simplifying assumption of a single value chain. However, as the level of detail increases, it is likely that a need for different roles will emerge. The objective is to identify the various roles that must be filled to meet the needs of all products, since all such roles must be filled to support all product lines. We discuss mechanisms for addressing the requirements of various products in Chapter 3 as an aspect of managing process variations.

A value chain should be viewed as a use case of enterprise capabilities. The variations in uses of similar capabilities provide the basis for defining the capabilities of shared service units. The roles define the contexts and associated requirements for which the service units will be used. More value chains and thus more use cases help define more robust and reusable service units.

Not every role defined in this decomposition will be filled by a service unit. The goal of this analysis is to break down the roles to a level of granularity that requires a distinct capability that either is appropriate for assignment to a single team or member of a team that does a type of work or is a capability that is provided by an external organization. So the important roles are the leaves of the tree where actual work gets done.

It is important to note that a level in this hierarchy does not establish a degree of complexity or magnitude of the underlying capability. For example, in a manufacturing hierarchy, "ship the product" might be a simple action at the end of the value chain, but it can invoke a variety of processes involving many facilities and personnel of external organizations to get the product delivered to the customer. The manufacturer views this as the use of an abstract capability that results in the customer receiving the product.

Each role is broken down into subordinate roles that would need to be performed to fulfill the requirement, and the capabilities needed to satisfy each of those roles must be considered. If a subordinate role capability requirement is reasonably consistent with the parent role requirement, it may be performed within the same service unit, but if it is a distinct capability, particularly if it requires different resources, disciplines, or independent control, it should be identified as a role for another service unit.

The size of an organization providing the capability is a factor to consider. A larger organization provides more opportunity to specialize and thus may be further segmented into different service units.

For example, in the job shop we described the routing of a job to different types of tool-and-die operations. In a small shop, all the tool-and-die makers and their machines would be in a single service unit because some would operate multiple machines and perform different tasks, depending on the workload. In a large shop with maybe hundreds of machines and personnel, service units might be defined for each type of operation, such as milling, grinding, shapers, lathes, fabrication, assembly, and so on. Service unit managers would then focus on the specialized skills and performance of their workers and the supports needed to achieve high levels of efficiency and quality. The enterprise might also offer specific tool-and-die services to outside customers.

Roles

A role defines a need for a capability. It defines what needs to be done and the context in which it is to be done. At an operational level, the context is specified in a request to a service unit. A participant in a role may be a service unit, a person or persons, or a machine (e.g., a computer application). Fundamental capabilities are satisfied by people or machines. That is where work actually gets done. The analysis proceeds iteratively to break down roles, to define supporting roles until fundamental capability needs are identified.

As the analysis proceeds, the following characteristics are captured for each role:

- An objective to be satisfied, or, in other words, the value to be produced
- The context in which its objective is to be accomplished, including relevant specifications and parameters
- An output that defines the resulting work product and the value produced
- A description of the capability needed to fill the role

- Input material used to produce the output; the material is often a work product of another service unit or business entity
- Qualifications, selection criteria, that characterize the needed capability; qualifications might include a person's job code and required credentials

The participant in a role may be required to have some or all the following types of capabilities to fulfill the role and achieve the objective:

- Intellectual capital
- Tools and facilities
- Raw materials or work product components
- Information resources
- Personnel with particular skills
- Proximity to related resources or business activities

Service Unit Consolidation

Roles that call for similar capabilities represent the potential for the needs of these roles to be met by the same service unit, i.e., a shared capability. Some roles may call for a similar capability, but the context and result are sufficiently different that they could not be satisfied by the same service (yet possibly by the same service unit). These similarities should be noted, but consolidation should be deferred to ensure that the implications of each of the services are considered in the further breakdown. Once the breakdown is complete, services that require similar capabilities can be consolidated into service units representing shared capabilities that may provide multiple services. When this consolidation is applied, the relationships of services are no longer a tree but a network where some branches are joined together to use a shared service unit.

The consolidated service units need not come from the same level in the hierarchy; in fact, there could be recursion where a higher-level service unit uses other service units and one or more of those uses the higher-level service unit again in its context.

This consolidation achieves two important objectives: (1) it identifies multiple contexts in which a shared service unit can be applied, and (2) it reduces the explosion of detail, since the detail of a consolidated service unit need be expanded only once.

It may be necessary to modify the definition of some roles to fulfill them with shared services. In some cases, a parent and peer nodes may need to be modified to provide a more appropriate scope or objective for a role and thus the shared service it uses. In other words, the groupings of what needs to be done are modified to achieve consistency of shared services.

When a role has no similar role, an associated service unit may not be shared. We might not define an associated service unit but instead include it within the service unit supporting its parent role. It may then be viewed as a subprocess within the parent role's service unit, but such subprocesses are not intended to be shared outside the service unit. They are essentially more detailed specifications of the way a capability may be applied. This could be fine if the required capability is similar. However, it may still be appropriate to support the role with a distinct service unit if (1) the responsibilities or capabilities of the host node or peer nodes are quite different from the target node, (2) the capability is such that it may be shared in future business activities, or (3) the capability should be managed independently for accountability, optimization, or control.

Services that require similar capabilities but are expected to require different processes should be reviewed for potential consolidation. Consolidation depends on the similarity of the capability and the work to be done. The service requirements should be compared to determine whether they can be reconciled to a single service request type, potentially with different request options, or whether distinct service request types are needed. If there is an opportunity for economies of scale, consolidation is more desirable. Consolidation also should be considered in the context of organizational design criteria, discussed in Chapter 7.

Work Management Service Units

Each service unit should have the business processes to manage its work. The design of the business process is often a major factor in the performance of the service unit, and the service unit manager should have as much discretion as possible to make internal improvements to service unit operations.

However, there is a need for some service units to manage work across other service units. At the enterprise level, this takes the form of customer order management. For major enterprise undertakings, there may be a program management office.

There also may be needs for intermediate work management service units. These work management service units coordinate and control the work of multiple service units to achieve optimization that cannot be achieved within the individual service units. The following are examples of factors to be considered for consolidated work management:

- Batch production, balancing setup costs against responsiveness and inventory costs
- Sequencing of requests as for an automobile production line, to avoid bursts of high work content at individual stations
- Sharing resources across service units
- Selecting operating location for utilization of special machines or product distribution
- Designing a solution and selecting contributing services
- Sequencing work to manage priorities
- Managing change and rework

Generally, the work management service unit will be in the same organization as the service units for which work is managed so that a single manager is responsible for achieving the appropriate balance between service unit optimization and customer service. Placement of work management service units in the organization must be considered in the organization design discussed in Chapter 7.

The work breakdown structure should not be confused with the management hierarchy. Though the high-level value chain responsibilities may correspond to major business units, the business unit responsible for a particular service unit in the work breakdown structure may use service units managed in very different parts of the enterprise organization.

The management hierarchy is essentially an aggregation of service units. Service units are brought together to achieve further economies of scale and flexibility based on their similarities and work management requirements. We discuss this aggregation in greater detail in Chapter 7, where we focus on the agile organization structure, and in Chapter 8, where we detail the implications of decision making and agility.

Service Unit Interfaces

The service units are further refined by definition of the service interfaces. This clarifies the nature of the shared capability or the need to define separate service units. This reconciliation of the interface specification may uncover the need for alternative services (i.e., different request types), some differences in the input and output content, or generalization of the objective. A service unit may involve multiple interactions or related requests (e.g., change or cancel). This analysis helps clarify the capability and performance expectations for the service unit. It is preferable for all users of a service unit to invoke the same primary service process, since differences in service processes increase complexity and coupling between the service and its users.

Once service units have been identified, it is useful to look at the existing enterprise activities to identify where the capabilities currently exist. This provides additional context examples as well as more detail for the specification of service unit interfaces. This may also help identify additional capabilities that are needed to fully address business requirements.

Service Unit Specifications

As service units are identified, developed, deployed, and integrated, the specifications must be captured, refined, and maintained in an enterprise repository. We refer to this as the *Enterprise Architecture Repository*, which is a component of enterprise governance (discussed in Chapter 9) and the Enterprise Business Model (discussed in Chapter 10). This is distinct from the service registry that supports operational selection of services.

Note that though the focus is on service units that are electronically integrated and rely on automated business processes and applications, equivalent information must be included for manual services and exchanges based on paper or voice communications.

The following paragraphs describe key elements of the service unit specifications:

- *Service unit name.* A unique identifier for the service unit, typically the name of the primary service offered by the service unit or its capability.

- *Offering description.* This is a description of the capability being offered. It should be sufficient to qualify the service for roles as defined in the service definition analysis previously discussed.

- *Interfaces and versions.* Every service unit must have one or more service provider interfaces through which services are requested by people, applications, or other service units. An interface includes specifications of service requests and choreography if applicable. A single version of a service unit implementation may have multiple versions of an interface to accommodate the transition of users of the service unit from one version to another. Interface versions should also have effective dates, both when available and when deprecated.

- *Versions and life-cycle status.* There may be multiple versions of a service unit implementation in different stages of their life cycles: There may be versions under development, multiple current versions during a rollout to multiple sites, or versions that are no longer active but could be restored if a serious problem is encountered with a current version. Distinguishing features should be described. Service unit versions include software, business process specifications, resources, skills, facilities, or other aspects of the service unit that change to achieve a new service unit implementation.

- *Billing specifications.* This defines the basis for computation of service charges to be billed to service users.

- *Level of service specifications.* These are the performance targets for the service, primarily response times, scheduled availability, and quality of results that are measurable at the service interface. These are equivalent to level of service agreements; they define the basis for performance measures and should reflect the requirements and expectations of service users.

- *Security and business continuity requirements.* The level of security and business continuity requirements of the services go beyond the interface and level of service specifications to address implementation considerations involving other forms of exposure or disruptions of service. This includes the security of stored data and the recovery time after a system failure.

- *Used interfaces and versions.* These are references to the interfaces of other service units used by the specified service unit. Different versions of a service unit may use different versions of interfaces of other services.

- *Scalability.* Capacity limits or nonlinear impact of changes in volume on cost, timeliness, or quality. Of particular interest is the extent to which the impact of change in volume of production reaches a hard limit or becomes nonlinear so that, for example, a higher volume increases the unit cost.

- *Strategic service architecture mapping.* The enterprise should have a strategic architecture for the ideal services structure of the enterprise. This structure should specify the way each current service unit maps to that architecture. The strategic architecture is an enterprise-specific framework that may have been developed based on an industry framework (discussed later) or through the service-oriented analysis we discussed earlier.

- *Access authorization policy.* This is a statement of who qualifies to use the services offered and the process by which authorization is granted.

Development of these specifications should evolve over time but increase in importance as the enterprise becomes increasingly service oriented. These specifications are a component of the Enterprise Business Model (EBM) discussed in Chapter 10. It must be linked to other aspects of the EBM to support effective governance. Agile governance is discussed in Chapter 9.

Outsourcing

Outsourcing is the use of an external entity to provide client services that would otherwise be provided by an internal service unit or service group of the client. The purpose of outsourcing is to realize economies of scale and specialized capabilities that cannot be achieved within the enterprise. As the enterprise organization is transformed, it is important to consider outsourcing as an alternative to the transformation of existing capabilities.

When a group of capabilities are outsourced, their roles in value chains must be examined. Services of an outsourcing provider will typically replace capabilities of the client enterprise. If the client capabilities being replaced were shared among some other client service units that are not outsourced, the implications of losing these capabilities must be resolved. The outsourcing provider can be viewed as a service group with multiple interfaces that may or may not be supported by multiple internal service units. Potentially these interfaces will provide access to the shared capabilities replaced by the outsourcing provider. Of course, it is unlikely that the interfaces of the provider's shared services are compatible with the interfaces of the client's replaced service units, so there will be adaptation requirements.

If outsourcing is already established, it is not useful to expand the detail of capabilities that are expected to be internal to the outsourcing provider unless the provider has defined services that can be shared in other contexts. Generally speaking, the service provider implementation will be a black box, preserving the capability of the service provider to change its implementation to address new business challenges and opportunities. Exposing more shared services will limit this flexibility. At the same time, the services that are offered by the outsourcing provider should be reconciled with the capability requirements of the value chain breakdown.

The enterprise must manage the outsourcing relationship primarily as a service user. Managers within the enterprise do not control the resources or the operations of the outsourced service units. The enterprise must manage the services on the basis of a service contract, costs, and performance metrics, along with assessment of the satisfaction of internal users with the outsourced service.

The service interfaces require close attention. The interfaces are more difficult to change because the same services are being used by other enterprises. In addition, all requirements must be reflected in the interface specification; otherwise, there is no basis for corrective action if the service is not meeting expectations.

The service interfaces should be based on industry standards, if available. The enterprise should be able to switch to an alternative service provider if the current provider is not meeting expectations. Furthermore, the ability to switch to alternative services maintains competition between service providers to drive improvements in cost and performance.

Obviously, if the same services are available to competitors, they cannot be a source of competitive advantage. At best it moves the enterprise to a best-practices level of performance. At the same time, the management of the enterprise does not have the burden of managing the implementation or ongoing operation of the service, although it is important for enterprise management to measure performance and enforce service agreements.

The risks and benefits of outsourcing are outlined in Table 2.1.

Table 2.1 Risks and Benefits of Outsourcing

Risks	Benefits
Inability to take direct corrective action in service operations	Economies of scale across multiple enterprises (cost savings and workload leveling, driven by competition)
Service provider failure could bring the enterprise to a standstill	Service can leverage and retain specialists to ensure quality
No service employee loyalty to the user client enterprise	Service should be able to absorb changes in scale
Burden of contract management—monitoring performance and enforcing service agreement	May enable entry to new markets (e.g., address regulations in another country)
No competitive advantage	Should implement best practices

Role of Industry Frameworks

Industry frameworks provide prototypical designs of enterprises in a particular industry, based on generally accepted approaches and best practices. The frameworks tend to define characteristic breakdowns of functionality and business processes similar to the conventional value chain discussed earlier. The structure and content of an industry framework can be helpful in defining the SOA for a particular enterprise. Note, however, that each enterprise may be different due to individual circumstances or manner of doing business.

Service Units

A primary contribution of industry frameworks is to guide the definition of service units based on industry best practices. These service unit definitions tend to align with implementations of service unit capabilities in commercial enterprise applications and outsourcing services. Though industry frameworks are based on best practices, these practices reflect current approaches to doing business in the particular industry. Frameworks must be considered in the context of the particular enterprise under analysis. Care must be taken to define service units that enable future changes to the business. Use of an industry framework does not mean that a well-defined conventional value chain should be abandoned; instead, together they define more use cases for the definition of service units.

Data Models

An industry framework should include an enterprise data model. The role of a consistent, enterprise logical data model is discussed in Chapter 4. Use of a framework data model should be strongly considered early in the development of an SOA for a particular enterprise, for two reasons. First, development of a good enterprise logical data model is a very large and time-consuming undertaking that will delay the SOA transformation and exceed the cost of acquiring a model. Second, the framework data model is more likely to be consistent with commercial software systems and outsourcing services as well as industry standards, so data exchanged between services have fewer data transformation problems.

Processes

An industry framework may include best-practice business processes. These processes should not be assumed to be the best for a particular enterprise but should be considered as a starting point or basis of comparison to current practices. The most important value of these processes is to put the use of service units into context. The design of service units is more robust when a greater variety of usages is considered. The processes may also help identify resource and skill requirements.

Rules

Some frameworks may include business rules, which are discussed in Chapter 4. As with business processes, business rules should be considered points of reference but not necessarily the right rules for a particular enterprise.

Rules expressing government regulations may well be useful as they are. Rules expressing tax computations may be directly applicable. However, regulations, in general, still require interpretation in the context of the particular enterprise.

Framework business rules provide a basis for development of business rules for the particular enterprise, by focusing attention on particular issues and decisions that affect the operation of the business.

A Framework Example

The enhanced Telecom Operations Map (eTOM) from the Tele Management Forum (TMF) is a widely recognized industry framework. It is a business process framework for all processes of a telecommunications service provider. eTOM defines a process hierarchy similar to that previously described for the service-oriented analysis. The TMF has also defined a companion enterprise data model called Shared Information and Data (SID) that supports the Enterprise Logical Data Model requirement discussed in Chapter 5.

Figure 2.9 illustrates the eTOM framework at the enterprise level. It is described as a process framework that defines the business processes of the enterprise in a hierarchy. There are three major process categories: (1) operations, (2) strategy, infrastructure, and product, and (3) enterprise management. These are described as level-zero processes.

The Operations category reflects the primary business operations. The Strategy, Infrastructure, and Product segment defines processes for changes to the business; that aspect of agile enterprise architecture is addressed in Chapters 8 and 9 of this book. The processes in Enterprise Management are typically viewed as support services—those processes that are part of managing the enterprise, such as finance and human resources, but are not a direct part of the value chain.

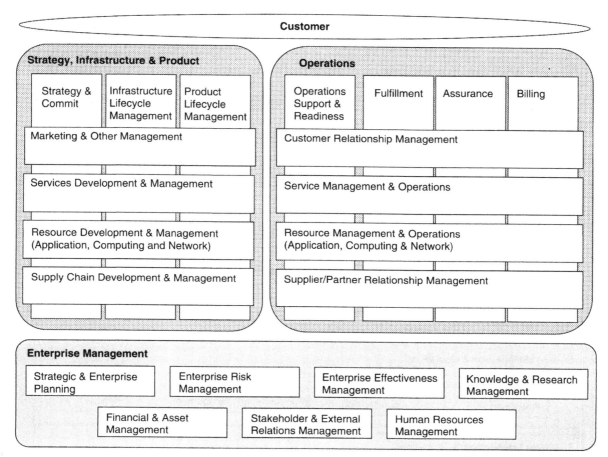

■ FIGURE 2.9 eTOM Framework.

The Operations and the Strategy, Infrastructure, and Product categories of Figure 2.9 are each divided by vertical and horizontal partitions described as level 1 processes. The vertical partitions reflect functional capabilities. The horizontal partitions reflect primary enterprise objectives that cut across the functional capabilities. For example, customer relationship management (CRM) is an enterprise objective that requires participation and support from each of the functional capabilities. These objectives are optimized operationally in the Operations segment and optimized from a business change perspective in the Strategy, Infrastructure, and Product segment.

Figure 2.10 shows more detail for the Operations process. These level 2 processes are shown at the intersections of the vertical and horizontal level 1 processes; each is in both a horizontal and a vertical level 1 process within the eTOM specification. Each of these level 2 processes is further detailed in subprocesses. Note that some level 2 processes span level 1 processes; these are effectively shared capabilities that may

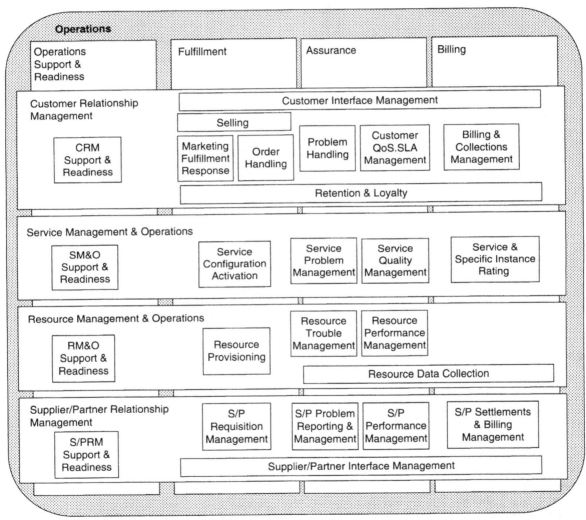

© TeleManagement Forum

■ FIGURE 2.10 eTOM Operations Level 2 Processes.

represent either shared work management service units or capabilities that can be further broken down to define shared operational service units. A similar breakdown is defined for the Strategy, Infrastructure, and Product level 1 process. More detailed breakdowns also exist for the Enterprise Management process. eTOM process models provide additional insights on capability requirements and the contexts in which they are used.

ROBUST VALUE CHAIN ANALYSIS

SOA brings added importance and rigor to the value chain concept. The general concept is to model the contributions of value toward the delivery of customer value. The value chain models that have been used for many years for enterprise analysis and strategic planning start with this general approach as a high-level abstraction, but as detail is expanded, they become essentially a work breakdown structure of capabilities needed to deliver value, but the chain of dependencies is lost.

We introduce a *robust value chain* (RVC) to be distinguished from the conventional value chain models and emphasize that it provides more rigorous support for strategic planning for new products as well as for improvement of existing products. It also supports better understanding of the consequences of operational problems. For brevity, we will refer to this dependency network model as a value chain or RVC model through the rest of the book.

Dependency Network

The RVC model is a dependency network of contributions to customer value where the customer may be an end customer of the enterprise or an internal customer. For example, value is provided for an internal customer when IT implements a new application or when human resource management enrolls an employee in a benefits program.

At a detailed level, the RVC is a use case of service units that contribute to the value delivered to the customer. We will refer to the participation of each of the service units as a value chain *activity*. The value chain is a dependency network because it depicts the dependencies of each activity (the service unit use case) on value provided by preceding activities. This is similar in concept to a PERT diagram of a project plan, where activities are shown as dependent on the work products of preceding activities. Unlike a PERT diagram, however, there may be no single start activity that enables the initial activities of a value chain.

■ **FIGURE 2.11** Value Chain Dependency Network.

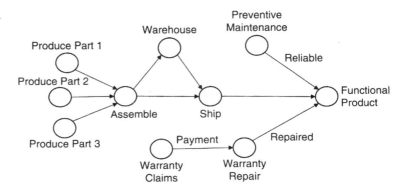

■ **FIGURE 2.11** Value Chain Dependency Network.

Figure 2.11 depicts a value chain dependency network. The value delivered to the end customer is designated a *functional product* in the diagram. The product may be maintained in reliable operation through a preventive maintenance program, and it may be repaired based on a warranty. The product, per se, is shipped by a shipping service unit either from a warehouse service unit or from the assembly service unit. The assembly service unit depends on parts manufactured by other service units.

The dependencies represent transfers of value. Examination of dependencies supports analysis of:

- The way capabilities impact customer value
- Significance of risks
- Product delivery weaknesses
- Significant sources of product costs
- Potential sources of identified problems
- Timeliness of customer response

Consequently, an RVC model is a valuable tool for management.

It is useful to develop the value chain starting with the completed value and working backward, just as it is useful to work backward from a completed project to develop a project plan. Generally this is not the way work gets done, although in some cases the dependency could be implemented as a request for the delivery of value and the request-response arrow would be in the opposite direction. For example, referring to Figure 2.11, warranty work generally gets done before the warranty repair organization receives payment. The warranty repair organization may actually request payment from the warranty claims processing organization and receive payment in return.

Abstract Activities

Except for the functional product, each of the activity circles in Figure 2.11 could be a service unit, or it may represent the contributions of several service units that have been aggregated to provide a higher-level abstraction.

We might provide a still higher-level abstraction by aggregating some of these activities, as indicated in Figure 2.12. These abstract activities look similar to the activities in the conventional value chain discussed earlier. It is desirable that these abstract activities correspond to organizational responsibilities so that there is accountability at higher levels as well as in the detail. For example, the Manufacturing organization should be accountable for the Produce Part activities and the Assemble activity. But note that the Manufacturing organization may do other things in other value chains or in the same value chain, so these aggregations are not comprehensive of the responsibility of the associated organization.

The objective of a RVC model is to develop the activity detail to the point where each value chain activity corresponds to a use of a service unit. Then, for each of the activities, the service unit should be able to provide a cost and duration for a service unit use case as a basis for product planning or analysis of operational performance for a particular product.

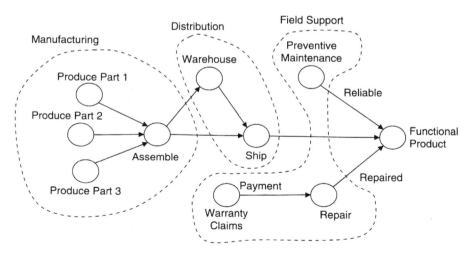

■ **FIGURE 2.12** Value Chain Abstraction.

These activity costs and durations can then be aggregated to provide an overall cost and time to deliver the product to the end customer. Note, of course, that some activities occur in parallel, and some activities may occur before a customer submits an order, for example, the parts may be produced in anticipation of orders. Consequently, not all activities are part of the critical path from receipt of order to product delivery.

The example value chain we discussed is a primary value chain—it focuses on the contributions of value for an end customer product. However, there are other value chains that contribute value within the enterprise. These value chains may contribute value for developing or maintaining service unit capabilities, or they may contribute value to the enterprise for effective management and governance.

Hierarchy of Value Chains

As the enterprise achieves higher levels of SOA maturity, the scope of service-oriented analysis and value chain modeling should expand. The models should not only encompass the activities directly involved in customer value creation, they should also address all aspects of the enterprise. Figure 2.13 depicts this "enterprise value chain" perspective.

The *production value chain* focuses on the services that contribute value to the individual units of production—the primary value chain that is the focus of initial analysis. The *product value chain* expands the scope to include the product or service life cycle, including one-time efforts

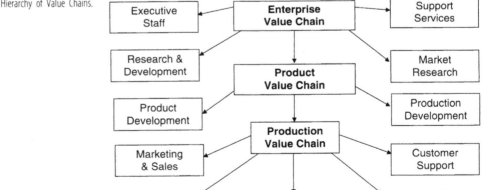

■ **FIGURE 2.13** Hierarchy of Value Chains.

to develop the product and the production capabilities. The *enterprise value chain* encompasses the entire enterprise, including the services that are not directly involved in providing value for a particular product or service but are required for the successful operation and viability of the enterprise.

We will return to discussion of the value chain later in this book, particularly in Chapter 9, where it has a direct impact on strategic planning and governance.

ENTERPRISE TRANSFORMATION PERSPECTIVES

Enterprise transformation requires significant business changes that may be disruptive to current business operations and are likely to involve significant investment in the transformation or development of information systems. This section briefly describes alternative approaches, first from a business perspective and then from an information technology perspective.

Business Perspective

Transformation to an SOA enterprise is a lengthy journey. It must be undertaken a step at a time, with each step along the way providing business value.

The ideal approach to transformation is to perform a top-down, service-oriented architecture analysis with reference to an industry framework, if available, to develop a strategic architecture, and then use the strategic architecture as a basis for defining a roadmap for implementation of service units with high business value. This ensures that all existing contexts for the use of service units are identified so that the definitions of these service units are more robust. It also ensures that full opportunities for economies of scale are realized and that service units are defined for optimization at the enterprise level.

However, a full, top-down analysis is very ambitious, takes considerable time and investment, and may be difficult to justify to managers who are not yet sure what a service-oriented architecture is or are skeptical about the benefits and risks. The SOA Maturity Model, discussed in Chapter 1, suggests that a top-down analysis is appropriate at level 3, where the enterprise has developed a capability, has established an infrastructure, and has realized business value from the implementation of some shared services.

Here we present several strategies for less ambitious efforts to start the transition to SOA. An actual undertaking may combine aspects of more than one of these approaches. All of them should take advantage of an industry framework to provide insight into the appropriate scope and capabilities of candidate services.

Note that any approach has the burden that some SOA infrastructure is needed to support a solution even of small scope, resulting in a higher cost for initial projects. Failure to invest in the strategic infrastructure in the beginning results in greater expense later, when the necessary infrastructure is finally implemented and must be retrofitted. Demonstration of the benefits of SOA to justify infrastructure investment, as well as minimization of retrofitting expense, should be factors considered in the selection and design of initial projects.

Departmental Scope

A top-down analysis may be performed on a division, department, or other segment of the business. Essentially this analysis defines how the department might be restructured to provide shared capabilities in different contexts. Of course, this does not identify other contexts outside the department for use of these services elsewhere in the enterprise. Therefore, the service definitions are likely to be less robust and more vulnerable to need for change as the scope of the SOA is expanded or the business continues to evolve.

Address an Identified Business Need

An identified business need may be associated with a business requirement to improve operations, replace a legacy system, or develop a new business capability. This can be approached from an SOA perspective, designing the solution as a composition of services. Since this is less likely to be within the scope of a single service unit, there may be significant coupling with other systems and business activities. Therefore, the analysis must consider the nature and number of points of integration to systems in other parts of the organization.

Identify an Opportunity for Economy of Scale

Particularly where an enterprise is a product of mergers and acquisitions, it is likely that there are capabilities replicated in the formerly independent companies. These may offer opportunities for significant economies of scale through consolidation. A service unit, or potentially a service group, may be identified as the best solution and adapted to provide appropriate service interfaces to the lines of business derived from the formerly independent companies. Depending on the number of implementations and scope of consolidation, this could demonstrate substantial savings from SOA.

Information Systems Transformations

Existing information systems can be a major barrier to enterprise transformation. Large enterprise applications have business assumptions and processes embedded in them, and it is likely that their scope spans multiple services that would better be defined separately. Most existing systems are not designed to accept electronic messages as requests and return appropriate responses, let alone exchange messages to use other related services. In addition, when a new service is created, other systems for which it accepts input or provides output must be adapted to behave like service users or providers.

Nevertheless, enterprise applications have evolved from traditional organizations that reflect some clustering of similar capabilities. So it may be possible to recognize potential strategic services, even if it is difficult to improve or adapt them independently. Enterprise application vendors have recognized the need to provide finer-grained capabilities to meet more specific customer needs, and the design of these more granular applications provides reasonable services designed for integration and gaining customer acceptance.

The following sections describe some information systems transformation scenarios. As noted, all scenarios require the implementation of an appropriate infrastructure.

New Application

Implementation of a new service unit application can provide the best alignment of the application to the service unit requirements. It can be designed to comply with the SOA infrastructure standards, it can utilize a BPMS for process flexibility, and it can be designed to make appropriate use of other services. However, it also is likely to be the most costly and risky approach.

Regardless of the approach used, a new service unit still requires implementation of adaptors for other systems with which it must communicate, as illustrated in Figure 2.14.

The new service application does not need to be adapted, but all the related services do. The nature of the legacy applications, the adapter

■ **FIGURE 2.14** New Service Integration.

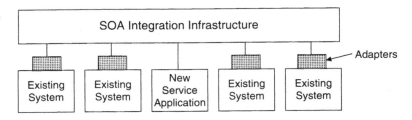

functionality required, and the number of adapters is a significant factor in the cost and risk of the project.

COTS Application

A commercial off-the-shelf (COTS) application could be available to support desired services. This substantially reduces the cost and risk of a new application, and, if it is designed to be service oriented, may provide a service interface that reflects industry best practices. It is important that the COTS application be designed to be driven by a BPMS, to provide maximum process flexibility and the ability to incorporate other services in support of the service unit activities.

Outsourcing

Outsourcing should be considered an option for commodity services—services that do not provide any competitive advantage. To implement outsourced services, the outsourcing service provider takes on most of the technical risk and much of the organizational risk by providing and integrating the needed capabilities as external services. Of course, there are other business factors to be considered when trusting an outsourcing provider to fulfill necessary business responsibilities.

Adapted Legacy Application

The primary reason to adapt a legacy application would be to consolidate operations that currently use different applications to perform the same business functions. This means that there are multiple legacy applications from which to choose. In addition to considering the functionality of the alternatives, the technology and architecture of the systems should be considered for flexibility, maintainability, and the cost of integration.

The legacy system may aggregate capabilities that should be available as separate services. If possible, it is desirable to provide separate service interfaces so that the services are available in different contexts, and users of the services are not affected if and when the legacy application is replaced.

Batch Process Legacy

Some legacy applications may be operating in batch mode rather than processing individual business transactions as they occur. Some applications should continue to operate in batch mode to achieve optimal results. For example, scheduling and distribution applications need to operate on a batch of transactions to optimize the relationships in terms of production sequencing, tooling change-over, vehicle loading, or timely delivery. Analysis and reporting activities generally reflect a point-in-time state of multiple transactions or elements.

For whatever reason, it may be appropriate to adapt batch applications to the service-oriented architecture. This effectively requires buffering. Input messages are held until a particular time or a threshold is reached, and then the batch processing is performed. Output messages go into message queues to be processed one at a time by receiving applications or services.

Rearchitecting

A variation on the adapted legacy application scenario is rearchitecting the legacy application. There are two potential benefits: (1) the application might be partitioned to provide more independent support of more granular service units, and (2) embedded business processes could be extracted and implemented in a BPMS for flexibility as well as service integration. Modernization tools are becoming increasingly powerful for analysis and transformation of applications. This effort could be limited to restructuring the application to provide better alignment with the strategic SOA.

Exposing and documenting business processes is a first step. Aligning business processes to SOA is fundamental to achieving the agile enterprise. In the next chapter we will examine the nature and role of business processes in greater detail.

Business Process Management

Business process management (BPM) is a management discipline that focuses on the design of business processes and continuous improvement of the speed, cost, and quality of business operations. BPM emphasizes the documentation of repeatable business processes as the basis for analysis and improvement. This includes both manual and automated business processes.

Information technology provides the ability to model business processes for more precise specifications and the ability to automate processes for controlled execution. Though not all business processes are automated, the speed, reliability, and discipline of automated processes suggests that most business processes should be automated, if possible. In particular, the processes that drive the integration and high-level execution of service unit activities should be automated to support consistent and effective operations. Consequently, though the agile enterprise includes manual business processes, our emphasis here is on the automated business processes that, for the most part, drive the operation of an agile enterprise.

In this chapter, we see how BPM complements and extends SOA to enable the definition, integration, and continuous improvement of services.

SOA brings a fundamental pattern to the design of business processes. Business processes do not exist independent of service units, and processes are confined to management of activities within an associated service unit. Business processes specify how service units produce value. For readers who are familiar with object-oriented programming, service units are like objects and business processes are like methods.

This represents a fundamental change in process thinking: A process is initiated with a request to accomplish some objective. The process and its associated capability belong to a service unit, and the process defines how a capability is applied to achieve that objective. Thus when a customer submits an order, order processing is the responsibility of a service unit.

In a small business, a service unit's responsibilities might include picking the products from bins and packing them and shipping them, whereas billing would likely be performed as a request to a billing process that is the responsibility of another service unit—possibly an outside accounting service.

In a large enterprise, the order-processing service unit has a more limited role so that various order-processing responsibilities can be fulfilled by specialists and may occur at different locations. So the order-processing service unit validates the order and maintains the order information and status but delegates other activities, such as a customer credit check, order fulfillment, and billing. The order fulfillment service unit may check inventory, delegate production to replenish inventory, and delegate packaging and shipment when the products are available. Therefore, from a customer perspective, the order-processing service fulfills the order, ships it, and bills for it, but internally these activities are performed by several different service units.

Each service unit has its own processes by which it receives and processes requests. Each service unit is responsible for the results, the management of the capability that it owns, and the use of other service units for delegated capabilities. Each service unit is a customer of the service units to which it delegates.

As a result, SOA provides an architectural context for business processes that support sharing of optimized processes and the associated capabilities in multiple contexts, producing economies of scale and improved enterprise agility. New standards for business process modeling support this architecture and provide a level of abstraction that enables businesspeople to understand and manage their business processes, including both those that are performed by humans and those executed by computers.

The work of the enterprise is performed by service units and driven by processes. The fully agile enterprise has been achieved when a significant new business opportunity can be addressed by specification or adaptation of a few business processes that extend, engage, or complement existing business services to develop and deliver a new product or service to customers. The introduction of information technology has enabled the execution of business processes to be automated, increasing the efficiency of process coordination and control and adding the ability to more quickly define and change business processes.

Since business processes drive the performance of work and relationships between services, they also are a major factor in the optimization of business performance. They determine the coordination of tasks and thus address factors that are beyond the scope of control of individual task performers. As such, business processes provide an important management perspective on the speed, cost, and quality of enterprise operations as well as the contributions of individual performers.

Information technology can greatly improve process visibility. Business process models expose the design of business processes. Runtime monitoring tools enable workloads and performance to be observed in real time. Operating statistics and audit trails support analysis of processes for process improvement and accountability.

In this chapter we begin by discussing business process concepts and modeling tools. We then consider how processes are used to implement different operating modes that consequently affect the design of services. We then focus specifically on the impact of SOA and the nature of choreography for the specification of service unit interactions.

BUSINESS PROCESS CONCEPTS

A *business process* is an orderly execution of activities to achieve a desired business result in response to a request or event. A process defines the work to be done, who does the work, when the work is done, and why (that is, the process objective). A process starts when there is a need to achieve the process objective in a particular context. We discuss processes initiated by events in Chapter 8.

Figure 3.1 illustrates the definition of a simple order process. The purpose is to respond to customer orders. The circle on the left designates the starting point. The bold circle on the right designates the end. The rounded rectangles in the middle represent activities to be performed.

■ **FIGURE 3.1** A Simple Order Process.

An *activity* is an element of a business process that defines a unit of work to be done. It may be work done by machine or human or delegated to another process. The arrows designate the sequence in which the activities will occur. The process has three activities: Edit Order, Fulfill Order, and Bill Order. We have not determined in this diagram where the order comes from nor whether the activities are fully automated or performed by humans. We might later decide that the activities use other services to fulfill their responsibilities.

This process is performed for each customer order received. If multiple orders are received, each order follows the same process. We may refer to each of the executions of the process as a *process execution* (that is, an execution of the process definition). The customer order is an input to the process and defines the context in which the process operates. Typically, instead of referring to the process execution, we refer to the order that is being processed, so order 101 may be completed while order 102 is being filled and order 103 is being edited.

We have not indicated any consideration of the management of resources to process these orders. It could be that each activity is performed by a single person, and thus orders are processed by each activity, one at a time. It could be that due to the cost of getting the orders from the Edit Order activity to the Fill Order activity, the orders are collected in batches. On the other hand, it could be that orders move through the activities, independently, as they are received. Such issues are considered in the implementation of the process based on the technology involved, the resources and optimization of timeliness, cost, and quality. We have not defined the technology used to implement this process; it could be electronic or it could be performed solely by people working with paper orders and voice communications and carrying the orders from one desk to another.

We have also not indicated what happens if the process cannot proceed as expected. For example, the order may have errors that must be corrected before it can be filled, or there could be insufficient inventory to fill the order. These issues must be addressed as the process is developed in greater detail.

Process Context

In Figure 3.1, the order defines the process context—who it is for, the products being ordered, data about the quantities, and prices. Though the process definition describes who, what, when, and why in general terms, the order contains specific data provided by the requester that further defines what is to be accomplished. We may think of this as a document with fields containing the appropriate data. The document has an identifier—for example, the order number—that can be used to refer to the request and the state of the activities performing the request.

As the order is processed, additional data may be accumulated about the manner in which it is processed. For example, there may be a translation of the customer requirements to the actual parts that satisfy the requirement, or there may be a reference to the storage bin from which a part is to be pulled. Such information may become part of the process context—that is, relevant information about the processing of each particular order.

Some of the context data is important for processing the order but is of no interest to the requester. However, the data that come with the order and the data returned to the requester must be meaningful to that requester. These data should be described by a shared data model so that there is no confusion about their meaning. Within an enterprise, these data also should be part of an enterprise logical data model so there is a common understanding of data exchanged even if a service unit implementation uses a different representation internally.

Roles

Processes don't actually do work; they direct the performance of work. To actually accomplish work, the process delegates responsibility to a person or team, to a computer application (for recordkeeping or computations), to a machine (for example, a manufacturing cell controller), or to another service unit that defines how the work is done in greater detail.

To delegate work, a process definition specifies a "role" for the performer. A role is the specification of a relationship that defines expectations, the capability required, and other qualifications that ensure the performer's ability to meet the needs of the process. For some roles, particularly where an internal, shared service is used, there may be only one candidate, but where people are the performers, there typically is more than one candidate. When the process is executed, the selection of performer may be further refined based on the specifications of the particular request.

Figure 3.2 depicts people assigned to roles (this is a non-standard notation for illustration purposes). This might be a process in a small

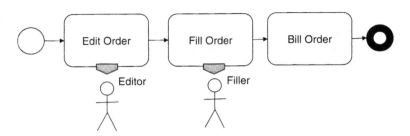

■ **FIGURE 3.2** Process with Human Roles.

enterprise where two people do the work of processing and filling orders. In this process the roles define the need for persons to do the work of editing and filling orders. There may be several people available to do this work, but the roles specify the qualifications of persons required to do the specific work.

For a particular order in a process execution, a particular person must be assigned to edit the order and a particular person must be assigned to fill the order. Typically, the need to fill a role is posted on work queues of qualified persons, and an available person accepts the assignment.

The Editor role qualifications might also be based on the context of the process execution such as the class of product being offered. So the qualifications might include a requirement that the performer be skilled in editing orders for the particular product group. The same concepts can apply when the performer is a computer application or another service unit. Different applications or specialized processes may be appropriate for editing different product groups.

Particularly where the performer is a human, we give the role a name; in our example, we might name the roles Editor and Filler. This is useful in dealing with humans as shorthand for describing an assignment. Where the performer is an application or another process, we don't necessarily assign a name to the role, because the selection may be predefined, so we just specify the participant (for example, the application or service).

Collaboration

Briefly, a *collaboration* is an interaction between peers to achieve a result with mutual benefit. We might describe the relationship between a business process and a person that fulfills a role as a collaboration, particularly if the person interacts with the process to perform multiple, related activities. It is more important to formalize the collaboration when the participants are not people but processes of other service units. In both these types of collaborative relationships, the service user's process specifies the role of a service provider and the service provider's process specifies the role of the service user. The collaboration specification defines the interactive relationship between these roles for exchange of information and delivery of value. The roles defined by the user and the provider may each define qualifications for the other participant.

Under some circumstances, the name of a role has additional importance within a single process. Suppose that the process in Figure 3.2 would be more efficient if both roles were performed by the same person for any particular order. We could specify this in the process definition by giving both roles the same name. So when the process executes, John Doe might be assigned as Editor in the first activity. When the process reaches the Fill Order activity, the performer role is specified again as Editor, and John Doe has already been assigned to that role for this process execution. As a result, John Doe is expected to perform the Fill Order activity as well.

John Doe may actually be working on several orders. Each of these orders is being directed by a separate execution of the Simple Order Process. When John is asked to fill an order that he edited earlier, he doesn't necessarily know which order he is now being directed to fill. The process context provides this information, specifically the order number. So John may have a paper file for each order, and when he's asked to fill an order, the order number directs him to the appropriate file. John's relationship with the process is no longer a request-response relationship that ends with completion of a specific activity, but rather we characterize it as a collaboration, a continuing interaction regarding a particular subject matter.

Applications and other processes may also engage in collaborative roles. Let's consider that the Simple Order Process is being used in a large company. The Edit Order and Fill Order activities each may be delegated to specialized service units that focus on particular product lines or geographical areas. The appropriate service unit for each activity can be selected based on request parameters and invoked when that activity is executed. Again, the same specialized service unit may edit the order and fill the order, so it interacts with both the Edit Order and Fill Order activities. The use of the specialized service unit is no longer a simple request-response; it has become a collaboration.

For further discussion of the nature of roles, see the discussion of choreography later in this chapter and role-based access control (RBAC) in Chapter 6.

■ **FIGURE 3.3** Expense Report Process.

■ **FIGURE 3.3** Expense Report Process.

Organizational Context

Processes not only direct the performance of work, they also provide the opportunity for control. Figure 3.3 illustrates an Expense Report Process whereby one of the activities is approval of an expense. This same process might be used throughout a large corporation. The Expense Approver role may be filled by many different managers. For a particular expense report, however, acceptable approvers are very limited because the Expense Approver role specification restricts approvers to people with a specific relationship to the expense submitter.

For expense approval, as with many other approval actions, the appropriate approver is determined by reference to the organization structure. Generally, the preferred approver is the manager of the person reporting the expense. If that person is not available, the manager's manager may be the alternative approver. Furthermore, the amount of the expense may be a factor. Approval may be required by the manager, and if the manager does not have sufficient authority, the expense may be referred up the chain of command for approvals until it reaches a manager with sufficient authority.

Thus approval is most likely a subprocess or a separate service. Different kinds of approval may involve different approval processes. Approval for a capital expenditure may require review of the details of the proposal by another organization and review of budget considerations by yet another organization. The approval process is a critical aspect of accountability and control. We might define the approval process as a process of a shared approval service to implement consistent controls throughout the enterprise. In the case of the expense report, the expense submitter and approver are participants in the approval process, but they are most likely not employees of the service unit that owns the approval service.

PROCESS MODELING

The design and refinement of business processes is fundamental to management of an enterprise. Managers should be able to participate in the design of processes and understand the operation of the business in terms of the process specifications. When something is late, a cost is excessive, or there are frequent defects in a product, a manager should be able to understand the source of the problem in terms of the processes and the service units responsible for those processes in order to ensure a prompt problem resolution.

Modeling Languages

Before computer-based modeling tools, managers and systems analysts would draw diagrams on paper with boxes and arrows to depict the flow of control or work products, or they would write "playscripts" expressing the sequence of "who does what" in a tabular structure. These models were cumbersome and inflexible.

Computer-based tools were developed to help design and manage these models. The computer can draw the boxes and arrows more quickly and precisely, the boxes and lines can easily be moved, and the computer can do some basic checks to see that the diagrams are consistent with process concepts.

These tools can provide specifications of processes that can be automated. Some tools provide high-level "business" views of processes. These high-level process models might be viewed as "requirements" for process automation specifications. Some tools are designed to specify process details, to resolve exceptions and abnormal terminations that must be precisely defined for automated processes.

Standards of the Object Management Group (OMG), an international standards organization, have been developed to provide robust modeling for business processes, including both those performed by humans and those that are automated. *Business process modeling notation* (BPMN) was developed to give businesspeople standard graphical modeling elements so that they could share and collaborate on business process diagrams.

The BPMN graphics have been implemented in many *business process modeling systems* (BPMS) for specification of automated processes. However, due to differences in interpretation and technical approaches along with proprietary extensions, BPMN diagrams are not entirely consistent from one tool to the next. Until recently, there was no standard for exchange of BPMN diagrams. XML Process Definition Language (XPDL) was developed by the Workflow Management Coalition for this purpose. However, though XPDL may repeat the same diagrams in the new tool, due to variations in interpretation of the graphics a process model transferred from one tool to another still may not produce the same runtime result.

The Business Process Definition Metamodel (BPDM) was developed by OMG as a computer-based representation of BPMN diagrams to provide a platform-independent modeling (PIM) language for business-level process modeling. The rigor of designing the computer language clarifies the meaning of BPMN graphics. Insights on modeling processes for SOA have made BPDM more robust than BPMN, particularly for reconciling an internal process with a specification for interaction with another process (that is, a choreography). Finally, BPDM supports XML for Metadata Interchange (XMI) a standard form of model exchange, so business process models can be exchanged between tools and interpreted consistently. At the time of this writing, an OMG initiative is under way to reconcile BPMN and BPDM to a single language specification, called Business Process Model and Notation (BPMN) 2.0, preserving the BPMN brand.

Some tools translate BPMN models to languages designed for automation. For example, Business Process Execution Language (BPEL) is an alternative language used for specification of automated processes. It is likely that tools relying on BPEL will be phased out in favor of tools that implement BPMN models more directly and display the processes in terms of BPMN graphics during actual execution. This will simplify BPMN application and will improve understanding and control of the business processes.

BPMN 2.0 will provide full representation and integration of choreography. Choreography provides a shared specification of the interaction between participants in a collaboration. BPEL and XPDL do not address choreography. There are currently two alternative choreography specification languages: Web Services Choreography Definition Language (WS-CDL) from the World Wide Web Consortium (W3C) and e-business Business Process (ebBP) from the Organization for Advancement of Structured Information Systems (OASIS). Both these languages are based on XML. It may be appropriate to transform the choreography specification of a BPMN model to a choreography specification in one of these languages for runtime specification of service interactions.

Process Modeling Notation

BPMN has been widely accepted as a business process modeling notation (that is, a form of expression) even though in practice there are some variations in the interpretation as well as some proprietary extensions. However, with the more robust capabilities developed through BPDM, it is unlikely that another standard graphical notation will emerge in the near future. The following subsections provide a brief presentation of BPMN that enables managers to participate in process design and understand the specification of processes that drive the enterprise.

Figure 3.4 provides examples of the use of some BPMN elements. Participants in the overall process are designated by the separated boxes (pools) with the names of the participants at the top. The focus of the diagram is on the process of the Seller. The Seller process (contained in the Seller pool) is started by a message from the Buyer. The Seller is partitioned into "lanes" representing different internal responsibilities. The Order Management organization (lane) edits the order, notifies the Buyer of acceptance or rejection, and obtains payment through the Biller after the order is shipped. The Warehouse (lane) fills and ships the order using the Carrier. Messages are exchanged between the Seller and the other participants. The Seller process ends if the order is rejected or after the Seller receives payment from the Biller.

Figure 3.4 indicates exchanges between participants that could be expressed in a choreography, but the sequence of exchange is defined

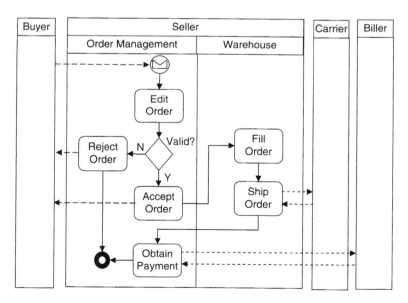

■ **FIGURE 3.4** Seller Internal Process.

by the internal process of the Seller, and a choreography would not expose that detail. In addition, a choreography would include the sequencing of exchanges of the Biller and Carrier with the Buyer along with the relationships of those exchanges with the Seller exchanges.

BPMN has 11 basic graphical shapes, as shown in Figure 3.5. The figure also shows examples of frequently used variations on the basic shapes. Each of these shapes and some of their variations are discussed briefly in the following sections.

■ **FIGURE 3.5** BPMN Graphical Elements (Abbreviated).

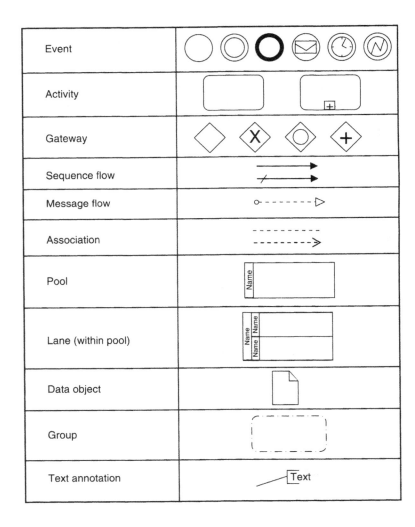

Event

An *event* causes a process flow to start or stop. There are three basic types: a start event designated with a simple circle, an end event designated by a bold circle, and an intermediate event designated by a double circle. A default process start is an empty circle, and a default process end is an empty bold circle. Icons appearing within the circle define specialized types of events—for example, an envelope designates a message, a clock designates a timer, a lightning bolt designates an error. A message can start, delay, or end a process. A timer can start or delay a process. An error can interrupt or end a process. There are other less commonly occurring events.

Activity

An *activity* is where work is done. The default is a *task*, which denotes that there is no more detailed specification of the activity. A *subprocess*, designated with a plus sign (+) in a small box, indicates that the activity is performed by a more detailed process. The process may be embedded and the activity can be expanded to show the detail, or the subprocess can be independent, meaning that it exists outside the current process and may be shared with other processes. Other activity specializations represent activities with repeated or concurrent executions.

Gateway

A *gateway* is a point in the process where flows converge or diverge. The default gateway (empty diamond) is an *exclusive or*. It provides for inputs from alternative paths to proceed on a single output path. If there are multiple output paths, only one can become active as specified by conditions on the outgoing paths. The *exclusive or* may also be designated with an X in the box. An *and* gateway, on the other hand, requires all inputs (from concurrent paths) to be active before it proceeds, and multiple outputs proceed concurrently, creating parallel paths. It may be called a *fork* for multiple outputs or a *join* for multiple inputs. The *and* gateway is designated by a plus sign (+) in the box. There are other less frequently used gateway types designated with other icons.

Sequence Flow

The solid arrow designates the *sequence* of execution of activities, events, and gateways. The arrow enables the execution of a target activity, event, or gateway when the activity, event, or gateway at the start of the arrow is completed. Where there are alternative paths, as from an *exclusive-or* gateway, the default path may be designated by a hash mark across the arrow.

Message Flow

A *message flow* is designated by a dashed arrow. A message flow comes into or goes out of a business entity (that is, a pool, discussed in a moment). Messages may be exchanged between processes or between a process and another system. With BPDM, the agreed-upon specification of the sequence of message flows can be expressed in choreography.

Association

A document or other object may be associated with the process elements using a dashed line or arrow. The arrowhead is optional and may be used to indicate whether the object is an input or output to the associated process element.

Pool

A *pool* designates a business entity responsible for the process contained in the pool. Processes are bounded by the boundary of the pool. Actions that cross pool boundaries must be represented with message flows. In Figure 3.4, Buyer, Seller, Carrier, and Biller are pools because they represent independent organizations. The Buyer, Carrier, and Biller pools are shown as empty because the focus of the diagram is on the Seller process, but the diagram implies that they have processes that send and receive messages, even though details of the processes are not known from the perspective of this diagram.

Lane

A *lane* is a segment of a pool that represents a organization or person within the pool organization that is responsible for the process elements contained in the lane. Lanes represent the roles of various participants in a process within a pool. In Figure 3.4, Order Management and Warehouse are lanes within the Seller pool. They represent roles within the Seller organization. The Seller has overall responsibility for the process. The Warehouse has responsibility for the activities in its lane—Fill Order and Ship Order—and Order Management has responsibility for the activities in its lane.

Data Object

A *data object* is a unit of information that may be produced or used by a process element within a pool.

Group

A *group* is a graphical representation of a shared characteristic of the process elements it contains. A group is not expected to have functional significance to the process flow but is used essentially for documentation.

Text Annotation

A *text annotation* is information added to a diagram to clarify the intent. It is documentation only. It is usually linked to a model element with an association line.

Attributes

BPMN also defines attributes associated with the graphical elements. These attributes are additional data that do not appear in the diagram but would typically be accessed in a BPMN tool by selecting the graphical element (for example, in a popup window).

Business Process Management Systems

BPMS manage the automation of business processes. Some of these have evolved from workflow management systems where the focus was replacement of paper flow for coordination of human activities. BPMS became the popular terminology as business process management (BPM) became a popular management discipline and automated processes became a more integral part of enterprise integration and electronic commerce.

Business processes should first be modeled at a business level where both manual and automated processes can be modeled without concern about the details of process execution in the particular implementation technology that is used. It is desirable to have a single modeling language to design business processes across the enterprise. A modeling tool that is BPMN compliant is recommended for this purpose. A tool that is also BPDM compliant supports robust modeling capabilities, where complementary executable processes (orchestration) and exchange processes (choreography) can be represented and where the models can be exchanged in a standard form between different modeling tools.

However, when processes are to be automated, it may be necessary to transform the process models to the language and design constraints of a particular BPMS product. Most enterprises already have one or more BPMS. Some BPMS will support BPMN and BPDM directly so that no transformation is necessary, and it will only be necessary to extend the process models to deal with all variations in the process that may result from unusual requests, violations of business rules, or error conditions. In other cases, the process models must be transformed to a proprietary language and may require adjustments to accommodate different design constraints imposed by the BPMS. With the development of BPDM, BPMS vendors are more likely than before to provide automated transformation capabilities from BPMN/BPDM models to their proprietary languages. There may still be manual involvement in design decisions required in the transformation as well as the development of additional process detail.

Where processes are not already automated or systems are being replaced, a BPMS should be selected that not only minimizes the work of transformation but also provides additional capabilities that improve the ability to analyze and improve business operations and to rapidly implement significant business changes. The following list highlights some important capabilities:

- Active processes can be displayed in a form equivalent to the models developed at a business level for monitoring current activities.
- A specific process execution (for example, the process for a particular customer order) can be examined and modified for that order, online if necessary, to resolve a problem.
- Statistics on process execution can be captured for process monitoring and analyzed to identify delays, bottlenecks, and possible sources of defects.
- Limits can be set on the duration of specific processes or activities to raise alarms when individual process executions are delayed.
- Process execution can be simulated using statistics derived from actual operations and assigned parameters, to evaluate problems or alternative process designs.
- Complex decisions should be implemented as rules (for example, order editing or claims processing). These rules may be incorporated directly into the BPMS, or a rules engine product may be invoked at points in the process where such decisions are made.

The BPMS marketplace is continuing to evolve as a result of emphasis on BPM, the development of standards, the need for integration of processes that span the enterprise, and the implementation of SOA.

Design Objectives

As an enterprise moves toward an implementation of SOA, business processes are analyzed, formalized, and redesigned. In addition to the design objectives specific to particular business activities, general process design objectives should be considered. Examples of process design objectives are as follows:

- *Process visibility.* Business processes should not be embedded in application code but should be expressed and deployed in a form consistent with the business process models that are meaningful to the businesspeople that own and use the business processes. The BPMS should expose the status of executing processes in terms of the processes as modeled.

- *Minimum coupling.* The purpose of a process should be clearly defined and should minimize dependencies on other processes, such as shared data or complex message exchanges.

- *Separation of duties.* An action that could personally benefit a participant must be approved by an authorized person who does not have personal gain or other conflict of interest associated with the action.

- *Service boundaries.* A business process must be owned by the service unit responsible for capabilities the process applies, and the process must begin and end within the service unit. The process may use other, shared, external services through defined interfaces, but the owner remains responsible for the overall result.

- *Continuity of roles.* A business process should minimize the transfer of responsibility among people within the same service unit, to reduce individual orientation overhead and improve accountability for results.

- *Participant discretion.* Actions delegated to human participants should avoid unnecessary limitations on discretion to enable the individual to optimize his or her performance and deal with circumstances that cannot be anticipated in the design of the process.

- *Accountability.* Individuals and external entities (for example, business partners) must be accountable for the actions they take and the data they provide when supporting or participating in a business process through electronic signatures.

- *Request-response structure.* In general, interactions between processes should be based on initiation by a request, with a response when the request has been satisfied or the action has been otherwise terminated. In this way the requestor retains responsibility and can take appropriate actions if the request is not satisfied or the response is not timely.

- *Process-level integration.* Integration of services and applications should occur only through the interactions of business processes. Service requests and responses are interactions between service requesters and service units and should be mediated by business processes that can be monitored and controlled by service unit personnel.

OPERATING MODES

Business processes can have different operating modes to achieve different kinds of business objectives. These modes affect the overall design of the process and may require specialized BPMS capabilities. Examples of a number of different process modes are discussed in the following sections.

Workflow

The traditional workflow mode moves a request through a predefined ordering of activities. This is typical of a paper-driven process in which an order moves from one activity to the next or often one desk to the next, where the necessary tasks are performed. Some workflow processes will provide for sequences of activities to occur in parallel.

Case Management

Case management represents a variation on the workflow mode. Here a case represents an ongoing, long-term obligation to manage services. The case manager may initiate a variety of processes (that is, services) as particular needs arise and is responsible for ensuring that the desired result is achieved in a timely manner. Typically, the process is tailored for the particular case and may be modified, ad hoc, as new requirements arise. Requests for services for a patient in a hospital might be handled in this way. The patient's hospital stay is an overall process that manages the specific services required for admission, diagnosis, treatment and discharge. The overall hospital-stay process is part of the inpatient service provided to the patient.

Job-Shop Mode

In a job-shop mode, a unique, one-time process may be defined for each incoming request. For example, let's say that a special machine tool is to be built, and sequences of tasks are defined for each part and for the final assembly. This may be viewed as a schedule of fine-grained services, each contributing their specialty as required to produce the desired, final result. Each of the services may be capable of a wide variety of outputs, defined by input specifications and confined to the associated resources and skills of that service.

Provisioning of some services in a telecommunications enterprise may take this form. In this case, the customer order may be translated to a schedule of installations and activations of service. Though the bulk of customer orders may be the same, the enterprise is capable of delivering a wide variety of service combinations.

This mode may be implemented using a rule-based system that configures a unique schedule based on requirements. This is distinguished from the rule-driven mode, discussed in a moment.

Production-Line Mode

In production-line mode, tasks are driven by the movement of the production line. The duration of each task is bounded by the length of production line allocated to the participant's station and the speed of the production line. Essentially, each station may be viewed as providing a service. Each unit of production may have specifications for the tasks to be performed at each station.

The ordering of units on the production line affects each participant's ability to complete his or her tasks since some units may require more or less work and some operations build on previous results. Production optimization is achieved by optimal "line balancing" of the order of production units so each operator can complete his or her work within his or her workstation.

Relay Mode

In relay mode, there is a defined sequence of services, but the overall process is driven by completion of processes. As each process completes, its work product is made available to the next service with no continuing responsibility. Typically, work products accumulate in buffers between services so that disruption of one service does not immediately affect continued operation of the other services. This mode is often used in combination with the production-line mode, where there are multiple production lines separated by staging areas.

There is an implicit process that drives the sequence of services, but there may be no organization responsible for managing the overall process to ensure timely completion of the sequence of services. Generally, progress will be reported to a monitoring activity that tracks completed orders at either the completion point or at relay points along the way. Orders not completed may be resolved by backtracking to identify the points of delay.

Rule-Driven Mode

Rule-driven processes use automated reasoning to determine the ad hoc ordering of activities based on requirements and circumstances encountered during the process. This might be viewed as managing a trip. As the traveler proceeds along the trip, different routes may be selected depending on road conditions, availability of overnight accommodations, and unforeseen problems.

A rule-driven process might be used where each customer order requires a unique product configuration that reflects consideration of dependencies between components such as configuration of a computer, an automobile, or an insurance policy. It also might be appropriate for field service operations where there may be a number of service requests outstanding and the work required for each may not be apparent until the technician arrives to diagnose the problem. In this case the focus of the process may be on managing the technician assignments to minimize travel time while ensuring a reasonably timely response to each service request.

Rule-driven processes are not common and require special tools, but they can be very effective where the operations are well defined but highly variable.

Development Projects

Development projects include product engineering and software development processes. These processes have the following characteristics: (1) each project has a distinct process, (2) they are typically long-running—months or sometimes years, (3) segments of the process may be iterative, converging on a solution, (4) specification changes may be common, resulting in rework, and (5) resource allocation is a significant management responsibility. Time and cost are subject to a number of factors, and completion is often driven by a target date. The process requires extensive planning and continuous monitoring and revision. The activities and processes are nonrepetitive so they are difficult to optimize.

The Systems Engineering Process Metamodel (SPEM) from OMG defines modeling elements for definition and management of such projects. Eclipse Process Framework (EPF), an open-source product from the Eclipse Foundation, is based on SPEM. These solutions support construction of projects from method libraries that specify common patterns. This is a still-evolving field.

Such processes apply to enterprise transformation initiatives. By structuring the enterprise as a composition of service units, SOA helps reduce the scope of transformation efforts and provides a structure, based on service units, to partition the work.

Product Configuration

Service units are expected to be shared by different value chains. The capability requirements may be the same, but the actual work done may differ. Product design often has a significant impact on process design. For example, in assembling a complex product, there is usually a logical order in which parts can be added. In some cases, there may also be collaborations with a customer or with other participants in the value chain where the collaboration requirements restrict the process design.

Differences in product configurations may be accommodated at three different levels: (1) the product components differ but operations are the same or equivalent, (2) each product has different requirements for the activities to be performed, or (3) different products or product categories require different processes. Some or all of these approaches may be required.

Where a single process is used for different products, the service unit accepts different request parameters and/or product specifications. The parameters and specifications may alter the process flow or the specifics of tasks performed. The objective of the service unit should be to support the implementation of product variations without tailoring processes for particular products.

The use of different processes for different products or product groups may be necessary, but it increases service unit complexity and reduces flexibility. Some of the operating modes discussed previously provide ways of addressing product diversity without defining specialized processes.

Note that service units may participate in different value chains and not all value chains produce end-customer products. Value chains for product development, support services, and executive staff services may also have variations that should be driven by request parameters and "product" specifications. Variation in purchase requests is a good example.

Generally, it is desirable for variations to be based on generic parameters either expressed in a service request or in referenced product specifications. Service parameters may be used to indicate differences in the context of the request, such as the originating country or language, whereas product differences should be expressed in parameters of referenced product specifications. The processes should be designed to operate correctly for all combinations of parameters unless some are defined as impossible or always unacceptable.

In all cases, agility is enhanced by the ability to change a value chain or create a new one by defining new parameter values and product specifications, but without changing the implementations of participating service units.

PROCESSES IN SOA

SOA brings new dimensions to the design, management, and technical support of business processes. The fundamental concepts of business processes have not changed, but SOA brings a discipline for composition, security, accountability, and sharing of capabilities. SOA brings the fundamental design principle that a process begins and ends within its associated service unit so it is under the control of the service unit manager. Capabilities delegated to other service units are engaged by requests to the other service units, invoking their internal processes.

While SOA defines an architecture for processes, processes define how services are performed and interact. A service unit is not implemented with a single process but is a bundle of processes that provide access to its capability in different ways, provide information to service users, and internally manage its capabilities. Processes support the exchange of messages between service units that is required for loose coupling and different modes of interaction. Finally, services sharing creates the need for control of access to processes. These concepts are discussed further in following sections.

Process-Driven Services

In general, the manner in which a service unit functions is driven by its business processes. These business processes, where appropriate, engage other services by initiating the business processes of the other service units. Consequently, the integration of service units is typically a relationship between business processes. Note that not all business processes are implemented with a BPMS—some may be manual and some may be embedded in applications.

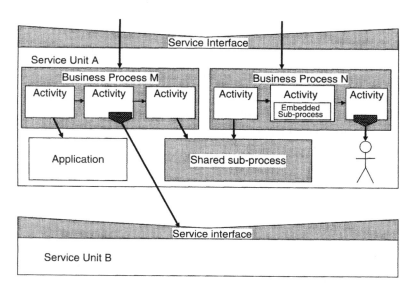

These relationships are depicted in Figure 3.6. Service Unit A accepts two kinds of service requests (two arrows entering from the top). These invoke two different business processes, M and N. Process M has an activity that invokes an application, an activity that invokes another service, and an activity that invokes a shared subprocess. The activity that invokes another service has a role filled by that service (designated by the small, pentagon element). The shared subprocess is used by different processes within Service Unit A but is not shared outside Service Unit A, so it is not a service offered by Service Unit A. It is not selected from alternatives, so it is not filling a role that would be selected based on a role capability specification.

Process N shares the subprocess with process M. It also has an activity that contains an embedded subprocess and another activity performed by a person. The embedded subprocess is essentially a bounded set of activities within Process N that supports treating those activities as a unit for such actions as termination and compensation (reversing the effects when a failure occurs). The person fills a role (again designated by the small pentagon element).

The key point of this diagram is to show the relationship of processes and service units. Service units contain one or more processes, and processes within service units may invoke other services, so the integration of service units occurs through processes. This is important for agility so that the use of service units can be defined and changed through the specification of processes.

Multiple Services of a Service Unit

The general concept of a service is commonly interpreted as accepting a request and providing a result. This is consistent with the concept of a process, in which a request initiates a process and a result is returned when the process is completed. However, a service unit provides a capability that may be offered in different ways; that is, requests may invoke different services. Different services initiate different processes within the service unit. So a service unit is not a single business process but rather a bundle of processes that provide access to a shared capability.

There may be one process that reflects the primary purpose of the service, but in many cases that is not enough, particularly if the requested process is long running or the same capability is used in different ways. The request requirements are more likely to change during a long-running process. For any requested service, the service user may want to change or cancel the request, or the user may want to obtain information on the request status. A service unit may offer the ability to obtain a price quote or forecast of delivery date prior to sending a request for its primary service. Complex processes are likely to involve specialized subprocesses within the service unit.

Services such as change, cancel, or status check, however, are dependent on a pending request. The initial request establishes a context and an identifier for reference to that context, such as an order number. Subsequent requests related to that original request contain the context identifier and are expected to perform appropriate actions in the identified context. The process maintains data regarding that context until the request is either completed or otherwise terminated. Afterward, historical data may be accessed using the same identifier.

A service may also accept different forms of request for different categories of customers or different product lines. Though this may increase the complexity of the service, it can improve the service's usability for service users. Different forms of request may also be used to enable a transition when technology or changing business requirements call for modification to the service interface. A new form of service request can be made available to transitioned service users while the old form of service request continues to be available for those service users who have not yet implemented the change. Internally to the service unit, it might be necessary to define different business processes for each of the input forms, but those may invoke shared internal business processes to drive the internal activities.

Loose Coupling

Loose coupling is commonly used to describe a store-and-forward, messaging linkage for integration where the relationship is defined by the messages exchanged. Service units generally interact through loose coupling to enable autonomy of participants. For a service unit to most effectively manage its resources and processes, it should not be driven immediately and directly by the processes of its users nor controlled by the processes of the services it uses. And from the service user's viewpoint, there may be delay between the receipt of a request and action taken on the request. Therefore, the service user should consider proceeding with related work rather than stopping to wait for the requested service to be completed. Loose coupling also enables a service user to abandon a request if there is not a timely response, although this assumes that actions can be taken to compensate for activities already completed.

Service users should anticipate that a service provider may encounter disruptions or delays and should design their operations to minimize the impact of these problems, depending, of course, on the level of service commitment of the service provider. In some cases, a service user may want to be prepared to switch to an alternative service provider to maintain desired levels of performance and continuous business operation.

Loose coupling also enables continuous improvement of a service. The expectations of service users should create minimal constraints on how the service is performed. The service provider should be able to design its internal processes with an understanding of the types of requests it will receive to support optimization, but it should not need to know how its users are performing their processes. The service provider should be able to continuously improve its processes without requiring changes by its users. It should also design its services to support future users addressing new business needs.

A higher degree of coupling implies limited autonomy. It may affect performance, quality, and flexibility of the user, the provider, or both. The following list describes aspects of a relationship that affect the degree of coupling:

- *Serialization. Serialization* refers to a relationship where the service must be completed before the user activity can proceed. This is often the case. The alternative is for the user to proceed and reconcile the result later. This may create a risk that the result of the service adversely affects the additional work done by the user, thus causing rework and possible defects.

- *Collaboration.* Collaboration occurs when the user and provider continue to interact during the performance of the service activity. This implies that some activities on each side are waiting for responses before proceeding and/or there may be a need for rework. Figure 3.7 depicts a collaboration relationship where the requesting process interacts with the requested service as the service is being performed. The dashed arrows represent messages exchanged between the processes executing in different organizations, depicted by *pools.* Changes to either the service requester or the service provider are constrained by the degree of coupling in this interaction. Such interactions may be specified with choreography, discussed later in the chapter.

- *Shared work product.* If the service user and service provider concurrently work on the same work product, there is a risk that there could be conflicting changes or competing access requirements that could delay progress. Certainly the processes of each are constrained by the need for cooperation and coordination.

- *Shared resources.* Shared resources could include equipment, people, or other facilities that must be scheduled or require coordinated use. It may be more difficult to ensure performance if a service unit does not control all its resources, but sharing can reduce costs through better utilization of the shared resource. Sharing is less likely to occur between a service user and service provider than is sharing between peer services that have similar capabilities or multiple executions of

■ **FIGURE 3.7** Collaboration Coupling.

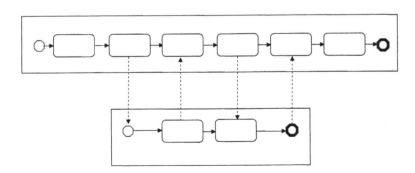

the same process. Requirements for liaison or progress review may involve sharing personnel and schedules for certain activities.

Transfer of Value

In Chapter 2, we discussed the relationship of a value chain to service units. The most straightforward transfer of value occurs when a service requester provides the required work product and materials with a request and the resulting work product is returned with the result. Then the value chain dependency corresponds to the request-response transfer.

However, service units often receive materials from sources other than a service requester—thus another dependency, and the resulting value or work product is often delivered to a recipient other than the service requester, in other words to a different destination than the service response—to satisfy another dependency. These transfers of value may take a variety of forms from a business process perspective. They are essentially exchanges with other service units.

The transfers could be implemented as request-response exchanges with the other services units. For example, a warranty repair service may receive a product with a request for repair and then after it is repaired give it to a shipping service to send it back to the customer. The response to the original request would confirm that the product was returned to the customer. To make the repair, the warranty repair service may diagnose a problem and then request replacement parts from other sources, potentially from a spare parts inventory activity or from an outside source. This is input of materials that did not come with the request but are required to comply with the request. These exchanges can be modeled with the business process modeling capabilities discussed earlier. Requests for parts can be assumed to obtain value to be added to the work product, but these are not explicitly different from the request for shipment except in the direction of movement of the physical work products.

On the other hand, a typical manufacturing operation does not use request-response exchanges for these transfers of value. Parts are produced in batches and delivered to designated assembly stations. The delivery of parts does not initiate a process to perform the next stage of production; the parts are available when the next stage of production occurs. A product being assembled is delivered to the next activity for subsequent work. This may or may not initiate a process in the next stage.

An operation performing assembly may have different instructions for assembling each unit of production, essentially a request for assembly, but probably not in the form of a typical service request. The completed assembly is then moved to the next station. These transfers of value are more like exchanges of business process events; the producer sends the work product to the next consumer.

In either case, these represent value chain links and service unit inputs and outputs. Each consumer depends on one or more producers to provide their work products before the consumer can proceed with its activity. As of this writing there is no standard way to represent these value transfers in a business process model.

A local convention can be adopted for designating messages or events that transfer input materials or output work products. These then provide the linkage from the business process models to the service unit inputs and outputs as well as the value chain dependencies. It may also be appropriate to distinguish the delivery of commodity materials. By viewing these as support activities rather than value chain activities, we avoid superfluous detail in the value chain model.

Security

Sharing services increases security risks. Services may be engaged by many more people from across the enterprise and possibly from business partners. Systems of many different organizations may submit requests, and a service unit may submit requests to services in many different organizations. Some of these other organizations may be external to the enterprise, and it is possible that service units that are internal today could be outsourced tomorrow.

A requester of a service as well as the provider should be authenticated to each other, their authorization to participate should be determined, data exchanged should have protection from disclosure or alteration, and accountability and control may require that electronic documents be signed. These issues are discussed in detail in Chapter 6. They affect both the requirements for BPMS support and the design of the processes.

CHOREOGRAPHY

Some services are used through a simple request-and-response interchange. The service user requests information and the information is returned, and there is no need to specify the interaction further. However, many transactions, particularly in an e-business context, are more complex and take the form of a collaboration. Often the exchange involves negotiation and possibly the participation of multiple organizations such as for financing and transportation after a sale.

Sequence of Exchange

In these more complex exchanges, it is important that participants in the exchange agree on the sequence of exchange and possible alternative responses. A specification of the agreed-on sequence of exchanges is called a *choreography*. A choreography is an essential part of a business-to-business agreement between service users and service providers. Again, the parties may understand the default choreography to be a request followed by a response.

Figure 3.8 depicts a choreography for a simple order placement. The notation is compatible with BPMN but is not yet adopted as a standard. The choreography is a description of the interactive behavior of the participants. The interaction is a product of the internal operations of both parties. The choreography is not executed like a typical business process but instead defines an agreement between the parties.

The choreography has a start and end the same as other processes. The rounded boxes designate interactions, that is, a message exchange as opposed to work being done. The solid arrows between interactions

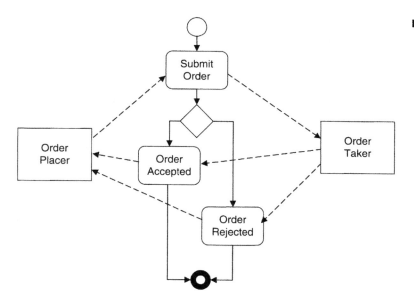

■ **FIGURE 3.8** Order Placement Choreography.

define the sequence of exchanges. A dashed line indicates the communication of a message from one participant to another. Note that BPMN also uses a dashed line or arrow to depict an association. Order Place and Order Taker are roles in the choreography representing participating entities. The choreography starts with a message containing an order from the Order Placer to the Order Taker. The Order Placer is the service user since it initiates the exchange and sets the context with the order content. The Order Taker receives the order and either accepts it or rejects it. The gateway (diamond-shaped) element in the choreography indicates alternative paths. The path taken is determined within the Order Taker's internal process that is private. The choreography only specifies that there are two possible responses to receipt of the order.

A choreography specification defines only the interactions between the parties and not how the parties perform their responsibilities, internally. Each party is free to define their internal processes as they like as long as they comply with the requirements established by the choreography. Of course, the content of the exchange or other agreements between the parties defines obligations of each as a result of the exchange, such as an obligation of the provider to deliver a product and the obligation of the requester to pay for it. This example choreography is quite trivial, but more complex choreographies may involve additional exchanges and participation of multiple parties that are coordinated to accomplish a shared result.

Complementary Internal Process

Figure 3.9 depicts an internal process of the Order Taker that supports the choreography of Figure 3.8.

Within the Order Taker's internal process, the Order Placer is a role. Up to this point, roles have designated the need for a capability to meet a requirement. Here, the Order Taker is the service provider, and its process interacts with a service user that takes the role of Order Placer. Although the Order Placer has initiated the exchange, the Order Taker may still have restrictions on the qualifications of the entity that fills the Order Placer role. The Order Taker's process is aligned to the choreography, but its internal process is actually more complex involving two decisions and fulfillment and billing activities.

This use of role may seem inconsistent with the earlier discussion of a role as a specification for delegation. Essentially the Edit Order activity depends on receipt of a message from an external participant.

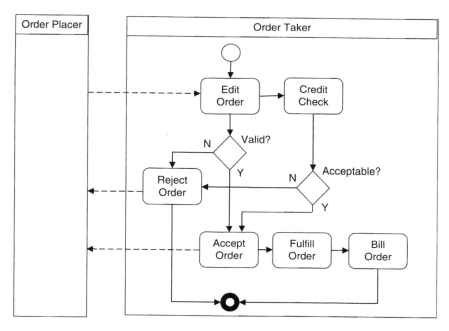

■ **FIGURE 3.9** Order Taker Process.

There could be different external participants involved, such as a transportation carrier, and they would each be assigned different roles for their interactions with the process. These are peer relationships, but they depend on each other and define roles to specify their expectations and relationships with each other.

The Order Taker internal process contains a determination of whether the order specification and customer credit are valid. This process is where the decision is actually made, and it determines the response to be sent to the Order Placer. These decisions correspond to the alternative flows of the choreography.

Extended Choreography

The Order Placement choreography may reflect only part of an overall business transaction. The complete service of the Order Taker, assuming the order is accepted, is to fill and deliver the order and receive payment. The Order Placement choreography may be viewed as a predefined component of a more complex choreography that we might call the Purchase choreography, shown in Figure 3.10. In the Purchase choreography, the Order Placer role of the Order Placement

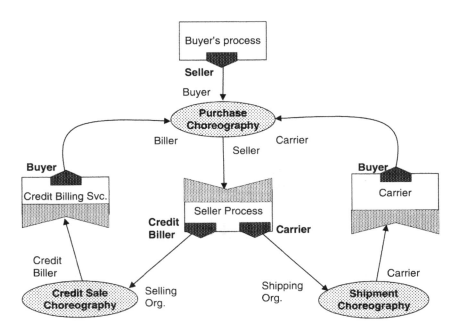

■**FIGURE 3.10** Roles in a Complex Choreography.

Choreography will be associated with the Buyer role, and the Order Taker role will be associated with the Seller role.

The Purchase choreography may involve additional roles. The product may be delivered by a transportation carrier, and the payment could be handled as a credit sale where the payment is collected by a bank.

Figure 3.10 depicts the Purchase choreography that includes the aforementioned Order Placement choreography, along with two additional choreographies: Credit Sale Choreography and Shipment Choreography. The illustration does not show the individual exchanges, but it does show the relationships of the parties to the choreographies and to each other. The component choreographies are depicted as ovals between the participants because they describe the interactive relationships between the participants.

The arrow goes from the Buyer (the service user), which initiates an order to the Seller using the Purchase choreography. The Seller fills the order and engages the transportation carrier using the Shipment choreography. The transportation carrier engages the Buyer identified in the shipment order for delivery of the product, thus filling its role as Carrier in the original Purchase choreography. The Seller also contacts the Credit Billing service for payment. The Credit Billing service sends a bill to the Buyer identified in the credit payment transaction, performing its role as Biller in the original Purchase choreography.

The complex Purchase choreography of Figure 3.10 involves participants in four different roles. The Credit-Sale and Shipment choreographies are independent of the Purchase choreography. The Purchase choreography contains three different pair-wise relationships: the buyer-seller relationship, the biller-buyer relationship, and the carrier-buyer relationship. In each case, a service user initiates the interaction and defines the context for the exchange. When the Buyer is contacted by the Carrier and then the Biller, the context of these relationships is tied back to the original purchase order, based on the order number, so the Buyer knows the basis for delivery and billing.

The Purchase choreography defines how these four participants interact to accomplish a sale, delivery, and payment. Three of the roles, Seller, Carrier, and Biller, could be performed by the organization acting as Seller. The Purchase choreography allows the Seller, Carrier, and Biller to be separate business entities but does not require it. The delegation of responsibility from the Seller to the Carrier and the Biller are not visible in the Purchase choreography, because those relationships are established independently. The Seller could perform the Biller and Carrier capabilities internally and still comply with the Purchase choreography, but there might be no Credit Sale choreography or Shipment choreography.

The three choreographies define interactive relationships between independent business entities. If these were interactions between service units within an enterprise, the interactions would likely be simpler, and there might even be informal agreements on the protocol. However, in a e-business relationship there must be a more formal basis for the collaboration. The choreography provides a formal specification of what is exchanged and when. The content of the exchanges or other business commitments must establish the necessary obligations and trust to support the business transaction.

Also notice in Figure 3.10 that the Buyer requests goods with an order and receives goods delivered by the Carrier, so the Buyer experiences the satisfaction of the request. This is not a simple request-response interaction with the Seller because there are several interactions through the Purchase choreography. However, the Buyer receives closure.

The Seller may have a somewhat different relationship with the Carrier. In this case, the Seller could transfer the goods to the Carrier with a shipping order and consider the delivery done, trusting the Carrier to complete delivery to the Buyer. This is often the case with goods delivered by mail. For some goods, and for time-critical deliveries, however, buyers may expect the Seller to keep track of the shipment and take action if delivery is not completed within a reasonable time.

The Seller has yet another relationship with the Biller. Here the Seller may request and receive payment from the Biller before the Biller takes any action to receive payment from the Buyer. The Seller's requirement for payment is satisfied, but the Seller has passed the obligation of the Buyer and burden of collecting payment to the Biller. The Biller must request payment from the Buyer, so the Buyer responds to the Biller's request with a payment and satisfies the obligation held by the Biller.

The Purchase choreography along with the Credit Sale and Shipment choreographies describe a complex set of relationships where choreography is essential to achieve orderly interactions.

It is important to note that although the examples have involved business-to-business interactions, choreography applies to interactions within an enterprise as well. Two departments may have processes that involve interactions over a period of time as the work progresses.

As noted earlier, simple request-response interactions don't require explicit choreography, but conceptually they have a choreography as well. Essentially, every relationship between processes has a choreography, though it may not be explicit.

Often a process interacts with the same person several times, as defined by the role assignment. This sequence of interactions with the person can be described as a choreography, and this specification may be useful for understanding the responsibilities of the person assigned to the role. Often, what at first appears to be a simple request-response relationship evolves to a more complex interaction, particularly if the request is not immediately followed by the response.

Choreography essentially defines the restrictions participants must observe to achieve a mutually beneficial outcome from a relationship. In the next chapter we will discuss business rules that are used to specify other forms of restriction on business operations.

Chapter 4

Business Rules

Business rules enable businesspeople to express requirements regarding *what* is required without needing to define the details of *where* and *how* the requirements are enforced in the operation of the business. Effective specification and management of business rules can ensure consistency in operating practices and compliance with regulatory requirements. The ability to change and quickly deploy business rules can have a significant impact on enterprise agility.

The value of rules in automated business systems is that they enable a businessperson to understand and express a requirement, based on understanding the business implications but without the need to understand the technology that applies it. Rules can also support complex decision making where all possible results are not explicitly programmed. For example, rules can be used to configure a product without explicitly defining all possible configurations, or rules might be used to load a truck with packages of different sizes and shapes. So rules can be used to enforce a spectrum of requirements, from configuring complex products to discovering a design defect. Rules are an important form of expressing knowledge and control.

There are significant differences between the various types of rules that may be called *business rules*. It is important that the types of rules be understood because the contexts of application, the forms of the rules, and the mechanisms of implementation vary. Based on consideration of the various types of rules, we consider the implications of SOA.

TYPES OF RULES

The term *business rule* has a variety of interpretations, depending on the context of discussion and the background of the participant. In general, a *rule* is a statement of truth of a relationship of two or more facts. So we might say "A customer must have an account number," or "A valid purchase order must have the signature of a person with appropriate authority." Or we might define an action to be taken when a condition is true: "If a customer does not have an account number, then one must be assigned."

Some rules may be incorporated in automated business processes or computer applications, and some rules must be applied to the behavior of humans. Where possible we should look for ways to manage and implement rules in automated processes and applications to ensure consistent application and improve control and flexibility.

The following subsections describe seven types of business rules: regulations, enterprise rules, production rules, diagnostic rules, event rules, qualification rules, and data integrity rules.

Regulations

Government regulations are effectively rules that define the bounds of legal behavior. Most regulations are expressed in a natural language (e.g., English), a form that requires some interpretation. In some cases regulations are intentionally vague to accommodate special interests or political pressures or to allow for a range of circumstances.

Regulations must be interpreted in the context of a particular enterprise, and the approach to application of the regulation may reflect consideration of risks of violation such as the likelihood of accidents, oversights, or mistakes, as well as the potential consequences to the enterprise and individual employees.

Some regulations are quite abstract, expressing an objective rather than a clear restriction on operations. The Sarbanes-Oxley Act, for example, requires accountability and control. Executives must ensure accurate corporate reporting. This requires measures such as separation of duties, disclosure of conflicts of interest, restrictions on spending authority, and independent review of operations. These measures are pervasive and must be addressed in the design of enterprise processes.

On the other hand, some regulations can be very specific. Tariffs, for example, define the rates to be charged for specific types of service. Taxes are usually very specific as well. Similarly, hazardous materials regulations can be very specific about precautions and prohibitions regarding use, storage, and transportation. It may be relatively straightforward to implement such regulations. But some regulations, such as the Corporate Average Fuel Economy (CAFE) regulations, are very specific but cannot be controlled directly since the target average depends on production schedules that are driven by market demand.

Most regulations are not published in a form that can be used directly by automated systems. There must be some transformation by humans to codify the required intent and identify where, if possible, the controls can be implemented in business processes or computations.

In the future, regulations may be codified so that they can be interpreted and analyzed by computers. The Semantics of Business Vocabulary and Rules (SBVR) specification from the Object Management Group provides a formal way to capture and express rules in a natural language-like form. In fact this facility enables the same rules to be expressed in alternative natural languages. The rules are represented in a computer model that can be used to analyze the rules for inconsistencies. The formal structure of the rules helps remove ambiguities. Eventually, it may be possible to use such rules to analyze business processes for potential risks and violations.

Enterprise Rules

Enterprise rules are those expressed by management to define constraints on the operation of the enterprise. These rules are referred to as *business rules* by a community of management consultants who specialize in the capture and application of rules expressed by executives. However, a reference to *business rules* is ambiguous outside that community.

An enterprise rule is a declarative expression of intent independent of specific business operations. For example, an enterprise rule might express that "any purchase of a personal computer or laptop computer must conform to an approved hardware and software configuration." The rule does not define an action to be taken but rather a constraint on business operations. At the same time there may be degrees of enforcement from a level of discretion, where deviation might be authorized under special circumstances, to a level of absolute compliance in cases where there could be civil or criminal liability. The computer purchase rule we mentioned might have a level of enforcement that allows exceptions with prior approval—perhaps approval by the manager of the personal computer support activity.

Enterprise rules are a mechanism for managing the enterprise. Other management directives such as strategic initiatives, high-level business processes, organization structure, and allocation of resources are important aspects of enterprise management, but they have only indirect effect on how the enterprise actually operates. Enterprise rules define management controls that can have direct effect on daily operations as well as longer-term activities.

Ideally, executive management should create and modify enterprise rules, and the rules should have immediate effect on the operation of the business. For example, consider an enterprise rule that "returns must be in original packaging, accompanied by the original receipt and received within 30 days of the sale." This rule might discourage some potential customers and alienate some current customers. The management might want to adopt a more accommodating return policy, such as "returns must be in original packaging suitable for resale, goods must be current stock items, and refunds are in the form of a company gift card." In a large retail enterprise, this not only has direct effects on the product return activities but also on advertising, and it should be expressed to customers when they are considering a purchase.

Technology for deployment of enterprise rules is still evolving. A major step forward was accomplished with the adoption of the previously mentioned Semantics of Business Vocabulary and Rules (SBVR) specification. SBVR defines a standard computer-based modeling environment for enterprise rules. This formal, computer-based representation of rules provides a basis for automation of deployment. Since the model can support multiple vocabularies, the same rules and the concepts referenced in the rules might be expressed alternatively in English, German, French, or other natural languages or vernacular. This can be important for proper understanding of the rules throughout a global enterprise, particularly if the rules must be implemented in human activities. In addition, the models support capture of the meanings of the concepts being modeled, independent of the language used to express them.

Using SBVR, we might express the personal computer purchasing rule suggested earlier in the following form:

> *It is obligatory that the equipment configuration of each personal computer is an approved configuration.*

Obligatory, as defined by the SBVR specification, indicates that the rule is expected to be true but may have exceptions. The key concepts are the *personal computer*, the *equipment configuration* characteristic of the personal computer, and the *approved configuration* that identifies one or more specifications. Though this rule might be enforced by the purchasing department, it should be applied wherever the purchase of new personal computers is being considered.

Application of this rule might be manual or automated. Evaluation requires the ability to access approved configuration specifications and the ability to compare the configuration of the computer to be purchased against the approved configurations. Since automated comparison of the configuration specifications might be quite complex, the comparison might be done manually, or the approved configurations might each have an identifier that is used to specify the configuration of the computer being purchased. Purchase requests that are not specified with an approved configuration designation could be assumed to be noncompliant.

Consequently we have an enterprise rule that may be applied in many places throughout the enterprise where purchase requests are being prepared while the rule is enforced in the purchasing department prior to issue of a purchase order. In the various departments originating purchase requests, the rule should cause a noncompliant request to be directed to an appropriate level of approval so that when it reaches the purchasing department, the exception has already been approved.

However, note that the action taken from the rule differs depending on the context. In the originating departments, the purchase request should be routed for appropriate approval. In the purchasing department, if the nonconforming purchase request does not have the required exception authorization, the request is rejected. This highlights the difference between enterprise rules and production rules, discussed in the next subsection.

Enterprise rules should be managed centrally, in a rules repository or repositories for specific categories of rules (e.g., operating rules, product rules, contract terms), and their deployment should be tracked for accountability and to enable reliable deployment of changes. This provides the opportunity to ensure that rules are consistent and to support traceability of rule applications.

Production Rules

Production rules define an action or result to be produced under specified circumstances. These can be thought of as *if-then* or *condition-action* rules. For example, "if a customer automobile order includes the exterior appearance option, then add chrome trim and decals to the bill of materials." Production rules might also be used to plan a trip or load a truck with packages of different sizes and shapes. In some cases, production rules implement enterprise rules in a particular context; in other cases they simply reflect the application of expertise, design requirements, or operating decisions appropriate to the particular situation. Where they implement enterprise rules, it would be desirable that there be traceability between an enterprise rules

■ **FIGURE 4.1** Production Rules Engine.

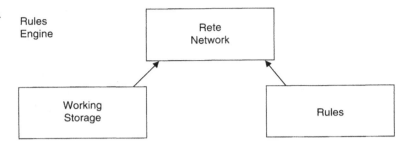

repository and the associated production rule to support change management and accountability.

Production rules are generally applied by a *rules engine*, as depicted in Figure 4.1. A rules engine is a software product that applies rules to a problem. Generally, the rules reside in the runtime environment and, on request, the data representing a problem to be evaluated is loaded into the rules engine *working storage*. A *Rete network* (pronounced *ree-tee*) is created to link the rules to the working storage for efficient processing. The rules engine determines whether any of the rule conditions are met. If the conditions of more than one rule are met, the rules engine has logic to decide which rule to "fire" (i.e., execute). When a rule fires, its action is performed. This action likely changes the data in working storage that defines the current situation; it may also cause some external effect. When the data changes, the conditions of a different subset of the rules may be met, and the rules engine again selects a rule to fire.

This general class of rules processing is called *forward chaining* because the action of each fired rule affects the selection of the next rule and the subsequent chain of actions. The generally accepted mechanism for evaluating, selecting, and firing rules is the Rete algorithm.

Production rules are used for planning and configuration. Most often they are used for complex configurations, such as computation of the payment for a health care claim or configuration of a complex product such as an automobile or a computer. For example, a rule may specify that "if a customer automobile order includes air conditioning, and if the order also includes an optional V-8 engine, then air conditioning compressor 1234 is added to the bill of materials." Another rule may specify that "if air conditioning compressor 1234 is included, and the order also includes power windows or power door locks, then the alternator must be replaced by a heavy-duty alternator."

Production rules might also be used for such computations as process planning, in-process inventory computation, design of experiments, or forecasting.

In general, a rules engine and an applicable set of rules are invoked at a particular point in a business process where there is a need for a complex computation to produce a desired result. This is typical of claims processing or product configuration. The rules engine is presented with all the relevant data, and the rules are applied. The rules engine returns a result, or it may return a failure to produce a desired result—the claim is invalid, the product cannot be configured, the solution cannot be reached.

The specification of production rules can be quite complex. The firing of some rules is dependent on the firing of other rules, as in the automobile configuration we mentioned. The rules engine defines a controlled environment in which the rules operate on a specific set of data that is affected only by the actions of the rules during the rules processing. For example, for automobile configuration, the rules engine would use the data that specify the requirements of the specific automobile to create a representation appropriate for rules processing, and it would produce a bill of materials in that specialized environment. It would not deal with other customer order information or other process variables. In addition, the rules engine introduces processing overhead for linking data to rules and rule selection. Consequently, a rules engine typically is not active throughout the execution of a business process but only at those points where appropriate, complex computations are required.

Alternatively, a process can be dynamically defined by rules. Where a process involves many variables and different actions for different results, production rules can actually determine the activities to be performed and their sequence as appropriate for the particular situation. Based on the state of the request and the work product, certain rules are available to fire. When one fires, it may perform an activity that changes the state of the subject matter, making other rules available to fire. In such a process, there is no obvious, predefined flow, just a set of rules. This differs from the typical rules engine because here activities are performed that are equivalent to activities in a conventional business process. Such processes can become very complex and difficult to manage, so this is not common practice.

Within conventional processes, *if-then* or *condition-action* rules are often applicable at many points in a process. These rules take the form of decision points, or *gateways*, of a process in BPMN terms. For example, a rule might state, "if acceptance of an order will cause the customer's credit limit to be exceeded, then the order must be rejected." This rule is quite straightforward and does not require a rules engine to perform the computation. Sometimes the same rule may be applied at multiple points in different business processes. For example, instead of rejecting the order in our example, the rule might be changed to offer the customer an alternative payment option. The credit limit rule might be applied in an order-change process as well, and a rule change should be reflected in both processes.

Today many production rules are embedded in application logic. When there are relevant changes to business operations, programmers must search program code to identify decisions that embody the current production rules. This can be expensive, time consuming, and subject to errors. There are application modernization tools available for mining business rules from legacy applications, but this still requires human analysis to distinguish business rules from less significant program logic. Even when these decisions are implemented in automated business processes, they may be overlooked when a change is required. Specification and implementation of processes and applications using computer-based models can provide this traceability, both to identify where rules are applied and to trace from the application of a rule back to the business requirement.

Diagnostic Rules

Diagnostic rules are used to search for an answer, such as to find a diagnosis that is consistent with a set of symptoms. These solutions are generally developed with *logic programming*. Prolog is the best-known language for logic programming. The rule-processing mechanism is also called *backward chaining* because it starts with a result and searches for an explanation.

We might think of the basic form of a logic programming rule as *then-if*. For example, the "result" might be, "the car won't start." We then look for potential reasons—in other words, things that, if true, would cause the car to not start. So, in a rather informal form, the rules might look something like this:

Car-wont-start(?) <=Battery-dead(?) or Flooded(?) or Out-of-gasoline(?)

Battery-dead(?) <= Lights-dont-go-on(?)

Flooded(?) <= Smell-gasoline(?)

Out-of-gasoline(?) <= Fuel-gauge-shows-empty(?)

Here the question mark (?) represents a reference to the particular vehicle under consideration. More complex rules might reference additional relevant entities or values.

If implemented as Prolog statements, the execution would start with the first rule, where we are interested in finding a potential reason that Car-wont-start could be true. In order for Car-wont-start to be true, one of the subsequent statements must be true, i.e., Battery-dead or .... If we consider Battery-dead, we see that the next rule evaluates Battery-dead. If Lights-dont-go-on is true, then Battery-dead is true and the cause of Car-wont-start is found. If Lights-dont-go-on is false, then Battery-dead is false and we return to the first rule (we backtrack) to examine the next possibility: Flooded. The nesting of rules can be very complex. The ordering and structure of the rules determines the order in which questions are asked. For example, if Lights-dont-go-on is true, we have completed the search and we need not ask about Smell-gasoline or Fuel-gauge-shows-empty.

The example is quite trivial; it fails to demonstrate many capabilities of Prolog, it does not cover all possible causes of nonstarting car, and the result is fairly obvious. Much more complex problems can be addressed; among the most sophisticated is mathematical theorem proving.

The following are examples of potential business application areas for diagnostic rules:

- Diagnosis of failures or malfunctions in complex products or equipment
- Diagnosis of problems and causes of variance in complex manufacturing processes
- Analysis of designs for identification of product defects
- Analysis of causes of market trends

Note that rules engines that implement production rules (forward chaining) also usually include backward-chaining capabilities where an evaluation of a condition requires examination of other conditions on which it depends. Thus, in the automobile configuration example, instead of adding a heavy-duty alternator when air conditioning and power windows are ordered, the analysis might add a heavy-duty alternator if the power consumption is high, and power consumption might then be defined in terms of multiple other alternative factors. These rules engine facilities may not include backtracking, so they would not be able to search for alternative solutions. The use of forward and backward chaining together may make the design and maintenance of the rules more complex.

Logic programming is important for implementing complex searches. The programmer can focus attention on defining the rules and does not need to deal with the mechanics of backward chaining and backtracking. Nevertheless, logic programming does require special skills and attention to the order in which statements are executed.

Event Rules

Event rules define changes of state that are of interest. There are an infinite number of events that occur in the operation of an enterprise, so it is essential that the multitude of enterprise events be filtered down to those events that require consideration. Rules can be used to accomplish that filtering.

There are certain events that are of interest outside the normal operating activity. These events may be of interest simply for reporting certain activity, or they may be *disruptive events*, which can reflect a failure, a variance beyond normal limits, an opportunity, or a trend. The implications of disruptive events are discussed in Chapter 8.

From an information systems perspective, an event happens when a system is updated to reflect an associated change of state in the enterprise. So completion of an order entry is an event, issue of a purchase order is an event, an account reaching a zero balance is an event, completion of a business process activity is an event, shipment of a customer order is an event, and a power failure is an event (if there is a power-monitoring system to sense it).

Event notices are often managed in a *publish and subscribe* infrastructure whereby sources of events send the event notices to an event notification service, which redistributes the event notices to interested recipients. So event rules should be considered at three levels: at the event source, at a point of distribution, and in a resulting action.

Event source rules identify events of interest and restrict the publication of event notices to those events that have been identified as being of interest. For example, an order entry event might be of interest if the order is greater than $1 million or the salesperson exceeds her quota. Rules must limit the event notices so that the system is not flooded with event notices of no particular interest.

When an event notice is forwarded to an event notification service, rules define which subscribers should receive the notice. Some notices may have multiple recipients; some may have none—for example, "notify sales manager John Jones if a $1 million sale occurs in his region." The notification service thus further limits the proliferation of notices and at the same time enables interested recipients to subscribe to notices of certain types of events, without the need to know where the notices originate. The distribution rules generally consider the type of event and associated information about the event.

Finally, recipients of event notices may use rules to decide what, if any, action is required. These rules might be characterized as *event-condition-action* (ECA) rules. They may consider the type of event and information associated with the event as well as other relevant information about the state of the enterprise or its environment and then perform an appropriate action. ECA rules are most often embedded in business processes or applications because they tend to stand alone. Rules may be used to evaluate the occurrence of related events, to infer the occurrence of a situation of interest. This is called *complex event processing* and involves specialized systems for event analysis. Complex events are discussed in Chapter 8.

In some ways these rules are similar to production rules because they are driven by changes in the state of the enterprise and they perform some relevant action. However, these rules operate in a loosely coupled, often distributed environment, and the actions taken are generally quite independent of the activity in which the precipitating event occurred.

Events generally drive side effects of primary activities. The primary activity is not concerned about others who are interested in the event. At the same time, the recipient is not required to know the source of the event notices. The difficulty of implementation is that though the recipient may expect to receive notices for all events of interest, (1) there may be unknown sources of potentially interesting events so that some events are not reported, and (2) a source may be applying an overly restrictive event condition so some events of interest are blocked.

Qualification Rules

Qualification rules define constraints on participation of people, services, or organizations in associated activities. These are of interest for process role assignments, for personnel assignments to positions in an organization structure, and for access authorization. Process roles are discussed in Chapter 3, access control roles in Chapter 6, and organizational positions in Chapter 7. Though rules can be used to express these various types of qualifications, the form of the rules and mechanisms of application vary. Qualification rules in an SOA context are discussed later in this chapter.

Data Integrity Rules

Data integrity rules are incorporated in data models and the design of databases. These rules may also be called *business rules* by developers of data models and designers of databases. These rules reflect constraints that exist in the real world. For example, a person cannot have a birth date in the future, and two people cannot have the same tax ID number. These rules do not change, and violation of these rules would indicate that the integrity of the associated database has been compromised. Consequently, in addition to being implemented in databases, these rules should be applied as data entry constraints and for validation of data received from other sources.

In some cases the rules incorporated in data models and databases are essentially enterprise rules—management decisions enforced by restrictions on data. This may be an effective way to enforce an enterprise rule, but rules embedded in database schema may not provide visibility and flexibility for the management of such rules. As discussed earlier, enterprise rules should be centrally managed and their deployment tracked.

IMPLICATIONS OF SOA

The primary implications of SOA are a result of two characteristics: (1) similar capabilities are consolidated and (2) users of services may come from across the enterprise as well as the extended enterprise. Consolidation provides better focus for the application of rules, whereas an expanded user community increases the need for well-defined controls. Application of the different categories of business rules in an SOA environment is discussed in the following subsections.

Regulations and Enterprise Rules

Regulations should not be applied directly to the enterprise but should be translated into enterprise rules appropriate to the particular enterprise. There should, nevertheless, be clear traceability between the regulations and the enterprise rules. This is not unique to SOA.

However, SOA makes it more straightforward to determine where an enterprise rule applies precisely because the affected operations are consolidated. In general, enterprise rules affect certain capabilities, so SOA makes it easier to identify the service units and processes that must be held in compliance. In addition, where an enterprise rule affects many capabilities, implementation may be facilitated through creation of a shared service that applies the enterprise rules and is invoked at key points in the processes of affected services. This parallels the use of purchasing, accounting, and personnel services to control vendor selection, ensure control of financial records, and achieve consistency in personnel administration throughout the enterprise.

Even more focused control may be realized where there is a service that manages relevant master data (see the discussion of master data management in Chapter 5). Changes in the state of the enterprise are reflected in the master data. Rules are relevant when changes occur that violate the rules. Rules can be evaluated at the point at which the database is updated.

Again, traceability of rule deployment should be maintained so that the effects of the rules can be assessed and changes to rules can be quickly and consistently implemented.

Production and Diagnostic Rules

Where production or diagnostic rules are used to solve complex problems, they are applied by a rules engine or specialized language (e.g., Prolog). Essentially they provide a specialized capability that must include the expertise to maintain the rules. Thus the specialized capability should belong in a consolidated service. In some cases the rules and associated engine should be provided as a distinct service that is used in multiple contexts. Diagnostic services, in particular, may be useful to a variety of users.

Rules implemented with rules engines are relatively easy to locate because they are already separated from the processes that use them. Rules that define decisions within processes are not so visible. However, the consolidation of capabilities within services should help identify the processes where certain rules should be implemented to narrow the search and reduce the number of implementations for changes of a single rule.

Consolidation of capabilities may also provide greater opportunity for the codification of complex decisions. Generally, a rules engine is used at a point in a process where a complex problem is to be solved. Consolidation may yield the economies of scale that would justify a rules engine solution. For example, computation of billing for specialized services might be a time-consuming manual process performed by individual, field service units, whereas consolidation of the billing function as a shared service might justify the development of a rules-engine solution.

Event Rules

SOA facilitates the identification of sources of internal events of interest because capabilities are more likely consolidated and processes more consistent. At the same time, the current approach to publication of events requires that each event be explicitly programmed. In other words, a process that is the source of an event must be designed to recognize the event of interest and publish a notice. The result is that either there are many unnecessary event notices published in anticipation of interest or there is a need to modify processes every time a new event notice is needed.

Events occur when the state of the enterprise changes, just as enterprise rules apply when the state of the enterprise changes. If there is a service responsible for master data management, then, like enterprise rules, event rules could be evaluated when the master data are updated. This would allow a generalized capability to implement event triggers when there is at least one subscriber and remove the triggers when there are no subscribers. The result would be a high degree of flexibility in the detection of relevant events, with no unnecessary overhead for either evaluation of rules or creation of network traffic for events of no interest. Of course, for rules that detect violations or errors, detection of the condition in a master data update may occur after the fact and result in more difficult corrective action.

Qualification Rules

SOA involves three different applications of qualification rules: people qualifications, service policies, and access control rules.

People Qualifications

In business processes that engage people to perform tasks, there are rules in the form of attribute requirements and constraints that determine who is qualified to fill a role. Typically, the qualifications are applied to a local group of people that are members of the department responsible for the process. The rules may focus on the experience, training, or job functions of the people involved. They may also focus on the process context and subject matter, such as where there is value in having the same person do a sequence of related tasks, or the same person cannot be assigned to multiple tasks where there is a requirement for separation of duties. The form of expression depends on the BPMS product.

In an SOA, people who are candidates for a process role may come from various parts of the organization, as opposed to traditional processes, where they are within the same department. As a result there is a need for a consistent representation of people qualifications so that qualification rules can be applied consistently, regardless of where the person is in the organization.

Service Policies

Where there is a choice of alternative services, such as where one enterprise is selecting from alternative vendors, there is a need to determine which of the alternative services qualify. In this case, there could be requirements and capabilities expressed by both the requester and the provider. Each potential participant must determine whether the other potential participant qualifies to fill its role.

WS-Policy from OASIS is a standard language for expression of these requirements and capabilities policies. Policy expressions might specify an encryption algorithm to be used or the time allowed for a response. A service may specify alternative policies from which prospective service users may choose. Both service users and service providers may have policies regarding acceptable participants and exchanges. To collaborate, the participants must have a combination of policy alternatives that are complementary. The service users and service providers also must have a common vocabulary for expression of policies.

Access Control Rules

SOA increases the population and diversity of persons or processes accessing each service. This requires role-based access control (RBAC) to enable managers to control access and grant authority, without the need to get into extensive technical detail. Each employee may require authorization to access many operations and data in many systems to meet their responsibilities. With RBAC, rules specify the access authority of roles. These rules are specified by the manager responsible for protecting the operations and data, and he or she is able to focus on controlling what can be accessed if a user has been assigned to a particular role. The manager of an employee can then assign certain roles to an employee and the employee then has the authority granted to these roles. RBAC is discussed further in Chapter 6, in the discussion of security.

Data Integrity Rules

SOA does not affect the implementation of database integrity rules except that each service should apply the same rules to data received from other services, just as it would apply them to data entered by a human. A service should be designed to be used in a variety of contexts and cannot assume that all data inputs are reliable. Similarly, a service may use other services that could be independently upgraded or replaced in the future, resulting in incompatibility.

RULES MANAGEMENT

There is a need to manage some rules at an enterprise level. Production rules, diagnostic rules, and qualification rules are generally applicable to specific activities and can be managed at that level. However, enterprise rules, event rules, and data integrity rules may be applicable in different activities throughout the enterprise. A rules repository provides a central source in which the relationships between rules can be analyzed, the rules can be found to be incorporated in appropriate activities, and links can be maintained to identify where the rules are being applied.

Figure 4.2 illustrates a basic data model for a rules repository expressed in Unified Modeling Language (UML). UML modeling is discussed briefly in Chapter 5. Each rule is parsed (broken down) to identify the entities, attributes, and relationships referenced in the condition part of the rule. Rules are stored in the repository based on these associated condition elements.

Rules are of interest to a developer when the rule condition depends on an entity, relationships, or attributes that can be changed by the process or application under development. So process and

■ **FIGURE 4.2** Rules Repository Data Model.

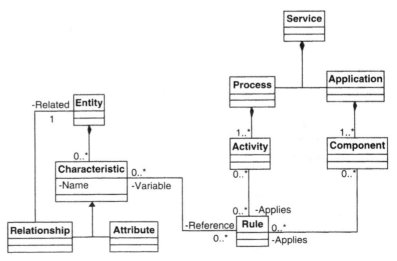

application developers can retrieve relevant rules from the repository on that basis. The developer should then identify the process activity or the application component where the rule is applied. This provides the ability to determine whether a rule has been applied in all the right places and the ability to change the rule in all those places, if that becomes necessary. Of course, this assumes the existence of an enterprise logical data model (discussed in the next chapter) so that the entities, attributes, relationships, and rules can be expressed in consistent terms.

As depicted, rules operate on data—the attributes and relationships of business entities. Rules that are deployed to various activities throughout the enterprise are meaningless if their references to data are not understood across the enterprise. The development of a consistent Enterprise Logical Data Model is discussed in the next chapter.

Enterprise Information Management

Information is the lifeblood of the enterprise. Without information there can be no coordinated activity, no record of accomplishments, no plans for the future. Management of information is a critical responsibility and becomes increasingly critical as enterprises become international and require greater agility. *Enterprise information management* (EIM) involves the validation, transformation, storage, communication, and presentation of data to provide information to support the pursuit of enterprise objectives. Data are the raw materials typically managed by computers; information is the organized presentation of data in context that has business meaning to humans.

In this chapter we first consider the information management issues of a service-oriented, agile enterprise, and then we discuss their implications for EIM. This chapter is not a comprehensive discussion of EIM requirements and methodology but rather a discussion of EIM from a business perspective and a focus on the aspects of EIM that require particular attention in a service-oriented, agile enterprise.

INFORMATION MANAGEMENT ISSUES

We focus on the agile enterprise as defined by the SOA Maturity Model discussed in Chapter 1. Briefly, an agile enterprise is one that has implemented SOA, automated business processes, business rules, and performance metrics and has established governance that optimizes and adapts from an enterprise perspective. The following sections highlight the information management issues.

Consistent Data Representation

Integration of service units involves the exchange of data. The sending and receiving service units must have a common understanding of the data being exchanged. The data exchanged often represent agreements regarding the exchange or consumption of assets. Many of the records exchanged must be recognized as business documents that should have legal effect. So documents must represent common understanding and be retained for accountability and enforcement of agreements in the future.

Optimization of enterprise operation requires the ability to integrate data from multiple sources in the enterprise to support planning and decision making. Agility also requires data integration, both to sense the need for change and to formulate plans for adaptation. The diversity of sources and uses, along with the need to combine data from different sources, requires that the enterprise have a shared understanding of the business meaning of shared data elements and relationships and that each data element value be expressed in a consist format and terms or units of measure.

Differences in format, terms, and units of measure cause incompatibility that is relatively easy to correct. For example, dates may be expressed in different forms, such as *dd/mm/yyyy, mm/dd/yyyy, ddd/yyyy* (Julian), or other variations. Different terms might be used, for example, to describe employee status, such as *temporary, part-time, salaried,* and so forth, where they might be expressed in different languages but have the same meanings. Units of measure might be feet and pounds or meters and kilograms. Again, these are relatively straightforward but necessary conversions.

More significant inconsistencies are with respect to identities, reference times, and scope.

The same business entities may be represented, but different identifiers may be used for each individual entity. Then there must be a cross-reference source to support a conversion. There can be problems if the records are historical and the identifiers from the different sources have changed over time.

Fields that provide information based on reference date and time or time duration must be based on the same date and time or time period. For example, if sales figures for one system are weekly and for another system are monthly, there is no way to convert weekly sales figures to monthly sales figures, or vice versa.

Also, if there are data based on groups, categories, or geographical domains, the boundaries of the groups must be identical. There is no way to convert statistics on groups in one system to the associated groups in another system if the members of the groups are not identical. For example, "shipping weight must be defined as the weight of material being shipped, including packaging, and must be expressed in pounds," or "periodic sales revenue is expressed in dollars worth of goods sold (but not necessarily delivered) Sunday through Saturday of each week."

Without this common understanding, inconsistent data may be combined or compared, resulting in misunderstanding of the business reality and inappropriate plans and decisions.

Note that it is not essential that the terms used to describe the data elements are the same throughout the enterprise, but the business concepts and the meaning of the data must be consistent. So data may be presented in a report or display in New York with English captions and annotations, and the same data may be presented in a report or display in Paris with French captions and annotations, and there need be no misunderstanding.

Multiple Links Between Service Units

Conventional business functions are supported by large-scale applications that automate the departmental silos. These large, departmental applications are often called *enterprise applications*. Integration of activities within a silo is accomplished by the processes and databases embedded in the enterprise application. Integration of the silos is accomplished with enterprise application integration (EAI) in which messages are communicated, primarily source to destination, between applications.

The agile enterprise breaks down these silos into relatively autonomous service units. The integration is not just a transfer of data between applications but request-response and collaborative exchanges. Message exchange relationships are not source to destination but many to one and sometimes many to many. A service unit can expect to get requests from multiple users in different parts of the enterprise organization or even outside organizations and return results to each of those requesters. It may, in turn, use multiple services to honor those requests, and it may select from alternative provider service units.

A service unit should be designed to anticipate requests from users currently unknown to it, including users addressing future business requirements. The exchange cannot simply be defined through an agreement between one user and one provider but must be designed for sharing, where the request and the response, as well as other exchanges, are meaningful in the different contexts of different users and for variations in customer products and services. In addition, the exchange should be designed such that the provider service unit could be replaced by an alternative provider in the future with little or no impact on the service user.

Cross-Enterprise Views

Conventional enterprises tend to operate in silos. Each department assembles the necessary resources to fulfill its enterprise role. Delegation is to employees and groups within the department, and accountability is up the management chain. The results achieved by the department are achieved, for the most part, within the department.

In an agile enterprise, service units respond to requests from other parts of the enterprise and may, in turn, delegate tasks to service units in still other parts of the enterprise organization. Accountability for performance is still up the management chain, but accountability for results also often crosses organizational boundaries. Optimization of results at an enterprise level is a consequence of the participation of multiple service units. Service units that are optimized in isolation may be suboptimized from an enterprise perspective. Service unit operating decisions may be based on data from other service units that either use or are used by the service unit. Managers and other decision makers must be able to access information through cross-enterprise views, to assess performance, resolve problems, make decisions, and plan for changes for enterprise optimization.

SOA drives centralization of many planning and decision-making activities to ensure effective integration of services, optimize performance from an enterprise perspective, and maintain or improve enterprise agility. This strengthening of enterprise governance requires that enterprise leaders have access to a wealth of data from many sources and the ability to combine data from those different sources to gain appropriate insights and ensure accountability and control.

Distributed Databases

Data that has been managed by an enterprise application in a large, shared database may, in an SOA, be distributed among several service units, managed in their separate databases. Some service units may be implemented with legacy systems or purchased software that has not been designed for compatibility with the enterprise view. Data from these different sources must be accessible and combinable to provide an consistent view of enterprise operations.

A unified enterprise view requires not only consistent format (the data structures and values) and semantics (the meanings) but also that the data in an enterprise view represent a consistent point or period in time. Conventional enterprise applications control the relationships between the data they manage so that, within the scope of the enterprise application, data retrieved for a particular view are consistent. In contrast, service units are loosely coupled and do not synchronize their database updates to ensure that they are always consistent in time.

Some data are replicated in the databases of different service units. Some data within a service unit database may be tentative working data or data that represent an earlier point in the development of a particular result. There must be a clear identification of the sources of data that represent the current state of the enterprise as well as reliable records of results.

In addition, because the enterprise is composed of a network of services participating in different enterprise endeavors, it is essential that managers have a consistent view of service unit performance and its impact on enterprise value chains.

Shared Knowledge

Enterprise agility requires access to shared knowledge about how the enterprise works as well as knowledge that provides the basis for competitive advantage. This includes knowledge expressed in documents and knowledge known by subject matter experts.

Traditionally, relevant documents and subject matter experts were managed within a departmental silo, often at a single office location. With SOA these functional capabilities are divided into more granular, shared services. The services may be geographically distributed and some employees may work from home. In addition, in support of adaptation initiatives, it is necessary to share knowledge more widely so that many factors can be considered to optimize from an enterprise perspective.

Business Models

Models would not be important if the enterprise were operating successfully, there were no problems, and there were no changes occurring in the ecosystem. Obviously, particularly in the modern world, change is constant. The agile enterprise must have a culture of constant change. Models are essential for understanding the current state of the enterprise as well as evaluating potential future states. Models that reflect the state of the business are built on data.

The agile enterprise requires top management to deal with greater complexity as a result of the multitude of relationships among service units, along with continuous change. In addition, due to increased competition, there is less margin for error. Strategic initiatives must get it right the first time.

We explore the need for business models in greater depth in Chapter 10, but here we recognize that models must be linked to the realities of the enterprise and its ecosystem. That means access to relevant, consistent, and reliable data and knowledge about the current state of the enterprise, capabilities, and trends as well as a wealth of knowledge about risks, regulations, threats, and opportunities.

LOGICAL DATA MODEL

Fundamental to these requirements is the need for consistent data for (1) understanding the state of the enterprise from different viewpoints and (2) communicating unambiguously between service units. A *logical data model* (LDM) provides the specifications for data that describe the concepts, relationships, and interpretation of values of data. It is a *logical* data model because it does not define the physical structures in which the data may be stored in files or databases or transmitted between service units—these simply reflect technical design considerations. An LDM is a business abstraction of the data specifications.

Metadata

An LDM is *data about data* such that it describes the form, relationships, and identifiers of data. This is commonly called *metadata*—data that describe data. Data models are metadata.

An LDM can define a wide variety of data. The data may be about many things, including people, orders, facilities, and products. The data may be about information, data in a business context. It may be about knowledge such as rules or reports, or it may be about wisdom in such forms models or strategies. From a computer perspective, it's all data in the sense that it is stored and manipulated with the same technology. The purpose, context, and meaning of the data determine whether is the data are simply raw facts or represents information, knowledge, or wisdom.

A customer order form provides metadata that describe the data fields. Data about the source, reliability, and timeliness of a record are metadata. Data about the structure of rules, neural networks, and business models are metadata. Computer programs are metadata, although they are not usually described that way. So computers not only capture, store, and communicate data that represent things about the enterprise; they also capture, store, and communicate data that specify what the data mean and what computers do with them.

Metadata that specify the meaning and relationships of data elements are often called *technical metadata* because they are used for the design and implementation of systems. *Business metadata* refers to metadata that defines the quality of the data, such as the timeliness, source, and reliability. These metadata are important to businesspeople because they can affect the quality of their interpretations and their resulting decisions.

An LDM focuses on technical metadata that specify business concepts; attributes of those concepts such as an identifier, a color, an age, or a value; and relationships between the business concepts such as ownership, parts of an assembly, or interactions. *Physical* data models are used by technical people to define how the data are actually stored in databases as well as the data structures that may be exchanged by services and used within applications.

As a practical matter, there are data inconsistencies within the enterprise. The business and supporting systems change over time; concepts evolve and new concepts emerge. Mergers and acquisitions require the integration and consolidation of systems of different companies. Commercial software products are installed with data definitions and formats that may not be entirely consistent with the rest of the enterprise. For these reasons, there must be a capability to transform data to achieve consistency.

Enterprise Logical Data Model

At the same time, there must be a consistent target for these transformations. There must be an enterprisewide understanding of the form and meaning of data to be exchanged, particularly since service user/provider relationships may be many to one or many to many and may change over time. This common form and meaning should be specified by an *enterprise logical data model* (ELDM)—a logical data model with enterprise scope. The ELDM provides the common language for the exchange of data between service units and for coordination, record-keeping, planning, and decision-making activities at all levels.

Development of an ELDM is a major undertaking, but some of the work has already been done. The enterprise would not function today if there were not some common understanding of the data in reports and records and the data communicated between systems. Sometimes the inconsistencies are not in the data per se but in what it is called in different departments. The current ability to exchange data requires that some degree of common understanding was developed in the past, although that may not have been captured in a shared data model.

From an industry perspective, understanding the data exchanged between enterprise applications was a major challenge of EAI. Suppliers of enterprise systems realized that the integration of their systems would be less costly and disruptive if they could exchange data consistent with a common data model, so they promoted the development of standards for exchange data. Many such standards were developed by the Open Applications Group, Inc. (OAGi).

Common data models are evident in industry standards such as those developed by the United Nations Centre for Trade Facilitation and Electronic Business (UN/CEFACT), XML Business Reporting Language (XBRL), and Human Relations XML (HR-XML). In the telecommunications industry, the TeleManagement Forum (TMF) has developed a substantial ELDM called Shared Information/Data (SID).

As the scope of electronic integration of the enterprise expands to include relationships with customers and suppliers, the scope of need for data consistency expands. When orders were exchanged and coordination was accomplished by human-to-human communications, the people involved were able to compensate for inconsistencies, translating the terminology and the data formats as required. Computers are not so forgiving. Thus, there is a need for a shared specification for data exchanged.

As a result of these forces, the world of information systems is converging toward a common LDM. Although new concepts emerge, we can expect this industry convergence to continue so that most differences will be only where innovative business solutions provide an enterprise with competitive advantage. For the most part, even significantly different business processes and product designs will use accepted data models.

To the individual enterprise, convergence on a common data model reduces the cost of developing data models and database designs; reduces the cost of developing, maintaining, and executing data transformations; and improves the ability to measure and analyze operating performance and key indicators from an enterprise perspective. Consequently, it is the interest of every enterprise to align as much as possible to the emerging global logical data model.

Logical data models that should reflect the emerging common model are available for purchase or as a basis for consulting and integration services. Work on an ELDM should not start from scratch.

Data Modeling

In the meantime, each enterprise must establish and maintain an ELDM as the basis for exchange, storage, and retrieval of consistent data. The primary form of enterprise data modeling is class models, generally associated with object-oriented programming. These models provide a relatively robust way of representing business entities, their attributes, and their relationships. Implementations of computer applications usually employ relational databases, so for database design, entity-relationship (ER) modeling is more suitable, but we do not get into that level of detail here. We focus on class models that are the generally accepted form of logical data models.

A *class* represents similar persons, places, or things in the business domain. Class models rely on a concept called *inheritance* whereby a class may inherit characteristics defined for a more general class. Figure 5.1 illustrates a class diagram for a customer-order example. A class may represent a generalization of similar things, such as Customer, or it may be specialized to represent a more specific type of things, such as Retail Customer or Wholesaler. The more specialized class is said to *inherit* from the more general class, so characteristics of Customer are inherited by Wholesaler, as indicated by the open-headed arrow from Wholesaler to Customer in the diagram. This is a Unified Modeling Language (UML) class diagram. UML is the generally accepted standard developed by OMG for modeling a number of aspects of an object-oriented application.

Inheritance provides a way to describe similarities between classes. Several different classes may inherit common characteristics from a shared parent class, or a specialized class may be defined as adding characteristics to a more general class. In the class diagram in Figure 5.1, the Order, Customer, and Order Item classes show attributes of the classes within the boxes. The Wholesaler class is a specialization of Customer.

■ **FIGURE 5.1** Class Model.

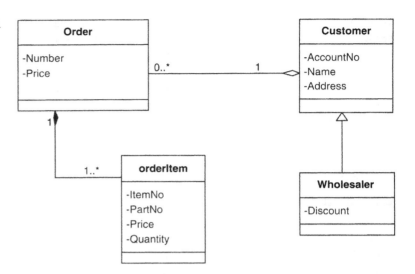

Wholesaler inherits AccountNo, Name, and Address from Customer and has an additional attribute that is a discount specification that presumably is not meaningful for most customers. Wholesaler implicitly has all the other attributes and relationships of Customer, so a Wholesaler "is" a customer with an additional attribute. A Wholesaler can occur anywhere in a model or database that a Customer can occur. The numbers on the relationships indicate the *cardinality*, e.g., an order must have one customer, but a customer can have zero or more orders.

Class models can express logical data models, but the data may be expressed in different forms for storage and exchange. Generally, data exchanged between services are expressed in XML. Data stored in databases are most often in relational tables. Data warehouses have specialized data structures to support retrieval and analysis. Transformations between these and other representations can be modeled with tools based on the OMG Common Warehouse Metamodel (CWM), discussed more later.

An ELDM should represent everything that may be the subject of data processing. This may be thousands of classes, but not all these classes are implemented in a single database. A database stores a subset of the data that are of interest to a particular application or group of applications used by a particular organization. Some classes are stored in more than one database but may not include all the associated attributes and relationships in each of the databases.

For example, in a manufacturing enterprise, orders are stored to capture sales data, then additional data are captured as the basis for production. The manufacturing database includes some associated customer information, such as the shipping address, but probably does not include financial information. The linkage between databases is the data exchanged between applications and the keys associated with the business entities, such as the order numbers and account numbers.

To get a comprehensive report on a customer, it might be necessary to query several databases that hold data related to that customer. When such reporting or analysis occurs, the ELDM ensures that the data from different sources can be combined to produce a consistent representation and the meaning will be generally understood.

Semantics

Class models do not provide a precise way to capture *data semantics*, the meaning of the data classes, attributes, and relationships. Definitions are captured in textual descriptions. The enterprise and interenterprise scope of data models calls for more rigorous specification of semantics. Standards such as Web Ontology Language (OWL) and Semantics of Business Vocabulary and Rules (SBVR) have been developed for the representation of semantics and should become incorporated in data-modeling tools in the future.

DATA EXCHANGE

Service units don't do anything without exchanging data to submit and accept requests, return results, and potentially collaborate, receive event notices, or issue event notices. Shared services exchange data with multiple users.

Data exchanged with a service unit must be consistent for all users so that the service deals with all requests in the same way. The data models of records exchanged should be subsets of the ELDM. These subsets are often called *views* because they represent that subset of the ELDM data elements that is viewed by the participants in the exchange for the particular subject matter. This is similar to a display or a report that shows selected data elements from a database.

The data exchanged among service units are generally communicated by automated business processes. Requests to a service unit should be received by a business process and results should be returned by a business process. Requests for status of a process as well as receipt and publication of event notices involve exchange of data with business processes. Electronic business documents are created and managed by business processes and must be archived for future reference. Though some service units may have their business processes embedded in applications, it is important to understand that, for the most part, the exchanges of data between service units are essentially exchanges between business processes within the service units.

eXtensible Markup Language (XML) was recognized fairly early in the 1990s as a useful form of data interchange. It has several important characteristics:

- XML documents (i.e., records) are somewhat self-documenting. Each element is tagged with a descriptive name.

- The fields are variable in length, with special characters designating the beginning and ending so that the format remains valid, even if the length of a field changes, and text fields can take whatever space is required.

- A receiving program can select fields of interest based on the tags and ignore any other fields that may have been added by the sender, so the receiver can continue to use documents that have been expanded for other purposes.

- XML is used to specify the structure of XML documents (using XML Schema) so that shared specifications can be used for computational validation.

- XML is also used to express the transformation of XML documents by using Extensible Stylesheet Language Transformations (XSLT) so that there is a standard, computer-interpreted language for document transformation.

- XML is independent of the computing platform and computer languages used to send or receive it, so there is compatibility between diverse sending and receiving technologies.

- XML can be exchanged using HTTP and HTTPS, protocols of the World Wide Web, so that existing ports are compatible and the data can pass through existing firewalls.

- A widely accepted standard for electronic signatures is based on XML. Standards for encryption and signatures for XML documents are discussed in Chapter 6.

XML, along with XML Schema, XSLT, HTTP, HTTPS, and related standards, has been developed by the World Wide Web Consortium (W3C). Though other forms such as electronic data interchange (EDI) are still widely used, XML has emerged as the preferred form for exchanging electronic documents between systems and enterprises. The flexibility of XML is a trade-off with the verbosity that increases communication overhead.

An example use of XML follows. This XML document is structured to contain a collection of customer orders—in the example there is only one order:

```xml
<?xml version="1.0" encoding="utf-8" ?>
<Orders>
    <Order orderID="103">
        <Customer customerID="1234"/>
        <OrderItems>
            <Item>
                <Product productNo="223445"/>
                <Description>
                    100-watt speaker, Mahogany case
                </Description>
                <Quantity> 2 </Quantity>
                <UnitPrice> 235.95 </UnitPrice>
            </Item>
            <Item>
                <Product productNo="234523"/>
                <Description>
                    CD Player, Mahogany case
                </Description>
                <Quantity> 1 </Quantity>
                <UnitPrice> 167.95 </UnitPrice>
            </Item>
        </OrderItems>
    </Order>
</Orders>
```

The XML expressions are indented for readability. Each expression begins with <*name*> to identify the data element (where *name* is the name of the data element) and ends with </*name*> (a slash prefix) to specify the end of the data element. An element may contain a primitive value (that is, a data type that is not defined in terms of other data types), another element, or multiple elements. A primitive element may be expressed with both a name and value together, for example the Product element in the example, by ending the value segment with />, and other attributes can be expressed with the name such as at the beginning of the Order element in the example. <*Orders*> could contain multiple orders, but in this case only one order is shown, which starts with <*Order*> and ends with </*Order*>. Within the Order are elements for Customer and Order Items. The Customer element only specifies the customer ID. There are then two order items, each containing several order-item attributes. XML structures are specified with a specialized XML language called XML Schema so the format can be validated by a generalized computer program.

Application adapters provided by integration middleware should provide for transformation between the application internal representation of data and an appropriate XML representation.

In many cases, these XML documents capture work products and decisions for which people should be held accountable, and some of these represent legal agreements. These implications are discussed further in Chapter 6 on security.

BUSINESS INTELLIGENCE SERVICES

Business intelligence (BI) refers to technical capabilities that provide information about the state of the enterprise and changes in the enterprise as well as in the business ecosystem. In Chapter 9, we will discuss the broader business requirement for enterprise intelligence that ensures availability of appropriate information and knowledge for management of the enterprise. SOA creates more sources for input to BI systems. In addition, the agile enterprise has a greater need for cross-enterprise data to support enterprise analysis, planning, and decision making for optimization and adaptation. Several BI technologies are described in the following sections.

Operational Data Stores

The current state of an enterprise exists in many databases throughout the enterprise. With the implementation of more granular service units, it may be necessary to integrate data from more databases to obtain a view of the enterprise's current state. In some cases the needs for cross-enterprise views are well defined and routine; in other cases, the needs are ad hoc, arising from disruptions in the business ecosystem that must be understood and resolved.

For routine views involving multiple data sources, the typical solution is an *operational data store* (ODS). An ODS receives inputs from multiple sources and updates its database for an integrated view of the data. The inputs are typically taken as periodic batch extracts from the production systems. The general assumption is that the cross-enterprise reporting is not time critical, so periodic updates provide data that are sufficiently current.

The mechanism for feeding an ODS, depicted in Figure 5.2, is often called *extract transform load* (ETL) because the relevant data must be extracted from the production systems, transformed to a common format, and loaded in an appropriate manner to be reconciled with data from other sources. The OMG Common Warehouse Metamodel (CWM) specification provides a standard for modeling the transformation of data from different sources and different format technologies; the Information Management Metamodel (IMM) specification currently under development at OMG will further enhance this modeling capability.

Transformation may include "cleansing" the data and merger of related data from different sources. A similar approach is used for feeding data warehouses, except that data warehouses typically receive data on completion of transactions, so, for example, a specific order would only be loaded into the data warehouse when completed.

The use of ODS databases generally limits the scope of possible views of the state of the enterprise, and there is often some delay between the

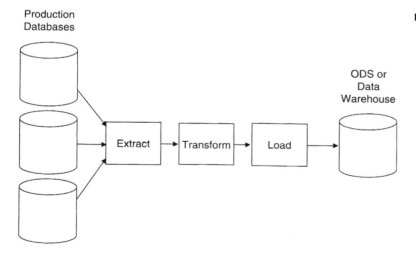

Production
Databases

ODS or
Data
Warehouse

Extract Transform Load

■ **FIGURE 5.2** Extract Transform Load (ETL).

occurrence of events and update of the ODS. There is an industry trend to shift from periodic batch ETL to updates based on events, so that the ODS is closer to a real-time representation of the state of the enterprise. The need for real-time data must be evaluated in the context of the kinds of decisions and actions that depend on the timeliness of the data.

Enterprise Information Integration

An alternative to ODS is to use an *enterprise information integration* (EII) tool. EII tools provide access to multiple databases based on a virtual database. In other words, the user submits a query expressed in terms of a shared data model, and the query is translated into appropriate queries in supporting databases. The data retrieved from the databases are then transformed and integrated to be a proper response in terms of the data requirements of the original query. The OMG CWM specification is also used to specify data transformations for EII.

For the agile enterprise, the virtual database should be consistent with the ELDM. Each service unit that maintains relevant data must also maintain the specifications for transformation of its database to a form consistent with the ELDM.

Though EII enables queries to access current (up-to-the-minute) data—operating data—it does not provide a mechanism to ensure that the data reflect a consistent point in time. Some databases may be updated more quickly than others in response to operational events. Consequently, the results may not add up. For example, a query might show that shipments from inventory are less than inventory reductions because the inventory records are updated more quickly than the shipment records.

An ODS provides the opportunity to improve the consistency of data by performing cleansing and filtering operations before updating the ODS database. Consequently, it may be desirable to have an ODS in addition to EII capabilities for different timeliness and accuracy requirements.

Business Activity Monitoring

Business activity monitoring (BAM) is intended to provide real-time tracking of enterprise activities. Occurrences of events such as completion of various activities are reported as they happen. This activity tracking may drive displays such as management dashboards and reflect the current status of key performance indicators (KPIs).

BAM may also utilize transformation specifications as for an ODS or EII system. Database extraction is not needed for BAM because notices are generated by the operational processes as the events occur.

However, BAM does not perform reconciliation the way an ODS or data warehouse does, because the notices are used immediately to update performance metrics.

In the agile enterprise, BAM should address performance metrics for services and support management dashboards at all levels. The fundamental mechanisms of BAM are not different for the agile enterprise, but the number of service units and performance-monitoring points should be more extensive, to provide more specific detail when required to resolve particular concerns, to provide cross-enterprise visibility in support of enterprise optimization, and to provide prompt and appropriate response to significant variances.

Data Warehouses

Data warehouses fulfill a different need; they provide historical data—data that reflect changes in the marketplace and enterprise operation over time. These data also come from mainstream systems. Again, ETL tools have been used to periodically extract data from the production systems, transform them to a consistent form, and load them into the data warehouse, typically merging them with data from other sources. This mode of operation is still appropriate.

The traditional approach, as with the ODS, assumes that analyses based on a data warehouse need not be real time and up to the minute. Usually the focus is on trends and relationships over a period of time, and the actions resulting from these analyses probably do not have immediate impact on enterprise operations. However, in some cases more timely analyses could have beneficial effects on current operations.

To support analysis of current data, service units can provide updates as relevant changes occur. This mode of operation is somewhat less efficient than batch processing, but the cost of this inefficiency is much less significant than in the past, and the pace of change in business is accelerating.

We'll return to concerns about monitoring business change in Chapter 8 with discussion of event-driven agility. In Chapter 9, we consider the broader concept of an enterprise intelligence service unit that has responsibility for providing access to information from across the enterprise and the enterprise ecosystem.

Business Metadata

The integration of data from multiple sources involves data of differing quality and reliability. Within a single service unit, the quality and reliability of that service unit's data may be well understood, but as the users of data become more remote from the sources, the users may not understand the inaccuracies that can occur in the data they are using for analysis, planning, and decision making.

The ELDM is an abstract metamodel, disassociated from the actual sources of the data. Business metadata describe the quality of the actual data in an ODS, EII query, or data warehouse database. Some descriptive data, metadata, are associated with individual records such as time stamps and source identifier. Metadata that are not stored with the data, metadata in a data model, should be provided as information associated with the display or reporting of the data. For aggregated data, it may be necessary to indicate the least reliable source or require that the user query the detail behind the aggregation, to understand the sources.

In addition, certain data may require special attention for protection of privacy, prevention of fraud, and retention for accountability. Security requirements should also be captured as business metadata, as a basis for restricting access and for ensuring users' awareness of their data protection obligations.

Business metadata are increasingly important in the agile enterprise because of the diversity of users and their potential lack of awareness of the credibility, timeliness, and sensitivity of the data on which they rely.

Query and reporting services may not always provide displays that integrate business metadata, but associated metadata should be available, and users should be advised to use it to ensure their awareness of potential inaccuracies and inconsistencies that may occur in the data they observe.

MASTER DATA MANAGEMENT

Master data are the primary sources of data that represent the current state and recorded actions of the enterprise. Unlike some definitions of the term, we include a comprehensive set of databases or other forms of data storage that represent the enterprise as a whole, not just relatively stable reference data. This is conceptually the "single version of the truth" that should be the common basis for enterprise planning and decision making. In most cases, each segment of the master data is owned by a service unit that provides related services whereby the data are captured or updated. Also, some master data may be managed by a commercial application or an outsourcing provider that has implemented a proprietary data model.

Many enterprise data are distributed in multiple databases across the enterprise, with overlaps and sometimes variations in semantics, format, currency, and accuracy. Master data management has the goal of defining the trusted sources and ensuring access to an integrated view of the enterprise, even though data may be stored in multiple databases.

SOA creates new challenges for ensuring that the enterprise operates on a consistent and reliable version of the truth.

Primary Source

A single service unit should have ownership of the primary source of each subset of master data for a well-defined domain. This service unit is responsible for ensuring the integrity and security of the data. It is the single version of the truth for these data. Typically, this ownership is aligned with the service unit that is the primary source of updates and either has the greatest dependence on the data or is best positioned to maintain alignment of the data with the realities of the business. In some cases, the master data service unit may be dedicated specifically to management of its master data.

Figure 5.3 depicts the common aspects of a master data service unit. The management of these data is a service to the rest of the enterprise. The stored data should not be accessed directly by outside applications or organizations for either reads or updates so that (1) changes are controlled to ensure integrity, (2) access is appropriately authorized, and

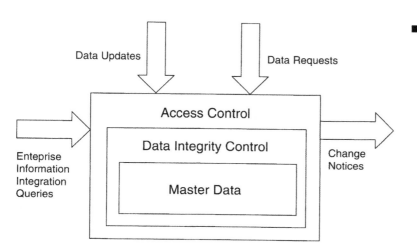

■ **FIGURE 5.3** Master Data Services.

(3) the database can be changed without affecting the data structures exchanged with other services. Data are requested as needed, and changes are submitted as requests for updates.

The service should support access through an EII facility and may issue update notices for coordination of related services and updating replicated data.

A master data service should maintain appropriate audit trails, back-ups, and controls to ensure the accuracy and reliability of the data and accountability for the content.

Data Hiding

In SOA, data are managed by each service unit, and the implementation of the service unit as well as its data are hidden behind the service unit interface. The interface is intended to minimize constraints on the technology employed and the design of the services, including the design of the databases. So the interface hides both the data managed within the service unit and capabilities delegated to other services, where some of the relevant data may be located.

It would significantly undermine the implementation flexibility of service units to expose their databases to direct access for other purposes. In addition, common business functions are increasingly implemented with commercial off-the-shelf (COTS) software and external service providers (outsourcing) that have their own versions of logical data models.

As a result, the data stored in a service unit may be in a quite different form from the way they are viewed outside the service unit. Furthermore, the form might be changed, independent of uses of the service unit, when the service unit is upgraded or even replaced. The goal is to enable such changes to occur without being burdened by the potential consequences to service users. The concept of a master data service, discussed earlier, provides the needed consistent version of the truth.

All updates should be submitted as requests to the service unit maintaining the master data. The service unit must determine whether the update is acceptable, and it may determine that consequential actions are required, such as related updates or issue of change notices.

Queries from external applications should be submitted as defined data requests. Responses to these requests should be through messaging using XML with the data format consistent with the enterprise logical data model. Necessary transformations should be internal to the service unit and designed for an appropriate balance between performance and flexibility. Users of the data can utilize data transformation services if their format requirements vary from the enterprise standard.

Where ad hoc queries are required, they should be supported by an EII tool, as discussed earlier. The owners of each of the master data services have a responsibility to maintain the mapping to the EII tool for its database and to define access authorization requirements.

Service Unit Granularity

Service units should be expected to be more granular than conventional enterprise applications so that they can be used in a variety of contexts— the larger a service unit, the more assumptions are built into its implementation and the less likely it can be useful in another context. Instead of a large enterprise application, the agile enterprise has multiple service units to provide the same capability but as separable components.

The traditional enterprise application is supported by a single database. Autonomy and flexibility of service units suggest that each should have its own database. At the same time, there are data that must be shared, and requests for data from another service unit could impact performance.

There are two ways to address this problem: (1) service unit clustering and (2) data replication.

Clustering

Service unit clustering brings together those services units that require high-performance access to a shared database. These service units will all be under the management of a single, higher-level manager. This common, higher-level manager has responsibility for the shared data and associated database. This cluster organization may be a reasonable performance solution if the responsibilities and objectives of the various services units are compatible. This may not be appropriate if there is a need for separation of responsibility to ensure integrity of the data. The risks of this approach are (1) a change to the shared data structure affects all of the clustered services, (2) the organization may not be as effective if the business roles of the various service units are quite different and require different management skills and organizational goals, and (3) as the number of services involved in management of the master data increases, so does the risk to data integrity, because responsibility for data integrity is shared by multiple service units. Essentially, the autonomy and accountability of the individual service units are eroded by clustering.

Data Replication

Replication accepts that the various service units each require their own database. Each of the service units then manages its own data along with replicas of data from one or more master data services. There are two primary technical approaches: change notices and distributed directories.

An application can maintain a copy of all or a portion of the master data and (1) subscribe to notices of updates and (2) request updates when its operations change its copy of the master data. There is some delay between update of the master data and updates to the replicas, and vice versa, so this approach should not be used where synchronization is critical.

If synchronization is critical, requests to the master data service may require that the data be retrieved with a lock (or "check-out" and "check-in") that prevents changes until the calling application has completed the associated operation. Locks should be avoided if at all possible due to the risk of performance consequences to other applications that would be locked out and the risk that release of the lock could be delayed.

Lightweight Directory Access Protocol (LDAP) has been used to provide distributed access to data that do not change frequently but where high-performance access is needed. There are two problems with using this technology for master data management: (1) the master data service may not be able to exercise adequate control of updates and (2) the stored data structure is shared by all users so that changing the data structure could be a major undertaking that would require synchronized conversion of all users. LDAP can be an appropriate solution if used for relatively stable data such as customer name and address.

With replication there is always a risk that the replica becomes out of sync with the master for more than a brief period of delayed update. Consequently there must be a capability to either restore the replica from the master or validate it against the master. These add to the complexity and operating responsibilities of the involved services.

Life-Cycle-Based Ownership

For some business data, the organization with the primary interest in accuracy and integrity of the data changes over the life cycle of the associated business concept. For example, as depicted in Figure 5.4, product

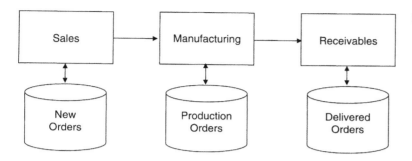

■ **FIGURE 5.4** Life-Cycle-Based Ownership.

orders are initially the concern of the sales organization, but they become the primary interest of the manufacturing organization for order fulfillment, and then they become the primary interest of the financial organization for invoicing and receivables. Product specifications are initially the primary concern of the engineering organization but become the primary concern of the manufacturing organization with regard to products actually in production. Responsibility for personnel records may change when an employee retires or leaves the company. Changes in the stages of the life cycle may correspond to changes in the level of access activity and frequency of change, resulting in different optimization approaches in the various areas of responsibility.

In some cases, there may be a clear change of responsibility so that only one organization is responsible for any one order, person, or product at a time. However, it is more typical that each retains responsibility for the records associated with the particular entity during certain phases of the life cycle. The sales organization continues to have responsibility for a record of the order as received, regardless of how it is built, but the manufacturing organization should be responsible for records about how it was built, particularly if there are safety or environmental factors and components must be traceable to delivered products. Generally, primary responsibility for the record at each phase is with the organization that performs the most frequent updates during that phase.

Consequently, data about a particular subject, such as a person, order, or product specification, may be managed by different organizations and have variations in associated content over the course of its lifetime. Some data for a particular business concept may be in the different databases at the same time. To some extent this may be replicas, but it may reflect the state of that business concept at that period in the life cycle. For example, the sales organization of Figure 5.4 may continue to hold the order data as received while the manufacturing organization may, for some reason, produce the order differently and reflect that in its record, while the receivables organization may record a final price that is different from the estimated price in the sales record. Though this may seem like multiple versions of "the truth," they are all correct in the context of their phases of the life cycle. The truth is a function of the context, and queries must be put into proper context to get the desired single version of the truth.

So the truth about a particular order, person, or product design could require queries to multiple databases. This is probably acceptable if the context of the query aligns to one of the databases. Otherwise, it may be appropriate to maintain a shared point of reference that would track the status of each subject so that the appropriate database can be queried. For example, it is probably useful to have a single source for the status of an order, for response to customer queries. This customer order database typically is the responsibility of the organization responsible for the subject matter during the initial phase. To keep it current, the service unit may receive updates as changes occur in the other databases.

In traditional enterprises, life-cycle-based data responsibility may not occur often, but with separation of data into more finely-grained service units, it is likely to occur more frequently.

Outsourced Services

Services may be outsourced at a variety of levels of granularity. For example, a service could be as simple as a stock market query about a current stock price, or it may be outsourcing of a complex set of services that provide a major portion of the human resources business function. Where the outsourcing represents a substantial business function, it includes management of enterprise master data, such as employee records in the case of human resource management outsourcing.

The objective for outsourced services should be the same as for internal service units. Services should have well-defined interfaces that are independent of whether the services are internal or outsourced. If the outsourcing is a substantial business function, it conceptually includes a number of service units within the business function characterized as a service group. If the outsourcing provider implements best practices, the conceptual service units should be consistent with service units the provider and its competitors either have or will have in the future. The outsourcing provider must then present interfaces to these service units for sharing the particular services that are needed by other users within the client enterprise. Service unit interfaces must also provide services associated with master data management. In the case of HR outsourcing, the client will need access to employee records along with a variety of services related to employment, benefits, compensation, and so forth.

KNOWLEDGE MANAGEMENT

Knowledge management involves the identification, retention, and retrieval of relevant insights and experiences. Much of this enterprise knowledge is in the heads of the enterprise's employees. Some of it has been captured in textual documents. Still less has been codified in business rules and models. Knowledge management is critical to enterprise agility because it provides insights for determining what changes are needed and how to make them.

We discussed business rules and business rules management in Chapter 4. We have also discussed some business models, and we focus on business models again in Chapter 10. Business models are generally developed to address particular problem domains and are incorporated in the tools and methods of specific functional capabilities. The primary challenge of knowledge management is to access the knowledge of people and the unstructured documents they have created.

Expertise of People

Though much of the routine work of an enterprise is automated, people and their relationships are still important for agility—adapting the enterprise to changing business needs. The expertise associated with a particular business capability is most often found with the people of the associated service unit. At the same time, relevant detailed and technical knowledge may be in the heads of those people that provide information systems development and support services. These clusters of people are primary knowledge resources.

However, when there are problems with a customer product or service, solution of a problem in one service unit may require insight into the capabilities of other service units and collaboration between people across organizational boundaries. In addition, when significant business changes are required, knowledge will be needed about how the business works beyond the scope of individual service units. Since experts will tend to be highly focused on their own service units, those with cross-functional expertise will be important resources in these exceptional situations.

People-focused knowledge management then requires identification of knowledgeable people and support for collaboration so they can exchange knowledge and develop new insights and solutions. With SOA, needed knowledge may be more scattered among a variety of service units and organizations. There are tools for cataloging and searching employee skills, but the skill classifications do not necessarily align well to the needs for finding knowledge. Currently, less formal techniques appear to be most effective:

- Establish mailing lists of interest groups to share information, and use them to solicit help using self-selection to identify people who can help.
- Establish mailing lists of service unit leaders to share information and use them to solicit identities of employees with relevant expertise.
- Catalog documents with authors and contributors so that when relevant documents are found, the authors and participants are identified for access to supplemental information.
- Maintain a searchable history of initiatives and the contributions of participants so that the participants can be contacted when similar initiatives occur.

These mechanisms help locate people with relevant expertise, but there also must be incentives for them to participate—both for the individuals and their managers. Service unit managers are heavily focused on optimization of their service unit operations. This is a strong disincentive to contribute their best people to other work. At a minimum, managers should be reimbursed for the cost of resources they contribute, but the incentives should go further. The incentives do not necessarily need to be financial; they may be motivations such as recognition or career opportunities.

In the long term, incentives may be the most important factor. With effective incentives, the people and their managers find ways to identify opportunities to contribute, both with their time and with documents. Then finding the right people is much easier.

Unstructured Documents

Unstructured documents, for the most part, are data in a form prepared by humans for human understanding. This includes textual documents, emails, spreadsheets, marketing literature, and some forms of specification. Though spreadsheets may seem structured, many have unique structures that cannot be easily transformed for database storage, and relevant metadata is typically in text expressions. These data are just as important to the operation of the business as are structured data and they consume larger volumes of storage, but they are often given little attention from an IT perspective.

A key issue for unstructured data is to make it available to the right person at the right time to address business needs. This requires that the unstructured data artifacts be stored in accessible locations and be catalogued, indexed, or searchable in a way that causes the right artifacts to come to the attention of a person in need of information.

As with other enterprise data, management of unstructured data should be provided as a service or services. These unstructured data service units should take responsibility for appropriate retention and access control. Critical enterprise documents are most likely already captured and catalogued to meet regulatory requirements. Other documents and records should also be captured and catalogued in an orderly way. This does not mean that all document storage should be consolidated, but documents that are of cross-organizational interest should be stored in a form that makes them accessible over the intranet. The centralized service unit should provide support for locating and open sharing of some documents rather than attempting to exercise centralized control.

A Wikipedia-like service can provide a forum for capture, development, and sharing of knowledge. It can also include links to relevant documents. This enables the development of consensus and integration of different perspectives. It will require the development of appropriate cultural attitudes and attention to incentives and disincentives to achieve a meaningful level of participation.

Some artifacts have a natural home. Product specifications, for example, should be accessible based on interest in specific products. Where there is knowledge that must be shared between service units, such as knowledge about manufacturing limitations for product engineers, appropriate classifications can be developed for identification of relevant documents based on the problem situation.

In some cases there is an ongoing need for sharing knowledge between particular service units or business disciplines. For example, product engineers need knowledge about manufacturing problems and limitations. They also need knowledge about customer preferences, cultural differences, and government regulations in various markets. Knowledge about these factors should be more formally captured, catalogued, and communicated, particularly when they change, so that timely and appropriate action can be taken.

However, the interest in many unstructured data artifacts may not be based on such predictable classifications. There may be ad hoc interest in documents related to a particular standard, a particular design pattern, a technology, an interaction, or various other concerns.

Search engines on the World Wide Web represent our best model for accessibility of unstructured data for ad hoc needs. The enterprise should have a comparable search service for unstructured data accessible on the enterprise intranet. Current search engines retrieve documents based on the presence of words or phrases. An enterprise should have an equivalent capability for access to unstructured data within the enterprise. It is still necessary to at least classify artifacts according to access authorization restrictions. A search engine should exclude from the search those artifacts the requestor is not authorized to see.

Captured knowledge is not valid forever. Records must be updated when circumstances change and deleted when no longer valid. We are starting to see the effects of aging records on the World Wide Web. When the Web was new, documents and other information that were posted were current. The historical scope of Web searches was limited. Now that knowledge is getting old and documents that predate the Web are being posted. A Web search can bring up documents that are decades old. The user must filter the knowledge, and there is a risk that the age of a document, not the relevance, may be the primary criterion used for exclusion.

Searches based on words or phrases in the artifact content have great value, but they still require some artful choice of words for the search, followed by a human search through the retrieved items. It is preferable to search based on semantic content—the meaning of the concepts addressed by the artifact. The semantic Web and associated capabilities are still emerging technologies. The need for better searches is not unique to the agile enterprise, but these technologies should be exploited as practical solutions become available.

Finding needed data is a fundamental problem. Protecting it is yet another. In the next chapter we will explore the security issues associated with the agile enterprise.

SOA Security

With the advent of the public Internet and the World Wide Web, security risks have increased dramatically. Systems are exposed to public access and email messages can carry or link to corrupting software. Automation and electronic communications have added new dimensions to security concerns. Electronic integration of services, extending beyond the walls of the enterprise, has created new security exposures. Fortunately, SOA technology and related industry standards have created new opportunities for accountability and control.

Many enterprises still have access control defined at an application level:

- *Identity management* uses local user identifiers.
- *Authentication* involves local user passwords.
- *Authorization* involves a local access control list for each user.
- *Access control* may be embedded in the application using the access control lists.
- *Accountability* may be implemented by tagging records with user identifiers and an application audit trail.

Such approaches are only suited to small, closed communities of users. The design of security mechanisms has been delegated to technical people and security administration has been delegated to clerical people. Managers often don't understand the nature of the risks and the necessary countermeasures until they hear about failures. For example, recently Societe Generale, one of France's largest and most respected banks, lost $7 billion in undetected fraudulent trades by an employee.

Fragmented security systems increase complexity, diminish control, and increase security risks. Government regulations such as the

Sarbanes-Oxley Act demand that managers take responsibility for ensuring accountability and control of enterprise assets and operations. Security is a fundamental aspect of accountability and control. Agility and efficiency require infrastructure consistency and thus consistency of security mechanisms. SOA improves accountability and control through clarification of responsibilities, and though SOA creates a number of new security concerns, its consistent architecture, technical infrastructure, and clarification of responsibility bring with them opportunities for improving the quality and consistency of security mechanisms.

The fundamental security issues have not changed and there are well-defined standards to support the capabilities necessary to address them. Nevertheless, the consistency, scale, and management participation necessary to an agile enterprise require significant technical investment and organizational transformation. Security is a major business issue for which top management and managers of each service unit must take responsibility and exercise control.

This chapter does not engage in a comprehensive discussion of information systems security but instead focuses on security concerns that arise or are amplified for the agile enterprise, particularly concerns raised by SOA. The chapter assumes that attention has already been given to such concerns as physical security, threats of intrusion from the World Wide Web, and virus protection. The purpose here is to provide an understanding of the requirements and approaches for optimizing security for services, from an enterprise perspective, so that management can plan for and commit to the necessary enterprise transformation.

In previous chapters, we made references to the security fundamentals of authentication, authorization, access control, and auditing. This chapter expands on these topics and goes on to describe the specific technical mechanisms that provide data secrecy (assurance that a message is not read by any but the intended recipient), data integrity (assurance that the message has not been modified in transit), and nonrepudiation (proof that the message was actually created or approved by the stated sender).

The following are primary sources of security concerns for a service-oriented enterprise:

- *Expanded number of access points.* When organizations are divided into finer-grained service units, each of the services becomes a point of access from other systems and people. Each must have appropriate access controls.

- *Expanded communities of users.* Each of the more granular service units also has more users and more people interested in accessing data. These people may be in various organizations that would previously have been denied access. Each person must be identifiable, and authorization may involve a greater variety of specific restrictions.

- *Perimeter security.* It is no longer sufficient to protect against intrusions by building barriers around the enterprise internal network. The internal network is typically accessible from many insecure sites, and there is an increasing number of internal points of access, particularly with SOA.

- *Dynamic service relationships.* Service units can be replaced when responsibility is assigned to a new organization or new technology is installed. Service users should be redirected without disruption of service, but there must be assurance that redirection does not give access to an imposter.

- *Access across trust domains.* Some services require access from business partner or customer organizations that manage employee identities, authorizations, and access control policies independently, so there must be a transformation from partner authorizations to appropriate local authorization.

- *Electronic documents.* Paper is being replaced by electronic documents, which serve as the medium of exchange for assets and commitments between organizations both inside and outside the enterprise. Documents must be protected and participants must be authenticated and accountable for their contributions and approvals.

- *Indirect access.* A user may request a service that in turn may access other services that the user might not otherwise be authorized to access.

In the following sections we describe the security technologies that most enterprises must upgrade or strengthen to achieve a security capability appropriate for an agile enterprise.

ENCRYPTION AND SIGNATURES

Encryption is a fundamental security requirement. Data are encrypted to protect them from exposure in an unprotected environment or medium of exchange. Encryption may also be used to enable a recipient to determine whether data have been changed.

Simple encryption can be performed by a transformation using a secret algorithm. Since it is difficult to define new, secret algorithms for every situation, current practice is to perform encryption with a standard encryption algorithm and a unique key. The key makes the encrypted data infeasible to decrypt simply by knowing the algorithm. Note that there is no perfect form of encryption; the more secure forms simply make decryption exceptionally difficult.

Secret key encryption, however, requires that both the originator and the intended recipient of the encrypted data know the secret key as well as the algorithm. That requires, first, that the two parties establish agreement on a secret key, and second, that a different secret key agreement be established for every exchange relationship. Secret key encryption is, nevertheless, a commonly used technique.

Public Key Encryption

In another form of encryption, called *public key encryption*, an entity possesses two complementary keys: a public key and a private key. The public key can be known by anyone, but only the owner knows the private key. The application of public key encryption is illustrated in Figure 6.1.

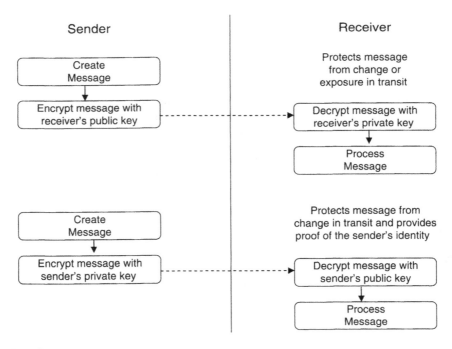

■ **FIGURE 6.1** Public Key Encryption.

Data encrypted with one of the keys can only be decrypted by the companion key. This allows a sender to encrypt data with a recipient's public key, and only the recipient can decrypt the data using the private key. Conversely, a sender can encrypt data with its private key, and a recipient can decrypt the data with the sender's public key; this assures that only the sender could have originated the data and the data have not been changed (but it does not keep the data secret). This system not only authenticates the sender, it establishes nonrepudiation of the content (in other words, the sender cannot deny sending it).

Public key encryption is the foundation of many industry security standards supporting Web services and SOA. A fundamental application is to create electronic signatures.

Electronic Signatures

The World Wide Web Consortium (W3C) has used public key encryption technology to define XML-Signature as a standard for creation and expression of electronic signatures in XML documents. An electronic signature is formed by first processing the data to be signed with a standard *digest algorithm* that creates a "hash value" that is unique (as a practical matter) for the digested data. A change to the data would result in a different hash value. The hash value is then encrypted with the signer's private key. To validate the signature, a recipient of the signed data applies the same digest algorithm to the data to recompute the hash value. This result is then compared to the signature value decrypted using the signer's public key. If the two hash values are the same, the signature is valid and the integrity of the data is assured.

Though public key encryption alone can ensure message integrity, the XML-Signature mechanism provides data integrity and nonrepudiation without incurring the cost of encrypting/decrypting entire documents.

The following is an example digital signature. Digest, key, and signature values are replaced with ellipses (...):

```
<Signature Id="SampleSignature"
xmlns="http://www.w3.org/2000/09/xmldsig#">
   <SignedInfo>
      <CanonicalizationMethod
      Algorithm="http://www.w3.org/TR/2001/REC-
      xml-c14n-20010315"/>
      <SignatureMethod
```

```
                         Algorithm="http://www.w3.org/2000/09/
                         xmldsig#dsa-sha1"/>
                         <Reference URI="#MySignedDocument">
                             <Transforms>
                                 <Transform Algorithm= "http://www.w3.
                                 org/TR/2001/REC-xml-c14n-20010315"/>
                             </Transforms>
                             <DigestMethod
                             Algorithm="http://www.w3.org/2000/09/
                             xmldsig#sha1"/>
                             <DigestValue>...</DigestValue>
                         </Reference
                     </SignedInfo>
                     <SignatureValue>...</SignatureValue>
                     <KeyInfo>
                         <KeyValue
                             <DSAKeyValue> ...</DSAKeyValue>
                         </KeyValue>
                     </KeyInfo>
                 </Signature>
```

A brief description of these elements follows:

- *Signature.* The signature element (includes all of the following):

    - *SignedInfo.* Specification of the information being signed (includes *CononicalizationMethod*, *SignatureMethod*, and one or more Reference elements)
    - *CanonicalizationMethod.* The algorithm used to structure the *SignedInfo* in a standard way.
    - *SignatureMethod.* The algorithm used to compute the signature.

- *Reference.* A link to the item being signed along with digest specifications (includes *Transforms*, *DigestMethod*, and *DigestValue*)
- *Transforms.* An optional set of transforms applied to the item being signed (includes one or more *Transforms* elements).
- *Transform.* A specific transform applied to the item being signed.
- *DigestMethod.* The digest algorithm applied to the item being signed.
- *DigestValue.* The value computed by the digest method.
- *SignatureValue.* The value computed by encryption of the *SignedInfo*, which includes the *SignedInfo* structure and the referenced content.
- *KeyInfo.* Optional information that may contain a key, certificate, name, or other key management information since the key may be available from other sources (includes *KeyValue* in the example).

- *KeyValue.* The public key of the signer (contains *DSAKeyValue* in the example).
- *DSAKeyValue.* The key value for DSA encryption as opposed to RSA encryption.

There may be multiple Reference elements for signing multiple objects. A reference may be to an element of the same document (which could be a complex structure) or documents referenced by URL.

ACCOUNTABILITY AND NONREPUDIATION

Accountability is a deterrent to undesirable behavior and a basis for enforcement of commitments. For example, employees are less likely to embezzle funds if they know they will get caught. A customer is more likely to pay for a service if the customer agreement cannot be repudiated and acceptance of a product or service can be proven.

In the past, and still today to a great extent, accountability is established through written signatures on documents. A signature on a paper document can be written in the presence of a witness, and the identity of the signer is established not only by the writing but by personal acquaintance of the parties and possibly credentials such as a passport or driver's license.

There are three important issues concerning enforcement of electronic documents: (1) documents as evidence, (2) compound documents, and (3) preservation of authenticity.

Electronic Documents as Evidence

Today, agreements and commitments are increasingly established electronically; many are in the form of XML documents. Traditional computer applications were developed for recordkeeping within departments. Users of these traditional application must establish their identity to access the system, and actions they take can be captured for accountability. Essentially the computer record of their input is their signature. However, this "signature" is meaningful only within the context of the application, and it is reliable only to the extent that the records cannot be changed to misrepresent responsibility.

When an enterprise records information or commitments from an external person or organization, the existence of the record in a system that belongs to the enterprise is not sufficient to resolve a dispute over the content. Enterprises are increasingly outsourcing business functions that have traditionally been held within the corporation. Without proof of message authenticity, a corporation cannot hold employees of outsourcing providers or the providers themselves legally accountable for the actions documented in electronic records. Even within an enterprise, where substantial assets are at stake, individuals should have greater assurance that their responsibility cannot be forged through tampering with electronic records, and the enterprise should have assurance that people really can be held accountable. In addition, government regulations are requiring greater assurance of accountability for operating decisions and controls.

For example, when an engineer submits a purchase request with an attached specification, the engineer must be accountable for the content of the request and the associated specification. When his or her manager approves it, the manager also becomes accountable. It should be possible to prove what the originator submitted and what the manager approved.

The solution to this dilemma is electronic signatures. The mechanism for applying and validating an electronic signature was discussed above. A signer is accountable and also protected from forgery because the signature could only have been created with his or her private key.

Electronic signatures should be used wherever written signatures would have been used in the past. This should include not only documents created with customers and business partners but documents created internally to authorize expenditures and transfers of assets. Support for signing and exchanging electronic documents should be incorporated into or associated with business process management systems so that signed documents can be an integral part of business processes. Few if any business process management systems currently support signatures on associated documents. An SOA infrastructure with support for public key encryption provides the necessary environment.

Compound Documents

The processing of business transactions frequently involves actions by multiple people or organizations; each of them contributes or approves aspects of the transaction, resulting in a compound document. The document defines the context and data associated with the particular business transaction. The document or portions of it move from one participant or service to the next to establish the context for activities and to capture results.

For example, extending our example, a purchase request and attached specification are originated by an engineer. That person's manager may be required to approve the expense and can add information regarding the approval. The request may then be directed to the purchasing organization to be reviewed and approved by a purchasing agent for compliance with corporate policies. The purchasing organization then proceeds to issue a purchase order (which may also be signed by the purchasing agent) that is incorporated by reference into the compound purchase request document.

Approvers cannot change what they received since it has been electronically signed by those who came before. Thus a compound electronic document may pass through different organizations for different purposes. The primary document may incorporate additional electronic documents by reference—for example, the specification attached to the purchase request might have been included by reference, and the electronic signatures would apply to the primary document and the referenced version of the specification.

Such situations are commonplace in paper-based systems. Current automated systems generally rely on records that are captured, processed, and retained in a single enterprise application with a defined set of authorized application users. With the automation of business processes and the movement of electronic documents among shared services, there must be consistent document integrity and participant accountability mechanisms that are effective across multiple business units as well as in exchanges with other enterprises.

XML-Signature allows each signature to apply to different portions of a compound document. Additional parts do not invalidate signatures on previous parts as long as the signed parts are not changed.

Preservation of Authenticity

Signatures ensure the integrity of the exchange of electronic documents; however, electronic business documents must remain valid for years. This fact places additional requirements on the handling of these documents.

First, a signed electronic document cannot be changed without the signature becoming invalid. In the signing and validation processes, a *canonicalization algorithm* is applied to ensure that the document is formatted in a standard way. This means that variations such as indentations and extra spaces produce the same signature value. But if the document is modified in any other way, the signature is no longer valid. This might occur, for example, if the document is converted to an internal computer form for processing and then regenerated for forwarding.

Thus a document cannot be transformed to comply with alternative data formats or element names required by a receiving application or service. If a transformation is necessary, the result must be considered a working document to be used by the recipient but distinct from the signed document. This creates some risk to the recipient that he or she (or the entity) may act on a misinterpretation or erroneous transformation of the original document as represented by the working document.

Signed documents should be archived in their original form. Note that documents included by reference must exist in their original form at the URL referenced in the composite document, since the reference is part of the signed data. This should be considered in the creation of the document so that the referenced documents continue to be available and the signature continues to be valid.

Over time, signatures may become questionable. A signer may claim that at the time he or she signed the document, his or her private key was compromised, so the document is a forgery. Records of a certificate authority (discussed later) can provide evidence to the contrary. If the signer gave no notice of revocation of the certificate within a reasonable time of signing the document, that would suggest that the signature was valid.

As a further measure, an "electronic notary" service might be employed. The electronic notary should be operated by a trusted third party. The notary can independently contact the signer to confirm his or her signature on the document. The notary signs the document as an independent third party. The notarized document and signatures can then be archived.

IDENTIFICATION AND AUTHENTICATION

Identification refers to associating a known identifier with a party. *Authentication* refers to determining if the party is legitimately using the identifier. There are three fundamental forms of identification and authentication: (1) what you know (such as an identifier and password), (2) what you have (such as a credit card, preferably a smart card with encrypted key), or (3) what you are (such as a fingerprint).

The traditional form of identification and authentication is through the use of an identifier and password. This approach has limited value. We refer to the entity to be identified as the *requesting party* and the entity requiring the identification as the *relying party*. The requesting party and relying party must first establish an initial trust relationship so that they agree on values of the identifier and password for the requesting party. For subsequent contacts, the requesting party's identifier is recognized by the relying party, and the password is a secret associated with the requesting party's identifier and known only to the requesting party and the relying party. If the requesting party uses the same password for other relationships, there are multiple relying parties that know the requesting party's secret password, and there is an increased risk of exposure where all relationships would be at risk. In addition, various recipients may require different identifiers for the same requesting party. Consequently, the requesting party must keep track of multiple identifiers and passwords.

The use of multiple identifiers also makes it difficult to recognize where the same person should be authorized to access the same business transaction from different applications or when a person is violating a separation-of-duties requirement by performing two mutually exclusive roles.

Digital Certificates

Public key encryption and electronic signatures provide a more robust and convenient form of identification and authentication. To establish an initial relationship, the identity of a participant is established with a trusted third party. The trusted third party provides a *digital certificate* that the third party has signed containing the identifier and public key of the participant. The participant can then establish its identity by demonstrating that it holds the complementary private key.

A standard form for a digital certificate is specified by International Telecommunications Union-Telecommunications Standards (ITU-T) X.509v3. A certificate authority (CA) is a trusted third party whereby entities can register their identities and public keys and obtain digital certificates signed by the CA. The CA also provides a certificate revocation list (CRL) of certificates for which the private keys have been compromised.

An X.509v3 digital certificate typically contains the following fields:

- *version.* V1, v2, or v3, designating the version of the certificate standard.
- *serialNumber.* A unique serial number that identifies the certificate.

- *signature.* Identifier for the algorithm used by the CA to sign the certificate.
- *issuer.* A unique identifier for the certificate authority that issued this certificate.
- *validity.* The valid time interval, two times indicating the earliest time the certificate is valid and the latest.
- *subject.* A unique name that identifies the entity for which the certificate is issued.
- *subjectPublicKeyInfo.* Contains the public key for the identified entity along with an identifier for the encryption algorithm used with the key (next two items).
- *signatureAlgorithm.* Identifier for the algorithm used by the CA to sign the certificate.
- *signatureValue.* The value of the certificate authority signature.
- *issuerUniqueID (optional).* A unique identifier for the CA that would resolve possible reuse of the issuer identifier used previously.
- *subjectUniqueID (optional).* A unique identifier for the subject entity that would resolve possible reuse of the subject identifier used previously.
- *extensions (optional).* Optional extensions that address special cases and restrictions, such as a certificate that identifies a CA and a certificate restricted to use for a specific purpose, such as for signatures only.

A *public key infrastructure* (PKI) is a set of facilities to support the use of digital certificates for identification and authentication. Minimally this involves a registration authority (RA) that validates the identity of entities seeking a certificate, a CA that issues and signs digital certificates and maintains a certificate revocation list, and directories where the certificates (containing the public keys) are available for access. An enterprise should implement a PKI for identification of its employees and service units.

Authentication of a party presenting a digital certificate is somewhat different from authentication with a password. The following steps describe an example exchange:

1. A requesting party submits its digital certificate.

2. The relying party validates the signature of the certificate authority. This establishes that the certificate is valid.

3. The relying party checks the validity time interval to ensure that the certificate has not expired.

4. The relying party checks the certificate authority revocation list to ensure that the certificate has not been revoked.

5. If the certificate is valid, it contains the identifier and public key of an identified party, but it is not yet established that this certificate belongs to the requesting party. The relying party may then encrypt a "nonce" (a unique bit string) with the certificate owner's public key and send it to the requesting party.

6. The requesting party returns a checksum computed with a standard algorithm and encrypted with its private key, using several established elements known to both parties, such as the requesting party's name, public key, the nonce value, and the requested service URL.

7. The relying party receives and decrypts the checksum and performs the checksum algorithm on the same elements to verify that the requesting party was able to correctly decrypt the nonce and encrypt the checksum (with the private key). The nonce prevents an imposter from copying an encrypted checksum from a different exchange by the requesting party.

At the end of this exchange, a valid link has been established for subsequent exchanges. If the requesting party is a person, essentially the link is established with the person's personal computer and browser, with the assumption that the person is in control of the computer. In high-security circumstances, it may be necessary to establish that the person using the computer is actually the owner of the certificate through other forms of identity verification, such as queries about personal information or use of biometric devices such as fingerprint verification. This is described as *multitoken authentication*.

Two-Way Authentication

The described protocol shows how a requester can be properly authenticated, but there are circumstances in which the provider must also be authenticated. On the public Internet, people are often victims of identity theft or other fraudulent activities because they are directed to interactions with an imposter of a trusted provider such as their bank. Within an enterprise, service users should be able to have their requests redirected when a service provider is replaced or upgraded with a new address, but there could be a risk of being redirected to a fraudulent service.

Where these risks are a concern, the service user should also authenticate the service provider. Service providers should provide a complementary protocol by which a requester can request and validate the provider's credentials.

Single Sign-On

A PKI provides the basis for single sign-on. An individual signs on to his or her personal computer to enable access to the private key; generally users are not expected to remember their private key but have an easier-to-remember password to sign onto their personal computer. On the basis of their certificate and their private key, they can be automatically identified and authenticated for multiple systems. Legacy systems can be enabled with adapters to accept the certificates for identification. The approach reduces security administration and improves security by reducing risk of exposure of conventional passwords, since the user never reveals the secret key.

For SOA, service units and personnel must have identities that are recognized throughout the extended enterprise. It should be possible to establish ad hoc interactions with services to support enterprise-level planning and decision making and to quickly adapt to changing business requirements. PKI and single sign-on are fundamental steps to achieve this flexibility.

Unified identification and authentication also enable one service to pass the identity of a requester through to other services needed to support the original request. This ensures that the requester does not do indirectly what he or she is not authorized to do directly. It also provides support for accountability back to the originator of a request.

The WS-Security standard from OASIS defines a generally accepted approach to integration of standard elements to convey authentication information and ensure message integrity.

AUTHORIZATION

It is not sufficient for a participant in an exchange to be authenticated and have a reliable identifier. The participant must also have appropriate authorization to participate in an exchange or access certain resources.

System access control is no longer a matter of defining which members of a department are authorized to perform particular operations or access certain data. Users of a shared service may come directly or indirectly from many different organizations, potentially outside as well as inside the corporation. Authorization and access control must be addressed at an enterprise level and, eventually, at an extended enterprise level, with an approach and administrative processes that work for all users and all services.

An example authentication and authorization exchange is illustrated in Figure 6.2. Central to this exchange is the use of Security Assertion Markup Language (SAML), a standard developed by OASIS that defines the form of expression of the authorization request and response in steps 6 to 9 of the exchange described at the end of this paragraph. Different security mechanisms may be used in conjunction with SAML, but a PKI is recommended. Note that in the diagram, arrows that loop back past the requester are redirections of the request through the requester, so responses always come back to the requester from the last-requested site:

1. The requester requests Service X.

2. Service X access control determines that the requester is not currently signed onto this service and redirects the request to the security service with an associated URL for the Service X artifact receiver that expects to receive a SAML assertion.

3. Security service access control determines that the requester is not currently signed on to the security service and issues a credential challenge to the requester. If the requester has already signed on to the security service, skip to step 5.

4. The requester responds to the credential challenge and the response is processed by the authentication authority.

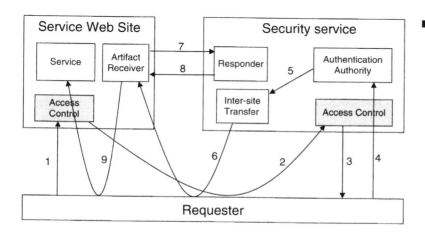

■ **FIGURE 6.2** Access Authorization.

5. The original request to Service X along with authentication information is directed to the local intersite transfer service.

6. The request is then redirected to the original service site artifact receiver function, along with a SAML "assertion" that specifies the requester's attributes, the "responder" (next step), and the URL for the original service request being forwarded from the security service.

7. The Service X artifact receiver submits a SAML authorization request, which includes the SAML artifact along with information about the request, to the security service's responder.

8. The responder applies appropriate policy rules to the SAML artifact and the request information and returns a decision.

9. An authorized request is redirected to the requested Service X; otherwise the request will be rejected as unauthorized.

This architecture separates the determination of authentication and authorization from the requested service. The attributes of the requesters and the services as well as the security policies are managed and evaluated by the security service. This allows these factors to be managed and controlled independent of changes to the requesters and services, and the overall permissions granted to individuals can be analyzed for consistency and appropriateness. Specialized hardware products, described as *XML appliances*, are designed for optimal performance of these access control functions.

Since this approach removes access control decisions from the resource being accessed, a legacy application may be protected by the same mechanism as current applications and services. This enables single sign-on within the scope of the enterprise and provides consolidated specification of access control for improved analysis, control, and accountability for authorization.

ROLE-BASED ACCESS CONTROL, EXTENDED

Role-based access control (RBAC) is a widely accepted approach to authorization. The general concept is that the "subject" (the person, system, or other business entity to be authorized) is assigned certain roles that associate authorization policies with resource access control rules. RBAC relationships are depicted in Figure 6.3. The roles have a user focus and effectively characterize the kinds of actions a user should be able to take to fulfill his or her responsibilities within the

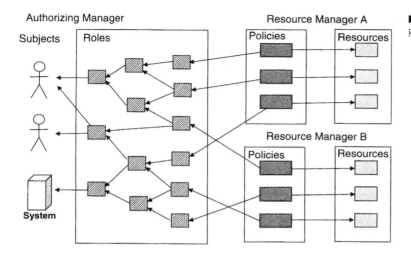

Authorizing Manager

enterprise. The policies and rules have a service focus and define the details of the authorization of specific roles to specific resources.

The exclusive use of roles to specify access authorization has some limitations. We extend basic RBAC by requiring that the subject have attributes that are relevant to his or her authorization, such as the subject's position in the organization. These attributes can be references within policies to further restrict authorization for particular roles.

An RBAC management facility should support a role inheritance mechanism, as depicted in Figure 6.3. Roles may be defined as incorporating the characteristics of other roles. Elementary roles are the most limited and specific, whereas compound roles incorporate the characteristics of less complex roles. So, in the figure, the subjects are assigned the roles that directly and indirectly point to them. This reduces the duplication of access control specifications and allows roles to be composed to more closely align to the access authorization requirements of job assignments.

These roles represent a different perspective from the roles in business processes and organizations. Process roles define a need for a performer, with selection based on attributes required to meet the need, and the process defines the bounds of required behavior—participation in the process. Organizational roles, or positions, define a more generic need, with qualifications (which may be more subjective), and the job description characterizes the bounds of required behavior. Security roles are assertions of the roles a person or system—a subject—is allowed to perform, and access control policies are the limits of expected behavior with respect to accessing resources. The security role assignments reflect consideration of the activities in which the subject is qualified to participate based on his or her responsibilities.

Security roles tend to be more specific than organizational roles and more general than process roles. So, a person in a given position may be assigned several security roles that characterize different types of activities, whereas a single security role may incorporate access authorization that is adequate for the person to participate in a number of similar process roles.

Sometimes security roles and positions can be identified as the same—for example, *manager* and *salesperson*—but these roles likely characterize only a primary responsibility of the position, so the same person will likely require other security roles from time to time based on assignments. Sometimes a process role and a security role can be identified as the same, such as *editor* or *reviewer*, but the process role designations are more likely to be meaningful only in the process context.

Note that the authorization specifications are also a protected resource, and managers must be authorized to make role assignments and specify resource security policies. This is discussed in more depth later in the chapter.

The definitions of these various roles should be considered orthogonal so that they can be managed independently; otherwise, a change could mean that each of the others would require changes. That is, job descriptions, process definitions, and security authorizations would be tightly coupled. At a minimum, references to roles should be appropriately qualified so that there is no confusion about roles that have the same name but different meanings.

Security roles are defined as required to address the access authorization needs of individuals and systems according to the nature of their business activities. A person likely has several roles that together define that person's authorization. The grantor of authorization, the person who assigns the roles to the person, should be able to think in general terms about the things the person needs to be able to do, and the roles should incorporate appropriate authorization.

RBAC is particularly important in SOA because of the expanded community of potential users of services and the need to authorize people as well as systems for appropriate access before their activities are disrupted and delayed by denials of access.

The manager authorizing access is not usually the manager of the service for which access is required. RBAC enables a separation of responsibilities so that the service manager can specify the access authorization of certain roles, and the managers of employees can assign roles to employees, giving them the necessary authorization to do their jobs.

Of course, assignment of roles, in many cases, is not a unilateral decision by an employee's manager but instead involves an approval process in which other managers, perhaps the service unit manager, have the opportunity to scrutinize the authorization.

Development of a specification for business-oriented modeling of RBAC specifications has been initiated at the Object Management Group (OMG).

Definitions of Roles

The following are a number of examples of types of roles to be considered:

- *Organizational role.* The position of a person in an organization determines certain types of authority, such as an expense authorization limit as well as hiring and firing authority, that are applied by approval processes. The position also implies certain access authorization required to perform in the position.

- *Financial role.* The relationship of a person to a budget account determines his or her authority with respect to that account. This authority is usually related to organizational position. For example, a person should only be able to approve expenditures against a specified budget account.

- *Process role.* A subject (person or system) may be assigned a role in a particular process. The subject should have authorization to access associated operations and data for that particular process instance but not other instances of the same process.

- *Process management role.* A person may have authority to make process role assignments, resolve exceptions, and approve variances in specified business processes.

- *Agent role.* A subject may participate in certain types of activity or agreements with specified authority to make commitments on behalf of another person, organization, or enterprise. This may reduce to authorization to participate in processes in which such agreements are being established and the context defines the principal of the agreement as a client of this agent.

- *Surrogate role.* A person (surrogate) performs as another person (grantor) in certain designated roles of the grantor that the grantor is authorized to delegate.

- *Proxy role.* A person grants authorization to another to act with the grantor's authority in a particular activity or process, so the authorization is restricted to a specified context, as opposed to all similar activities or processes.

- *Employee role.* Any employee should have authorization to access certain personal information, submit time and expense reports, and access other enterprise information related to employment and employee benefits. Similar general controls may be defined for contract employees and employees of business partners.

The goal of this complex set of role definitions is to improve the ease and accuracy of authorization. A new employee is assigned one or more roles that are typical of the job. It is not necessary to examine each person's responsibilities and authority with respect to everything they may do and every system with which they might interact. The result is that the authorization is actually more considered and complete because it is expressed in appropriate business terms. The same applies when the employee gets a new assignment. Furthermore, as systems change or new systems are implemented, it is not necessary to change the authorization of every potential participant, only to redefine the authorization specifications for the affected, elementary roles.

Role Authorization Requirements

Each type of role discussed previously places different requirements on the rules that specify the access authorization of a role. The most straightforward specifications of authorization grant access to service operations including requests for data. Rules for data access might restrict access to certain classes and attributes or relationships on those classes. However, there are often further restrictions on authorization, such as those discussed in the following sections.

Attributes of the Subject

The subject (person or system being authorized) may have credentials, such as a license or certification, that qualifies them for access to certain resources, regardless of the person's organization position or current assignment. This can be addressed simply by assignment of a role that reflects the necessary authorization in its access policies.

The Subject's Organizational Relationships

The policies associated with an organizational position may define authorization based on the relationship of the position to people in other positions. So a manager can access personnel records of subordinates but not personnel records of other employees such as subordinates of other managers. (This also requires reference to context data, for example, the employee in the record.) For financial records, a subject might be restricted to records pertaining to the organization in which the subject has a managerial position.

Note that a person may be assigned to multiple positions at the same time, such as department manager, member of a task force, and project leader. Each of these positions may bring a different set of roles.

The Subject's Relationship to a Process

A subject may be a requester of a process, a participant in a process, or a manager of a process. A requester may have authorization to initiate a process, but then, for an active process, access is restricted to process instances he or she requested. A participant in a process generally is restricted to access of processes and associated data for process instances to which he or she is assigned to a role. Generally, a process manager has administrative access to all instances of a process type, but in some cases different organizations may use the same processes and a manager might be restricted to administrative access to process instances initiated within his or her department.

In all cases where the subject is restricted to less than all instances of a process, the rules must refer to context data of the process instance, to establish the subject's relationship. For example, the rule for a process participant must find that the participant identity matches the identity of the person assigned to the process role. Rules may then authorize access to data associated with the context, such as product data for the associated product.

The Subject's Relationship to Data Being Accessed

A subject's access to data may be restricted to data that is in some way related to the subject. For example, an employee is authorized to read but not update his or her personnel records. In this case the requester's employee identification must match the employee identification of the record. A general policy might authorize an employee to read any document that he or she signed.

Grant of Authorization by Another Subject

Each grant of authority is made by someone else with authority to make that grant of authority. A subject's authorization should be by reference to the authorization of the grantor. A grant may be constrained by (1) the role(s) the grantor intends to delegate, (2) the role(s) the grantor is allowed to delegate, and (3) additional restrictions imposed by the grantor. This includes surrogates and proxies where the authority to designate surrogates or proxies may be restricted to certain persons and certain contexts. As in other situations, the subject should be accountable for his or her actions, but here the grantor should also be accountable for actions taken by the subject under the grantor's authorization. In all cases, an audit trail should identify the grantor of authorization and when the grant of authorization was effective.

Runtime Authorization

At runtime, a service unit should not need to deal with the details of the participant's roles or the details of the policies. Those data are maintained and applied by the security service, and the authorization determinations are made by the security service.

When a participant requests a particular service operation, a request is sent to the security service, specifying the participant, the type of request, and context data. The security service retrieves the participant's role specifications, evaluates the relevant policies against the roles and the context of the intended action, determines whether permission should be granted, and returns that result to the requesting service.

Note that a request for authorization evaluation may occur not only when the participant accesses a service but could occur when the service is about to take a protected action or return a result that might have different restrictions from the initial request.

When a party invokes a service and that service unit invokes another service, the actions of the second service unit must be based on appropriate authorization. This may occur in two ways: (1) the original party may authorize the intermediate service unit to act on its behalf, so the access to the second service is based on the party's credentials, or (2) the intermediate service unit acts on its own behalf on the basis that its actions are authorized to fulfill authorized requests it receives.

The first alternative creates the risk that the intermediate service unit could use the originating party's credentials to access resources it would otherwise not be authorized to access. This could be addressed by requiring both the originating party and the intermediate service to have appropriate authorizations. The second alternative relies on the intermediate service unit having an understanding of appropriate limitations on use of the second service and the results it returns.

XACML POLICIES

eXtensible Access Control Markup Language (XACML) is an OASIS standard for specification of policies and rules that define access authorization. Figure 6.4 depicts an abstraction of an XACML authorization structure.

A *PolicySet* contains one or more policies and may contain *PolicySets*, making it potentially recursive. A Policy contains rules for determination of authorization.

A *PolicySet* contains a *Target* element, and a *Target* element may also appear in a *Policy* or a *Rule*. The *Target* element limits the number of policies and rules that must be considered for an authorization request based on the context.

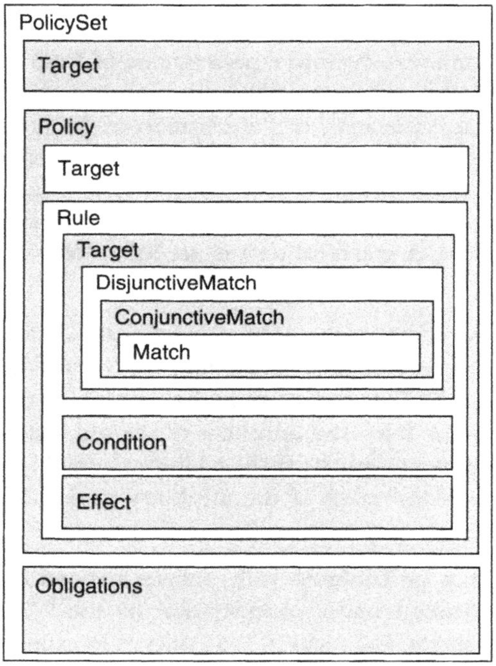

■ **FIGURE 6.4** XACML Policy Set Structure.

A *Target* defines circumstances and things for which the associated *PolicySet*, *Policy*, or *Rule* applies. It contains *DisjunctiveMatch* (logical *or*) elements that in turn contain *ConjunctiveMatch* (logical *and*) elements that each contain *Match* elements. The result is a set of alternative sets of *Match* conditions that apply to one or more subjects (that is, participants) of the authorization request and the resources, actions, or environment to be accessed. Each *Match* contains an attribute value and a reference to an attribute in the context or subject attributes. When the target matches, the policy set, policy, or rule is further evaluated.

A *PolicySet* or a *Policy* may contain *Obligations*. These are specifications of required actions to be taken at the point of authorization enforcement. There are currently no standards defined for obligations.

Within a policy, each *Rule* contains a *Condition* and an *Effect*. The *Condition* contains expressions that evaluate to true or false. These operate on attributes similar to those of the *Match* elements, but there are more complex functions that may be applied to determine the result. The *Effect* is the associated result if the condition is true and returns a value of *Permit* or *Deny*. Policy qualifiers can determine whether rule evaluation stops when the first *Permit* or *Deny* is encountered.

This discussion has been an oversimplified representation of XACML policy specifications. *PolicySet* and *Policy* have a number of other elements that qualify the interpretation and application of the policies. Rule conditions can also be very complex. The language is capable of expressing diverse authorization policies. The difficulty is that, as an XML form, it is quite verbose and the intent of the policies is obscured by the XML details. A graphical tool is needed to provide appropriate abstractions.

XACML 2.0 is expected to complement SAML 2.0 so that XACML expressions can operate on SAML subject attributes. Of course, the attributes referenced in an XACML policy must be present in the authorization request and the roles and attributes of the associated subjects, and the attribute names must match. Additional qualifiers can determine the action to be taken if the attributes cannot be found.

XACML policies should not be confused with policies defined by WS-Policy, another specification under consideration by the W3C for definition of service policies. The focus of WS-Policy is to express requirements and capabilities of services so that service users can determine whether potential providers are compatible. The WS-Policy assertions are essentially service specifications, whereas XACML policies are rules that must be evaluated to determine whether access is allowed or denied.

ACCESS CONTROL ADMINISTRATION

Roles and policies must work together to achieve the desired access control. Responsibility for access control policies is primarily the responsibility of managers of the services to be accessed. Responsibility for role specifications for a subject is primarily the responsibility of the individual's manager. When a service unit acts as a subject, it also needs role assignments that, for the most part, are the responsibility of the service unit manager.

Administration of roles and policies is a highly sensitive capability and must be protected by appropriate access controls. For administration, the access control roles and policies must define authorization to create or change roles and policies of others. Managers with authorization to assign roles or define policies must be restricted regarding the roles they can assign, the entities to which they can assign roles, and the services for which they can define access policies.

Changes to roles, role assignments, and policies should be managed through appropriate business processes. In the course of their work, individuals encounter needs for access authorization and should have a defined process for requesting authorization. The request should be given appropriate approval, the change should be defined by a qualified person, and, depending on the nature of the authorization, the proposed change should be reviewed and approved by other managers.

Many of the changes are required only at the time a new service is implemented or a person is assigned to a new position in the organization. However, other changes, particularly to role assignments, may occur more often. Primary examples are delegation of authorization such as the surrogate and proxy roles and temporary assignments such as participation in a project or task force.

A surrogate role requires that the primary individual grant authorization to their surrogate to perform with certain authorization defined by the organizational position of the primary individual. The grantor must be able to redirect requests to the surrogate and define the roles the surrogate is authorized to perform.

A proxy role is similar to a surrogate role except that the grant of authorization is restricted to a specific context such as a process, a project, or a design review. In this case, the delegation must include an attribute that specifies the particular context.

Both these delegations require supporting policies. In general, security policies should be generalized to avoid identifying specific personnel, organizations, resources, or processes and should relate variables in an authorization request to attributes of participating entities and the context in which they seek authorization. So there should be general rules to authorize the grant of surrogate and proxy authorization, and there should be general rules to enable the surrogate or proxy to exercise their restricted authorization at runtime. In addition, there must be accountability for changes to role assignments and policy specifications. It should be possible to determine who granted authorization for an entity to take a specific action, and grantors should be able to periodically review the authorization (that is, role assignments) they have granted.

Clearly, the development of roles and policies is a complex undertaking. Special skills and tools are required to establish the initial framework, to define administration processes, and to enable businesspeople to manage routine changes such as assignments of roles by managers. This may require assistance from a person skilled in the specification of policies, but the managers have clear responsibility and the policies should not change very often.

On the other hand, assignment of roles to people does occur frequently, and certain roles may be assigned frequently throughout the enterprise. The assignment of roles, itself, must be the subject of formal business processes that ensure appropriate criteria are applied and appropriate approvals are obtained.

Modeling tools are needed to appropriately specify grants of authorization. Managers must be able to easily express role assignments and policies and to periodically review all the specifications for which they are responsible as well as the subjects that have been granted authority to access their resources by other managers. Modeling tools are discussed further in Chapter 10.

FEDERATION OF TRUST DOMAINS

A large enterprise may have separate divisions or subsidiaries that each manage security data about their personnel separately—that is, those in different trust domains. At the same time, there is the potential for shared services that personnel from multiple divisions or subsidiaries should be allowed to access. In addition, an enterprise may have close relationships with certain business partners where business partner personnel should be allowed to access certain enterprise systems and services, and conversely, enterprise employees should be able to access certain business partner systems and services.

For example, a business partner employee may represent the business partner in a business transaction, and the receiving service must determine whether the employee has the authorization to act on behalf of the business partner organization. Similarly, different customers may submit requests in the form of product or service orders. These requests may be submitted by authorized customer personnel. The receiving enterprise must determine that the customer is trustworthy and that the request is appropriately authorized by the customer organization or other trustworthy entity.

Essentially, these participants come from other trust domains. They are not known to the enterprise. Their trustworthiness must be established by another source that has been previously established as sufficiently trustworthy.

An extended enterprise may involve a number of suppliers and customers. Each of these has mechanisms for identity authentication and authorization of their employees and others who are expected to access their systems and services.

There is currently no industry standard for federation. A WS-Federation specification has been proposed and is the subject of an OASIS technical committee formed in May 2007.

Federation involves a cooperative relationship between trust domains so that participants known to one domain can obtain access privileges in another domain. The following steps are an example of the type of exchange required for service of one enterprise to allow access to an employee of a trusted business partner.

1. The relying domain security service locates the participant's home trust domain.

2. The home trust domain provides the participant credentials that specify attributes for relevant roles. These may be restricted to roles and attributes that are allowed to be shared with other trust domains.

3. The relying domain security service must accept the identity of the participant, probably as a temporary entity for the duration of the login, to support subsequent authorization requests.

4. The relying domain security service must transform and filter the participant's credentials to its local requirements (including limitations on acceptable roles), and the subject's credentials must be made available for subsequent access decisions.

5. The relying trust domain then proceeds with its normal response to the initial request using the subject's ad hoc identity and security assertions.

The requested service subsequently requests authorization(s) that apply the local policies and rules to the request context and the participant's credentials.

There may be different approaches to step 1. For example, the Liberty Alliance has defined an approach to work with Web browsers. This approach requires that a participant first log in at a home trust domain. The authentication service calls a common domain server to send a cookie to that participant and create a record that the user is logged in. The common domain server is accessible from all affiliated trust domains.

The relying security service acting in step 1 sends a request to the common domain service, which has access to the participant's cookie. (A cookie is only accessible to the domain that created it.) The common domain then returns the identity of the user's home security service to the relying security service. The relying security service must then obtain the participant's credentials as described in steps 2 through 5. The common domain service tracks the domains in which the participant is signed in so that it can propagate a logout or expiration of the session.

The Liberty Alliance protocol only works with Web browsers, involves more message exchanges to establish access authorization, and relies on a common domain server that represents a potential single point of failure for all participating trust domains.

In the absence of an industry standard, the most straightforward approach is to establish partner employee identities within the enterprise security system and grant restricted access similar to that granted to contract personnel. This results in some increased administrative effort but avoids the need to develop and implement custom strategies and techniques that require continuing attention as business partners or their systems change.

PERIMETER SECURITY

Enterprise security has focused on access control at a protected perimeter, between the internal systems of the enterprise and the outside world. In early data centers, the perimeter was the walls of the data center. As the scope of access was expanded to remote access, the perimeter expanded to controlled use of online devices. As access was expanded to the Internet, firewalls controlled access from outside the enterprise.

Although the Internet does represent a major threat to security, there are nevertheless threats within the enterprise from both employees and from nonemployees who gain access to the intranet. Internal networks are often accessible from conference rooms or other less secure sites. The sheer size of internal networks and number of systems accessible from the enterprise intranet represent a significant security risk.

Enterprises that implement the high degree of integration, accessibility, and flexibility represented by SOA have an increased risk of intrusion. This risk can be reduced by creating smaller protected domains within the enterprise network.

SOA enables compartmentalization. Each service unit represents a compartmentalized capability that is integrated through well-defined interfaces. Service unit applications can be isolated behind their Web servers. An access control perimeter with firewall and proxy server can be established around each service unit that manages highly sensitive data or operations. Consequently, access to service units is still limited when there is intrusion into the enterprise intranet.

VULNERABILITY SCANNING AND INTRUSION DETECTION

SOA increases the number of access points for enterprise systems, and many of these access points are exposed to the public Internet. XML technology provides a common target for identification of vulnerabilities by potential intruders. The widespread use of popular middleware products, XML appliances, and XML processing algorithms all increase the risk of exposure by enabling intruders to exploit vulnerabilities in those products. Of course, critical business transactions provide a very appealing target to intruders.

For requests from known requesters, strong authentication and accountability mechanisms provide a deterrent. In addition, a new class of product has emerged: XML hardware in the form of a firewall or appliance. These are hardware products that scan XML messages for known problems essentially equivalent to the scanning of email messages for viruses. The XML firewall extends traditional firewall capabilities to address these XML concerns. By implementing these capabilities in hardware, the performance impact can be minimized.

Increased exposure also results from efforts to detect and respond to disruptive events from various external sources as discussed in the next chapter. Fraudulent events could trigger false alarms or emergency response that would disrupt business operations or worse.

MONITORING, LOGGING, ALERTS, AND AUDITS

Monitoring, logging, alerts, and audits are not new business requirements—they were common practice before computers. What has changed is the volume of activity, the number of participants, the obscurity of business operations occurring within computer systems, and the exposure of systems and communications to Internet access.

The security service unit should produce a log of restricted activity and provide reports for periodic review by the application or process owners so that monitoring and analysis span the enterprise. Managers should be aware of the ways in which their employees are using their grants of authorization. Monitoring and query capabilities should be provided for observation and investigation of potential improprieties. The level of tracking accesses should reflect the level of sensitivity of the resource and the type of operation so that queries about the status of a purchase order are not tracked with the same level of concern as queries against personnel records. It should also be possible to program various alerts to provide notice when certain unusual operations are performed or the occurrence of certain requests exceeds normal thresholds. Periodic audits should be conducted to assess controls, analyze authorization criteria, and sample current activity.

Monitoring, logging, alerts, and audit support should be incorporated into sensitive business processes and applications as well as the security infrastructure. Commercial products are available to support monitoring and logging at an access control level, but standards are needed for monitoring and assessing process activity to identify questionable business transactions. Such capabilities should be incorporated in business process management systems (BPMS), discussed in Chapter 3, and business activity monitoring (BAM), discussed in Chapter 5.

Though organizational roles are orthogonal to security roles, organizational roles define responsibility for resources. Consequently, reporting of access activity should be directed to the management chain of the protected resources. Furthermore, reporting of denied requests for access to sensitive resources should be reported to the management chain of the individual making the request. Thus the organization structure is an important consideration in the monitoring of security as well as the implementation of access controls. We will discuss the nature of the agile organization structure in the next chapter.

The Agile Organization Structure

An enterprise organization structure defines the relationships among people, along with their respective responsibilities and authority, as the basis of their collective efforts to achieve enterprise objectives. It also defines the chains of command through which enterprise management exerts leadership, accountability, and control. An agile enterprise changes these relationships by breaking down departmental silos into sharable service units and driving performance based on an SOA. The participation and relationships of people continue to be important in the agile enterprise, but the focus has shifted from performing production tasks to managing exceptions and resolving needs to address business challenges and opportunities.

Viewed from the bottom up, SOA is an approach to consolidation of duplicated capabilities to achieve economies of scale or control. However, when we view SOA as a fundamental approach to design of the organization, it yields a different vision. The enterprise becomes a network of services, contributing to value chains that achieve enterprise objectives. Essentially, service units are enterprise capabilities that can be engaged in a variety of enterprise pursuits. This is a sort of "hyper-matrix" structure because the cross-functional drivers are not restricted to a single dimension, such as products, customers, or markets. Instead, any new "matrix" can be established through the implementation of a value chain that engages the needed services to achieve particular business values.

In addition, people in the organization may have multiple roles and functional relationships, as depicted in Figure 7.1. This diagram depicts a hypothetical service unit and various relationships of personnel in that service unit. They are all part of a traditional management hierarchy, but they will participate in various other collaborative activities to

■ **FIGURE 7.1** Organizational Relationships.

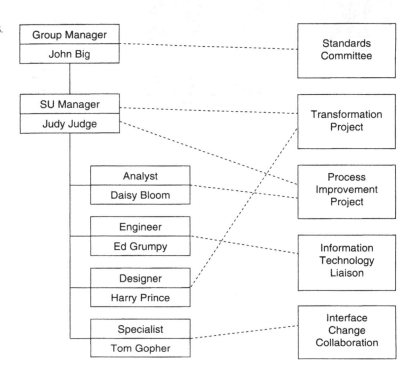

implement changes or resolve issues that go beyond the interests of their individual service unit.

Some of these collaborative activities are with representatives of service units that are users of or providers to the subject service unit—to resolve service problems or negotiate changes in a service interface or level of service specifications. Some collaborations, such as the Information Technology Liaison, are to obtain support services from other service units. Still other collaborations involve participation in executive staff initiatives to design enterprise capabilities or implement changes. A number of these relationships are discussed further in Chapter 9 on governance. The diagram does not express the organizational aspects of role assignments for access authorization or management chains for approvals associated with the collaborative activities.

In the following sections we begin by examining design principles for an agile organization. Then we discuss several high-level categories of services that suggest primary departments of the organization structure. Next, we discuss design factors for grouping service units into an organization hierarchy. Finally, we consider a general approach to transforming an existing organization to achieve the agility and performance potential of a SOA.

DESIGN PRINCIPLES

Several design principles are important to the design of an agile organization structure.

Centralization for Enterprise Optimization

A major design goal is enterprise optimization: economies of scale and leveraged capabilities. This requires centralized management to address the following requirements:

- Definition of shared services must overcome resistance of organizations that experience loss of local control.
- Changes to a service interface (specification of interactions with a service) require consideration of the impact on related services and the potential replacement by alternative services.
- Investments in development and improvement of capabilities require setting enterprise priorities and balancing enterprise objectives
- Agility requires the ability to retrain and redeploy personnel for shifts in workload and transformations to address new business capabilities.
- Technical standards must be enforced, including product, production, and information technology standards, to support both economies of scale and enterprise flexibility.
- Purchase of equipment and facilities must be considered with respect to optimal utilization of assets and shared support services.

These considerations are explored further in Chapter 9 on governance.

Management Hierarchy

The management hierarchy of an agile enterprise is, in many ways, similar to the management hierarchy of traditional organizations. However, in a service-oriented enterprise, every manager is a provider of services. He or she is responsible to the service users for the cost, quality, and timeliness of the services provided (i.e., what is done) and to the management chain for the effective management of resources in compliance with government regulations and requirements for enterprise optimization (i.e., how it is done).

Managers higher in the management hierarchy have responsibility for an aggregation of services that generally have some similarities or common objectives, as discussed later. These service groups may include specialists and support services for services units in their area of responsibility. For example, a manufacturing manager may also have materials management, machine repair, and product repair service units to support the value chain operations for production.

The management chain has direct control of the way services are performed but must negotiate service requirements to optimize utilization of resources while meeting current and future needs of service users. The manager must pursue continuous improvement and adapt to changing business challenges and opportunities, to maintain at least an industry best-practice level of performance, if not a competitive advantage for the enterprise. In a sense, each manager is responsible for a subordinate enterprise that must meet the needs of its customers and achieve stockholder objectives.

Service Units as Building Blocks

Fundamental to the agile enterprise is the identification of service units that provide distinct business capabilities. These capabilities, for the most part, should survive changes in the business to deliver new products or pursue new markets. A service unit should be able to apply its capability in a number of business contexts as requests are received from different users of its services. As stable components of the enterprise, they are the building blocks of current and future business endeavors.

Note that a service unit is an organizational unit that applies a capability to deliver a result. The manager of a service unit has direct responsibility for resources except to the extent that management of some operations is delegated to other service units. The manager retains responsibility to ensure that either those operations that are delegated meet requirements or that alternative providers are considered. An organizational unit that is formed to manage other managers is not a service unit at all but rather an organization formed to improve management of resources and pursuit of enterprise objectives among the service units under that management.

Service Unit Autonomy

A service unit manager should have autonomy to improve the cost, quality, and timeliness of the service within the constraints established by enterprise-defined specifications for services, enterprise policies, and budget. As a stable, enterprise-building block, a service unit should have clear, long-term objectives and an expectation of adequate and stable staffing. The service unit manager and the personnel of the service unit should be the experts for the particular service, and they should be empowered to pursue improvements so that the enterprise realizes the benefit of their knowledge and their support for the implementation of change. The service unit manager should be able to plan and pursue process improvement, technology changes, and innovation within reasonable budgetary constraints. Where more substantial investment or broader-scope changes are needed, they should be proposed to higher levels in the management chain. Conversely, new business requirements may be defined at a higher management level, and requirements for adaptation may be delegated to individual service units for implementation.

Accountability

An agile enterprise has new mechanisms of accountability. Service units are accountable to their service users and to enterprise leadership for meeting service cost, quality, and timeliness requirements. This results from well-defined service specifications, performance reporting, visible contributions to value chains, and the responsibility of every service unit for its performance.

Though a service unit is directly accountable to service users for the result of a request, it is indirectly accountable to additional service units up the chain of requests along with the original requester. This accountability can be important in decision making regarding delivery of a service. For example, a customer order is received by an order-processing service that directs a request to an order fulfillment service, which directs a request to a shipping service. The shipping service requires a decision regarding transportation mode, which should be resolved by the original customer. This resolution might be accomplished by direct contact with the customer based on customer order information, but it should be accomplished by referring the decision back up the request chain so that appropriate controls and possible side effects (for example, a change in shipping charges) can be applied to the customer's specification. The latter approach is more adaptable since it does not cause the shipping service to make assumptions about the order, the options available to the customer, or proper identification of the decision maker.

In addition, from an enterprise perspective, every service unit contributes directly or indirectly to the enterprise value chain. The impact of each service on the success of the enterprise should be periodically evaluated from this perspective. This should be an important factor in the performance evaluation and incentives for the management of each service unit. The performance of some service units should be evaluated against similar activities in other enterprises and potential performance of equivalent outsourced services.

Collaborative Relationships

In general, service units should be expected to have consumer-provider relationships with services that are in separate management chains so that where there are issues involving these relationships, most should be resolved without appeal to a common manager—both because of the delay in resolution and the fact that managers at a high level probably lack the necessary expertise. Consequently, the issues must be resolved through collaboration. An agile enterprise relies heavily on collaboration to resolve problems and adapt to new business requirements.

These collaborations may vary in duration and intensity. Where the duration is longer or the level of participation is more intense, particularly where participation involves an employee on a full-time basis, the relationship should be formal and visible so that other members of related organizations know who has responsibility. Where significant resources are required, as with a full-time employee, participation should be viewed as a service to a responsible organization, and the cost of participation should be billed to that organization, assuming it is not the employee's home service unit that is the primary beneficiary of the initiative.

Collaborative relationships, particularly those of greater duration and intensity, often create alternative chains of command for review and approval. For example, persons who incur expenses as members of a project team probably need to have their expenses reviewed and approved by a project leader and possibly the manager responsible for the project. These relationships then provide the basis for business processes to engage individuals for review and approval.

Development and support of IT applications typically involve a variety of collaborative relationships. In general, these involve assignment of IT personnel as service providers and liaison persons to other organizations that should be billed to the organization requesting the participation and support as an investment in improvement.

SERVICE UNIT TYPES

From an enterprise perspective, services may be classified into several types based on their participation in value chains:

- Line-of-business service units
- Value chain service units
- Support service units
- Product development service units
- Master data service units
- Work management service units
- Transformation service units
- Portal service units
- Executive staff service units

These service unit types affect the cost and performance of value chains in different ways. In general, the differences in focus and planning horizons of these service types suggest that they should be in separate branches of the enterprise management hierarchy. However, though this is a significant factor at a high level, it is one of many considerations in the design of the organization; additional considerations are discussed later. In the following subsections we discuss the distinguishing characteristics of each of these service unit types.

Line-of-business Service Units

A *line of business* is a collection of similar products that are managed together for production synergy, economies of scale, or focus on a market segment. A line-of-business service unit is responsible for management of the full life cycle of the associated products, from concept through obsolescence; each product life cycle can be modeled and evaluated as a product value chain and managed as a product life-cycle project. The life cycle of a product is initiated by a management decision to develop a new product. For example, a manufacturing line-of-business service unit uses product development services to develop its products, uses operations engineering service units to develop the production capability, uses marketing and sales service units to promote and sell its products, and monitors production service units to ensure that the products are competitively produced and delivered. The line-of-business service unit may be viewed as a special case of the work management service unit, discussed later.

Line-of-business service units must respond to the marketplace to refine products or develop new ones. They engage various services from across the enterprise to support the product life cycle. They are concerned with the life-cycle value of the product to the enterprise—the return on investment.

Production Value Chain Service Units

A *production value chain* defines the contributions to units of production to achieve end customer value. Production value chain service units are those directly involved in adding value to a unit of production. This has been described as a *line organization* or an organization providing *direct labor*. These services are distinct because they directly affect the time to deliver the product or service as well as the cost and quality of the product or service. Each participating service unit provides specialized capabilities required to produce the product. These service units are the focus of initial SOA analysis because they are usually the primary sources of enterprise costs and because they directly affect the enterprise's ability to optimize and adapt to new business opportunities.

The goals and performance measures of a production value chain service unit must be aligned with its contributions to the value chain. The performance of value chain services rolls up, through the network of service usages, to the production value chain, independent of the organization hierarchy under which they are managed. Consequently, the managers of these service units necessarily focus on their contribution to value chains, and particularly contributions to cost, quality, and response time.

Production value chain service units are a primary target for automation and process improvement because that is where much of the cost of running the enterprise is incurred, they have direct impact on customer value, and the operations are typically highly repetitive.

Support Service Units

Support service units come in a variety of forms. They do not engage in activities that have a direct impact on a product value chain but instead provide ancillary services that ensure the effective development, availability, and management of the capabilities provided by the service units they support.

At the enterprise level, there are support service units that consolidate management functions from across the enterprise and enforce management controls. These services are generally organized into functional groups or departments. They include finance and accounting, human resources, purchasing, and information systems services. These enterprise support roles are discussed in greater detail in Chapter 9.

At an operational level, there are support service units that may be specific to particular segments of the business such as machinery maintenance, inventory management, quality control, and facilities management, but there are also operational-level aspects of the enterprise services, such as finance, human resources, purchasing, and information systems.

Support services essentially provide separation of control, economies of scale, or specialized capabilities that are more effective if managed separately.

Support services may interact with employees at all levels, depending on the nature of the service. In many cases, service unit managers are their customers. Managers or employees, depending on their roles, may request services and may be called on to participate in support services, i.e., respond to requests for inputs or approvals. The manager-customers may have different service expectations at different management levels.

Though these services do not directly affect the value produced by the user service unit, they are, nevertheless, part of the cost of adding value and can indirectly affect the performance of their internal customers. The cost of these services, like other services, must be recovered through a chargeback mechanism.

Product Development Service Units

Product development includes any activities that establish the capability to deliver a new or improved product (or service). Product development service units contribute to an internal value chain that provides value by developing a new product for a line of business. The product development value chain is a component of the broader product value chain that comprehends the entire product life cycle. A new product design changes the enterprise capability to deliver a new product. The cost defined by this value chain is associated with a particular product and is an investment that should be recovered through sales of the product.

Product development services define the product specifications and production requirements—requirements for adaptation of the enterprise. They effectively define what the production value chain services deliver. As such, their planning horizon is relatively long and their success is measured by the timely availability, market acceptance, and profitability of the new product.

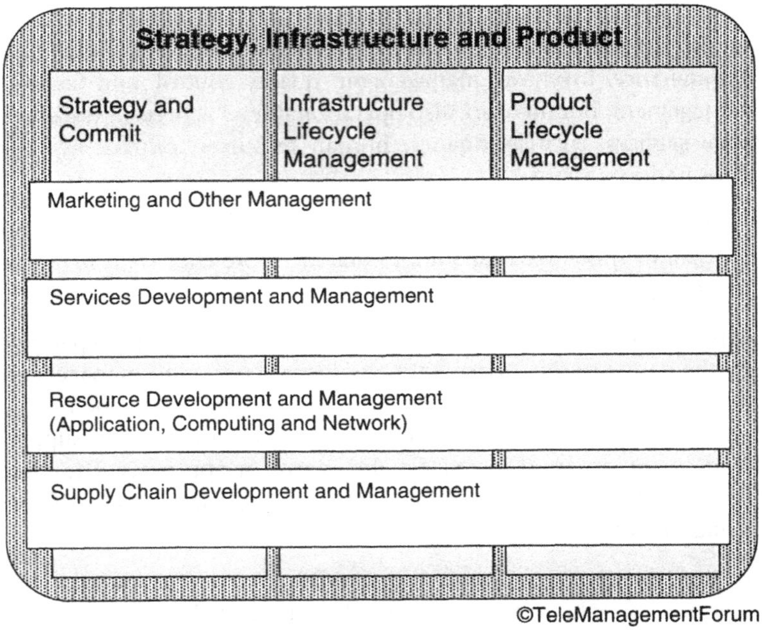

■ **FIGURE 7.2** The eTOM Strategy, Infrastructure, and Product Segment.

©TeleManagementForum

Product development includes product research and may include development of special production tools, methods, specifications, and processes to produce a new product.

The eTOM framework was introduced in Chapter 2. The Strategy, Infrastructure, and Product segment is illustrated in Figure 7.2. In this context, product life-cycle management is shown as one of the vertical functional capabilities. It changes the enterprise capabilities to support production of a new product. The development of new products, as well as the adoption of new technologies and methods, is driven by the broader Strategy and Commit segment. We talk more about strategic planning and the development of enterprise capabilities in Chapter 9 on governance.

Master Data Service Units

Various service units throughout the enterprise have responsibility for some segment of enterprise master data; the collective master data records are the current truth about the state of the enterprise. These service units are responsible for the integrity and confidentiality of their segments of the master data. They control updates and access to it, and they must ensure that it is available as needed to support other service unit operations.

A service unit need not be dedicated to master data management. Often the service unit that manages the most changes to the master data will include master data management responsibility. Nevertheless, the master data resource and effective management of it are key capabilities.

Work Management Service Units

We discussed work management service units in Chapter 2. The purpose of a work management service unit is to achieve a business objective involving several service units that cannot achieve an optimal result on their own. Most typical is a need to share resources to achieve economies of scale across the multiple service units.

In general, the optimization conflicts with the optimum that would be achieved by each of the service units acting on their own. So, manufacturing production scheduling is a work management service unit responsibility to optimize efficiency while minimizing the impact on delay of individual orders. Examples of the objectives to be pursued by work management service units were discussed in Chapter 2. Because the work management may adversely affect some of the performance of individual service units, the work management service unit generally reports to a manager who also has responsibility for the participating service units, so optimization is pursued from that manager's perspective.

Customer order management may be viewed as an enterprise-level work management service unit that is intended to optimize performance of business operations to serve the customer.

Transformation Service Units

Transformation services are not focused on particular products but instead on changing the way the enterprise does business. They develop and implement changes to the capabilities and potentially the design of the enterprise. These service units are separate from the other service types because the other services and their interactions become the work product of the transformation services. They need to bring an enterprise perspective and typically operate across organizational boundaries, sometimes making trade-offs and resolving role disputes between services and their users.

The scope and impact of transformation can vary widely from process improvement to large-scale reorganization. However, these services probably are not applicable to changes for a new product if the product impact is limited to variations in specifications, components, and configurations. They are applicable if the new product requires a new value chain, significant changes to an existing value chain, or major investment in service unit capabilities.

Enterprise transformations that involve multiple services and substantial enterprise investment or optimization must be managed by the Enterprise Transformation service group. The Enterprise Transformation service group is effectively both a transformation service and an executive staff service (discussed in a moment). This service is also discussed in greater detail in Chapter 9 on governance.

Large-scale business transformation occurs when there is a need for fundamental change in the enterprise capabilities and organization. These changes are driven by executive management as a result of strategic planning.

Service unit managers have primary responsibility for process improvement. This responsibility is generally limited by the scope of their service unit. Beyond the service unit scope, analyses must identify changes that optimize performance from an enterprise perspective, and proposed changes must be subject to enterprise-level review and approval.

The IT application development service units are transformation service units. Their responsibility is to ensure effective utilization of the technology and optimization of information systems and communications services. The application development services are utilized by individual service units to improve their capabilities and adapt applications to new business needs, and they are used by the enterprise transformation service to apply information technology in support of enterprise transformations.

In the eTOM framework, shown in Figure 7.2, some transformation services are represented by the Infrastructure Life-cycle Management capabilities. This framework does not explicitly address fundamental transformations to the design of the enterprise. It is focused more on the replacement and upgrade of telecommunication facilities. As with product development, the Infrastructure Life-cycle Management segment is driven by the Strategy and Commit segment.

Portal Service Units

A portal service unit provides services to a community of stakeholders, typically employees, customers, suppliers, or stockholders. These services may include call centers along with Web pages. The portal service unit provides a single point of contact from the stakeholder's perspective, directing requests to appropriate internal service units and tracking resolution of problems. The service unit tailors the portal to the particular needs of the stakeholder community.

Executive Staff Service Units

Executive management and the board of directors are served by executive staff service units that achieve coordination, control, optimization, and economies of scale at an enterprise level. These service units may respond to a variety of requests from executive managers and may have a number of defined services to serve the rest of the enterprise. For example, an executive staff process would review and authorize deviation from standards or review and approve changes to service interfaces. Strategic planning is an executive staff service.

Executive staff services must report to the CEO or a person reporting directly to the CEO to ensure that they function with an enterprise-wide perspective. The executive staff services provide the mechanisms for governance and transformation of the enterprise. These services are discussed in Chapter 9.

HIERARCHY DESIGN FACTORS

Design of the organization hierarchy is a complex ongoing task involving many factors.

Current-day organization hierarchies often reflect groupings of people engaged in functionally related activities. However, in some cases the clustering is based on business operations required decades ago, the remnants of mergers and acquisitions, or the independent evolution of various product lines.

In an agile enterprise, all management hierarchies are responsible for managing services. The leaves of the hierarchy are where the work of services is actually done. The hierarchy, for the most part, brings together service units that have similar capabilities and objectives. The primary objective of the management hierarchy is to optimize the operation of the service units and adapt the service units to changing business requirements.

A blank-slate synthesis of an organization hierarchy would, ideally, be both top down and bottom up. Top down, the service unit types discussed in the previous section, along with general functional groupings, provide a starting point. Bottom up, highly synergistic service units should be brought together at the operating level; then less intense synergy should bring together these clusters into larger organizations. The analysis and aggregation should be repeated, iteratively, to build the detail of a hierarchy.

Aggregation Factors

The following sections describe factors that suggest which service units should be grouped in the same organization. The aggregation factors suggest grouping at a lower level. Separation factors, discussed later, suggest grouping only at a higher level.

Functional Similarity

A basic factor in service unit clustering is still functional similarity—particularly the similarity of skills and knowledge of members of the service units. Similarity of work products suggests functional similarity. This yields flexibility in the allocation of people to service operations, and it yields other economies of scale for management of the clustered service units in terms of improvement of personnel capabilities, process improvement, and possibly sharing of resources and facilities.

The resources may include people, facilities, tools, data, and intellectual property. There are two primary goals: consistency and economies of scale. Consistency leads to improved performance by enabling problems and improvements to be resolved once and monitored for compliance. Economies of scale come from better utilization of resources and potentially the opportunity to develop specialists and acquire specialized tools. Some resources may be shared among multiple services for high utilization, or may be reallocated when workloads shift. Specialized support services may achieve economies of scale across multiple service units that have similar capabilities.

Thus, we tend to bring together service units that perform engineering functions, customer support functions, manufacturing functions, accounting functions, and so on.

Measures of Performance

The services brought together in an organization hierarchy should have compatible measures of performance. Two different service units are not expected to have the same service objectives, but the metrics relating to quality, timeliness, methods, resource management, and responsiveness to users should be compatible, particularly at lower levels in the hierarchy.

Higher-level managers also need consistent measures of performance for the various services under their responsibility, but the measures may be more generalized on service levels than the performance of particular resources. Where possible, metrics should roll up the chain of command so that the performance of different services and departments (groups of services) can be compared. Managers need to be able to define policies and issue directives without the need to significantly tailor the policies and directives to the differences between service units.

For example, a manager might expect all service units to meet certain metrics for employee satisfaction, employee turnover, salary levels, and absenteeism. This allows the managers to employ common performance measures and leverage improvements across multiple service units. At higher levels in the hierarchy, there are broader scope goals and fewer common operational performance measures.

Degree of Coupling

Traditionally, a high degree of coupling between business activities suggested that these activities should be organizationally affiliated. This was at least in part due to delays in communications between organizations, particularly the formal communications required between organizations that share only a high-level manager. With electronic communications and automated business processes, the degree of coupling should be a much less significant factor.

Today there may be relevant couplings whereby there are concerns about setting priorities or using complementary methods that may need to be resolved by a shared manager. For example, a manufacturing machine repair service unit and production operations should be affiliated closely enough to ensure that preventive maintenance, machine repair techniques, and response to failure are appropriate to minimize production downtime. The degree of coupling between production engineering and production operations probably overrides the potential consolidation of engineering capabilities between product engineering and production engineering based on functional similarity.

Outsourcing

The relationship with an outsourcing provider must be "owned" by a manager within the client enterprise so that there is a single point of contact for negotiations and contract enforcement. The management of the contractual relationship might be assigned to the purchasing organization, but it would be more appropriate to assign it to a manager positioned where the associated service units would be positioned if they were internal. The primary responsibility in either case is to ensure that the needs of the internal users are met with appropriate cost, quality, and timeliness.

There will be a need for adaptation and thus some negotiation of service interfaces provided and used by the outsourcing provider. Additional issues may arise in the future as the provider introduces operational improvements or changes for regulatory compliance. These issues should be addressed at an enterprise level, as with other transformation initiatives.

Separation Factors

The following sections describe factors that suggest that service units should be in separate branches of the organization hierarchy.

Independence from Users

As much as possible, all users of a service should be associated with the management of the service unit at the same management level so that all current and future service users have equal influence over the satisfaction of their requests. Close affiliation of some users can be a problem, particularly when a shared service is created from a segment of an existing organization and remains under the same management. Other service units that are expected to use the shared service are likely to believe that they are receiving lesser priority due to personal relationships, even if the joint manager does not exercise such influence.

Separation of Duties

It is appropriate to separate service units that implement critical controls from the service units to be controlled. This ensures that management policies and controls can be quickly, reliably, and uniformly enforced. This separation is evident in the separation of accounting, human resources, and purchasing services from the services that they support. Funding is controlled by the accounting organization, and business units must establish budgets and obtain disbursements through accounting services. Generally, accepted accounting practices define requirements for separation of duties for financial controls. Hiring, along with administration of personnel compensation and benefits, requires the use of human resource services. Purchasing of materials and equipment must be done through purchasing services to ensure objective supplier selection and negotiations.

Similar services might be implemented for such activities as customer quote preparation, application of certain government regulations, or allocation of expensive resources.

Separation of duties may also be needed where there are competing objectives. For example, it is appropriate to separate inspection operations from the manufacturing production organization or testing services from a product development organization. This also applies where critical records must be maintained or valuable assets could be at risk.

Differences in Service Request Life Cycle

A service request life cycle is the time and activities required to respond to a request. A machine repair life cycle usually is completed in hours or days, depending on the level of urgency and complexity, whereas a product development life cycle could take months or years. Service units and service groups should generally avoid combining services that have short request life cycles with services that have significantly longer life cycles because demands for immediate action on short life-cycle services are likely to divert attention from longer life-cycle services. In addition, performance metrics are likely to be significantly different.

Service Delivery Locations

Generally, we think of services as consolidations of similar activities at one location so that the resources can be shared and economies of scale can be realized. This is not always the best solution, and with the Internet and collaboration services, colocation of personnel may be unnecessary. In some cases, it is necessary for the service personnel to have face-to-face contact with customers or others or to work on a customer site for product maintenance and repair. These personnel should be geographically distributed. It may be important to perform the same services in different countries in a way that is more culturally sensitive. Government regulations may be best addressed by providing certain services in specific political jurisdictions. Some services may be distributed to different time zones to utilize daytime work hours while providing around the clock services.

These circumstances can be addressed in three ways: (1) a distinct service is located in each area, (2) service personnel work remotely from a central service unit operation, or (3) a single service unit has operations that are in multiple locations.

In all cases, there should be a consistent service interface. Where there are distinct service units in different areas, the implementations might not be the same in all locations. This might be a function of differences in infrastructure, culture, regulations, or resource availability.

If there are strong differences among the various locations, it is likely that a decentralized organization of separate service units is more appropriate. Some services still may be brought together based on their geographical proximity. At the same time, these services may utilize centralized, shared services that achieve economies of scale and consistency in certain aspects of their operations. This model is typical of retail operations.

Where the activities are primarily individual employee activities, there could be a single service operation that manages and coordinates the field activities, but the field personnel work remotely, interacting with the service applications for support, assignments, and data entry. This is typical of sales operations, where salespeople spend most of their time visiting customers.

Finally, a single service unit may have distributed operations so that the service users make requests of a single service and the service determines where the activities are performed. This could be a model for an engineering service where different specialists are located in different operating sites. For a service that delivers a complex product, various aspects of product development or production might be located in different countries, to optimize the use of expertise and variations in levels of compensation. Some service units may simply operate with employees who participate remotely from home or client sites, thus avoiding the need to relocate new employees and making assignments to employees based on their proximity to clients.

ORGANIZATION MODELING

In traditional organizations, the organizational hierarchy defines the primary responsibilities and authority of individuals and organizations. Interorganizational communications are formalized at an operating level, and managers collaborate to make interorganizational decisions.

In a modern enterprise, most employees are knowledge workers who must often collaborate across organizational boundaries. This is particularly true of an agile enterprise in which employees must collaborate with both users of their services and providers used by their service. To be effective, individuals must be able to identify the persons in other service units with whom they need to collaborate. The traditional organization chart no longer does the job.

In addition, business processes that require review and approval of certain actions or agreements must be able to identify appropriate reviewers and approvers. These are not identifiable simply by reference to the organizational hierarchy. They may involve roles in workgroups, task forces, projects, and committees.

New organizational modeling tools are needed to complement the design of processes and services and represent the relationships discussed earlier. Extended modeling capabilities could assist in more effective alignment of service units within the organizational hierarchy. Management of a multitude of service units, coordination of changes, management of risks, and optimization of enterprise performance will require that managers have more robust tools for dealing with this complexity. At this writing, initial work on a standard for organization modeling is under way within the Object Management Group (OMG).

The organization model must reflect multiple management chains. In addition to the conventional management chain, individuals will be engaged in projects, task forces, or other initiatives that cut across traditional organizational boundaries, and they will have a leader and associated management chain appropriate to the particular initiative. These alternative management chains may have responsibility for expenses, access authorizations, or other processes where review or approval is required. The organization model must provide the information needed for such processes to direct requests to the appropriate managers.

ORGANIZATIONAL TRANSFORMATION

Development of a service-oriented enterprise seldom starts with a blank slate but must deal with the realities of an existing organization. The approach should change as the enterprise becomes more mature with respect to the SOA Maturity Model discussed in Chapter 1. Organizations at level 1, Explored, and 2, Applied, should focus on the creation of individual shared services that realize business benefit with reasonable return on investment. In most cases this should result in service units that achieve significant economies of scale through consolidation. Alignment of these service units with the organizational hierarchy should give consideration to the design principles and hierarchy design factors discussed in this chapter.

At level 3 the enterprise should have a strategic view of needed service units. This may focus on the product value chain and enterprise governance requirements for creation of service units and development and integration of service capabilities. Planning for transformation of support services may be deferred except that consideration should be given to outsourcing. The plan for services developed at level 3 may not include a comprehensive plan for the organizational hierarchy since that evolves as services are developed, and the evolution depends on business priorities and the order in which service units are established.

At level 4, much of the organization should be transformed, particularly those elements involved in product and production value chains. Service specifications should be formally defined, and the capture and reporting of performance metrics should be supported by the infrastructure, enabling greater empowerment of service unit managers and their people to pursue improvements. The organization structure should be evolving to a strategic design.

At level 5, the organization structure should be optimized based on the design principles and hierarchy design factors discussed earlier in this chapter. The executive support services described in Chapter 9 should be fully implemented to support continuous change and more effective governance.

In the next chapter we will discuss how the organization structure aligns with the management of disruptive events to adapt the enterprise to challenges and opportunities.

Event-Driven Agility

Enterprises are not only driven by requests for services but also by events that occur both within the enterprise and in the business environment in which the enterprise functions. In this chapter, we focus on how events drive change in the enterprise. As depicted in Figure 8.1, the enterprise must recognize relevant events, analyze the threat or opportunity to determine a resolution, and implement appropriate changes to its business operations to maintain or improve its role in the ecosystem.

Not all events drive change. There are many events that occur in the normal course of business, such as receipt of a customer order, a payment became overdue, a defect was detected, a machine failed, a shift ended. However, *disruptive events* are those that suggest that a change has occurred in the enterprise ecosystem that impacts the ability of the enterprise to achieve optimal value now or particularly in the future.

Some disruptive events, such as departure of a skilled employee, storm damage to a production facility, or a shortage of a critical production resource, have only a temporary or limited effect. These are part of the spectrum of disruptive events, but of greater concern are those disruptive events that signal the need for a permanent change in the operation of the enterprise, such as introduction of a new product by a competitor or a new government regulation.

There has been considerable industry attention and confusion related to *event-driven architecture* (EDA). For some, EDA means systems that process business transactions as they occur in contrast to batch processing. To others it means initiating business processes based on events. From a technology perspective, it may be viewed as a publish-and-subscribe integration model in which event notices are

■ **FIGURE 8.1** Event-Driven Agility.

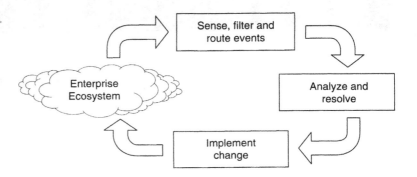

forwarded to applications or processes based on subscriptions rather than request-response exchanges or explicit addressing by an originator. To still others, it means sensing relevant business events and resolving associated challenges and opportunities.

We avoid reference to EDA and focus on this last perspective—sensing and responding to disruptive events, which can be resolved without information technology support, but in today's world, a timely response requires automation.

Response to disruptive events is essential to enterprise agility. Events drive enterprise actions to resolve changing business circumstances that may not otherwise be adequately recognized and resolved within mainstream operations. As the enterprise extends its business processes to respond to various exceptions, some events are anticipated in the normal operation of the business. For example, an enterprise normally anticipates that customers change their minds and unauthorized persons attempt to access protected resources. So some formerly disruptive events become routine events, resolved through well-defined processes. Disruptive events remain those that require some analysis and management planning or decision making. Management planning and decision making are the sources of transformation—adapting the enterprise to address business exceptions, challenges, and opportunities.

SOA can make an enterprise more flexible, accountable, and efficient, but it does not necessarily make it agile. The agile enterprise must be responsive to disruptive events. At the same time, an enterprise that is responsive to disruptive events is not agile if the responses are not timely and effective. SOA enables changes to be implemented more quickly and efficiently because (1) capabilities are consolidated and consistent, so changes can be more easily defined and deployed,

(2) service units can change their capabilities with minimal impact on other service units, (3) automated business processes can be more quickly changed, and (4) the impact of changes on related products, services, and capabilities can be more easily understood and optimized from an enterprise perspective.

In this chapter we consider how disruptive events drive agility. In Chapter 9 we see how change is managed through governance.

EVENT RESOLUTION BUSINESS FRAMEWORK

Event-driven agility, in a sense, requires a second-order enterprise architecture because it requires an architecture for changing the enterprise architecture. Increasingly, management attention must turn from managing resources for performance (a control focus) to managing how the enterprise must change (an adaptation focus).

We begin with the premise that the enterprise is currently designed to operate in the current state of the world. The enterprise must adapt when there are relevant changes to the state of the world, including changes that occur within the enterprise itself—changes to the enterprise ecosystem.

A disruptive event may be a discrete change of state, such as a discovery, a new regulation, a natural disaster, a new product announcement, or a major sale. An event may also be the occurrence of a variance of a business variable outside a normal range or exceeding an expected rate of change. Such events may be based on business variables such as market price, inventory level, customer complaints, or economic indicators.

Figure 8.2 depicts an event resolution business framework—a management framework in which the enterprise should resolve issues raised by disruptive events. The framework assumes that an affected manager becomes aware of a disruptive event. Later we consider how managers can become aware of disruptive events.

A manager at any level may become aware of a relevant event. If the event can be resolved at a lower level, within the scope of specific service units, the implementation may be delegated to those service units. If the resolution requires more extensive change, the event resolution may be escalated. The planning horizon is longer and the solutions more significant when it is necessary to resolve the event at higher levels. Management controls, business processes that initiate change,

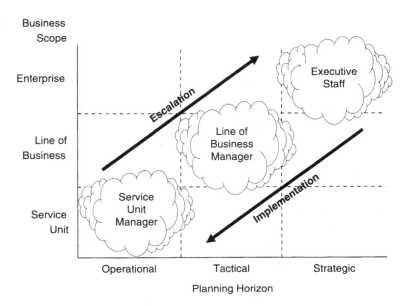

■ FIGURE 8.2 Event Resolution Framework.

and service unit manager incentives must be appropriately applied to achieve a balance between local initiative and enterprise optimization.

By clarifying the allocation of responsibility for enterprise capabilities, SOA helps frame the responsibility for resolution of disruptive events. Transformation, when required, involves changing one or more service unit capabilities or the way service units are used. In the following subsections, we consider the roles of service unit manager, line-of-business manager, and executive staff within this framework.

Service Unit Manager

For a service unit manager, a disruptive event is one that either interferes with the efficient and responsive operation of the service unit or that may put the service unit at a competitive disadvantage—that is, it might not perform as well as similar service units in competing enterprises or as well as it has in the past.

Some events have an effect specifically on the operating activities of a particular service unit. Resolutions of these events can be implemented immediately by the service unit manager unless they require substantial investment or will adversely affect service cost, quality, or timeliness. In a service-oriented architecture, the approach to implementation of service operations is internal to the service unit, as long as it does not adversely affect service users or services used. If changes to internal operations affect the cost, quality, or timeliness of the service, the service unit manager might need to negotiate with service users to justify the change. Changes that do not affect the interface and do not increase cost or degrade the level of service should not be a concern to service users.

When faced with a disruptive event, the affected service unit manager must consider solutions and determine whether there is an operational solution, one that can be implemented internally. The operational solution could be, for example, to hire a new employee, reallocate or train personnel, change internal business processes, acquire new equipment or use another service. The service unit manager's responsibility is to optimize the operation of the service unit, so in general terms resolving disruptive events is his or her responsibility.

In some cases, there may be a need to change the service interface. Figure 8.3 depicts relationships between service users and service providers. Service unit X is both a user of service unit Y and a provider to service units A, B, and C. A change to the service interface of service unit X may require changes to all the users of service unit X, here represented by service units A, B, and C. If an event impacts the competitive position of service unit X, it affects the competitive position of service units A, B, and C, because A, B, and C must bear the cost and depend on the results of service unit X in the delivery of their services. Consequently, the solution should be the result of collaboration between the service unit manager of service unit X and the managers of the user service units A, B, and C. Consideration of changes must include adverse effects on service units up the request chain as well as affected products.

Note that enterprise governance should require that changes to service unit interfaces be approved at an enterprise level to ensure that the solution is optimal for the enterprise, particularly for future needs that might not be represented by current service users.

A service unit may require changes to a service it uses. In the diagram, service unit X may need changes to service unit Y. If so, the service unit X manager should work with the manager of service unit Y to develop the changes. However, service unit Y may have other users, such as service units M and N, that are not apparent to service unit X. Thus service unit X may need to engage both service unit Y and all the users of service unit Y to accomplish the change. The change should occur easily if all users see a net benefit; otherwise, they either agree that it has value to the enterprise or the decision must be made

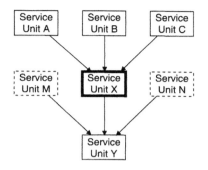

■ **FIGURE 8.3** Change Propagation.

at a higher level in the organization. This includes consideration of the cost of change as well as any increase in operating cost as compared to the business value of the change.

If a change to a service provider increases the cost or degrades the performance of a user, that user is in turn accountable to its users. In the diagram, suppose service unit Y makes a change to improve the quality of its product, but this causes a cost increase. This cost increase is incurred by service unit X along with the other services that use service unit Y. This affects the obligation of service unit X to its users, A, B, and C. This effect propagates up the chain of users until it becomes evident in one or more value chains or otherwise affects enterprise performance. At that level, the impact on the enterprise and the ultimate customer can be evaluated.

Even if a service unit manager makes a change that reduces cost over time, there may be an investment, and thus an increase in costs, incurred in the short term. It would not be desirable for all improvements to be impeded by opposition to cost increases by users. This should be addressed with an appropriate funding mechanism. For example, the cost of change might be recovered over time, so improvements that would be recovered within a certain number of years would be authorized and amortized for cost recovery. The service unit management chain has primary responsibility for making such changes. Changes that would increase the unit cost of services to users should be approved by the service user managers and/or the affected line of business managers. The enterprise must establish appropriate procedures to ensure an appropriate level of budgeting, approval, and concurrence by affected managers.

For example, a machine repair service unit may determine that an investment in a diagnostic tool would reduce the cost of repairs. If the return on investment is acceptable, the cost of the tool can be prorated, reflecting the return on investment so that there is no net cost increase to service users. This would not affect the service unit interface. On the other hand, shifting from a failure-response mode of machine repair to a preventive maintenance mode requires a different relationship with service users and thus a change to the service interface—which may put an additional burden on service users while reducing the impact of failures on the operations of the service users. This also requires a change in the cost model. This can be resolved through collaboration with service users but should still require enterprise-level approval of the interface change.

For a particular event, there may be no solution that can be implemented within a single service or through a collaboration among the service manager and service users. This may be because the disruptive event has long-term consequences or significantly impacts the enterprise product or service. The resolution of these disruptive events must be escalated to the line-of-business manager or managers. In some cases the disruptive event may come to the attention of a service unit manager but not have a direct bearing on his or her operation. Notices of these events should be posted for distribution to more appropriate recipients. Posting should involve a formal mechanism for reporting event details and classification of the event for distribution. If appropriate recipients have not been predefined, the event notice must be escalated up the management chain.

Line-of-Business Manager

The line-of-business (LOB) manager has a broader perspective on needs for change. The LOB manager is concerned about the competitive development and delivery of the products or services he or she manages and thus can assess the implications of the disruptive event in a market context. All LOB managers should be able to view the delivery of customer value in the context of a product life cycle for their line of business.

As with the service unit manager discussed previously, the LOB manager may be able to work with one or more service units to resolve events of limited impact. These are essentially operational adjustments.

Events that indicate a change in market demand or an opportunity for competitive advantage should be primarily directed to LOB managers. They must translate a change in market demand to a change in sales forecasts, and then, using their value chain, they must determine the implications to the services used to deliver their product or service. This may have a significant impact on the workload of service providers, but it might not require any change in functionality.

Some events call for significant changes to the product or service or need to be coordinated across a number of services that are only indirectly related. For example, a new product technology may require changes in product engineering activities, production activities, field service activities, and supply chain relationships. The design and implementation of these changes requires cross-organizational co-ordination and control. Management of cross-enterprise change is discussed in detail in the next chapter on governance.

The cost of such changes must nevertheless be determined and considered in the decision to change. Change implementation may be owned by the LOB manager but managed and performed by transformation service units. The affected provider service unit managers have the primary responsibility for change implementation. If the change adversely affects their other users, the impact on those users is part of the cost of change and could be an increased burden on other product lines. Unless the affected product lines agree, the issue should be escalated to the executive staff level in the organization.

Value chain relationships in a service-oriented architecture make it possible to determine the full cost of change as well as the full cost of a product, including the indirect impact on related products and services. Each product is the result of contributions of value and cost from the services used to develop and deliver the product. Each service must report its true cost, including the cost incurred in using other services and the recovery of costs for improvements.

In some cases a disruptive event has effects that reach beyond the responsibility of the LOB manager. This may be an opportunity for a new line of business, a severe competitive disadvantage, a need for substantial realignment of business operations, a need for a merger or acquisition, or a technology change that exceeds a threshold for investment in new capabilities. These disruptive events should be escalated to the executive staff.

Executive Staff

The term *executive staff* refers to the enterprise's top management team and their staff that supports them in managing enterprise strategic planning, business design, and decision making.

The executive staff should be aware of any disruptive events that can cause significant and sustained change in operating costs, personnel, investment, and supply chain relationships. To ensure that operations are optimized at an enterprise level, the executive staff should be informed of transformation initiatives that require new capabilities or make significant changes to service unit capabilities or interfaces. This coordination and optimization of change is a management responsibility addressed in the next chapter.

Though the executive staff may be aware of the effects of disruptive events and the changes being undertaken, the implementation of many such changes can be delegated to the LOB managers or the individual service managers, as long as the solutions are not suboptimal from an enterprise perspective.

At the same time, the executive staff should be sensitive to patterns of disruptive events that suggest more fundamental or pervasive problems.

In Chapter 9 on governance, we examine in more detail the enterprise-level impact of disruptive events and the potential planning, decision-making, and enterprise transformation actions that may result.

ORIGINS OF EVENTS

The enterprise must sense relevant changes in the enterprise ecosystem to drive appropriate changes in the enterprise. The enterprise cannot respond to events if it is not aware of them. Here we consider the origins of events, to provide perspective on the broad range of events that may be of interest and to stimulate thinking about how these events might be detected. Later we will consider analyzing and responding to events.

It should also be noted that event detection may still be sufficient if it does not capture the specific events of interest but instead captures events that suggest the likelihood that an event of interest has occurred or will occur. For example, a property and casualty insurance company can infer from reports of an approaching hurricane that it will be getting damage claims and may want to suspend issue of new policies in the area until after the storm has passed. A news report of a death or serious injury attributed to a product defect could suggest the occurrence of an engineering or production problem; it could also be an indicator of an impending sales slump.

Business Environment Events

Business environment events are the most difficult events to capture because they occur outside the control of the enterprise. Today, much relevant information exists on the World Wide Web. The occurrence of events of interest may be evident directly from certain Websites or Web services, but for other events it may be necessary to refer to Websites that reflect causal or consequential events. For example, an increase in the price of crude oil will be of interest as a causal event if the enterprise is affected by the consequential increase in fuel prices. News feeds may provide information on causal events such as a hurricane and consequential events, such as an increase in property damage claims or supplier shut-down, can be anticipated.

Though many events in the business environment are the root cause of changes, many may be precipitating events that have no immediate impact until the emergence of a new market that reflects changes in attitudes, applications, or synergy with other external changes. This is particularly true of new technology. The "invention" of the World Wide Web did not transform our view of the world for several years. Nevertheless, it is important to be aware of root-cause events and consider their strategic consequences so that the enterprise can be prepared for a timely response.

Some origins of events are highlighted here:

- *Customers.* Customers are of interest with respect to the business they may bring to or take away from the enterprise. A change in a customer credit rating may represent an increased or decreased ability to buy product. A change in customer satisfaction may also suggest a likelihood of increased or decreased business. Customer satisfaction may require a periodic survey or personal contact to determine whether there has been a change.

- *Supply chain.* The supply chain affects the capability of the enterprise to deliver value to customers. Changes in vendor product quality, price, or timeliness are of concern. A disruption or potential disruption of business operations of a supplier could stop or impair operation of the enterprise. Similarly, if the supply chain depends on transportation or communication carriers, disruptions of these services could stop or impair enterprise operations. In addition, changes in price or availability of raw materials used by suppliers or carriers could have a significant impact on the enterprise. For example, the price of crude oil and limitations on refinery capacity have resulted in significant increases in the cost of fuel, affecting transportation costs and indirectly affecting the costs of other products and services.

- *Economy.* A wealth of economic data is available on the Web. The current values of these variables may be of interest, but what's important here are changes in these indicators. These include stock prices, consumer confidence, interest rates, balance of trade, unemployment, and currency values. It may not be necessary to monitor all such indicators but rather those that indicate when a significant change has occurred. Even if all such indicators were monitored, it is likely that further investigation would be required to identify the root cause and implications of a change.

- *Competitors.* Actions by competitors that might gain competitive advantage are certainly events of interest. There are a wide variety of possible actions, but most reduce to new products or product improvements, pricing changes, marketing campaigns, joint ventures, or mergers and acquisitions. Most if not all of these are revealed in news releases. Though the news releases may be readily available, it could require human interpretation to determine the exact nature of the event.

- *Political.* New regulations are an increasing concern for business, particularly in a world market with many political jurisdictions. Issues raised in political campaigns can influence the marketplace. Military conflicts, regime changes, and boycotts can affect markets, suppliers, and enterprise operations in affected countries.

- *Social.* Fads can very quickly create new markets or shift market demand. Civil disturbances, particularly terrorist attacks or threats, can distract consumer attention and change patterns of behavior that can affect demand for products and services.

- *Nature.* Natural disasters such as storms, droughts, floods, earthquakes, and volcanic eruptions can have significant effects on local markets, and they may affect the ability of the enterprise's local operations to function. The risk of spread of disease has been heightened by a shrinking world. Individuals can carry infections diseases around the globe, overnight. Concerns about a bird flu pandemic have faded, but such risks remain. A pandemic could have a major impact, not only on the marketplace, but on the ability of the enterprise to function.

- *Technical.* Technical discoveries and inventions are the root cause of many changes in the way of doing business and in the products and services delivered. Patents should be noted as potential indications of initiatives by competitors that may result in competitive disadvantage to the enterprise. Scientific discoveries may take much longer to affect business operations and markets, so they probably affect strategic planning or research and advanced development activities. They may become tactical issues when they are reflected in announcements of new products, materials, methods, and tools.

Operational Events

Operational events are those that occur within the enterprise. Often these are consequential events resulting from an external event that has affected the operating capability or marketplace. Several categories of disruptive operational events are described briefly here:

- *Order volume.* Significant changes in the volume or content of customer orders received should receive attention.

- *Customer delivery times.* If times from receipt of an order until customer delivery change significantly, this can be cause for concern. Note that the average may remain stable while selected orders experience significant delays.

- *Service response time.* An event may be triggered when the response time of individual, internal services varies beyond an accepted threshold or level of service commitments are violated.

- *Inventory levels.* Inventory levels that are unacceptably high or low should be identified.

- *Defect rates.* An increase in defect rates should be cause for concern. A decrease in defect rates may suggest an opportunity to sustain a lower rate.

- *Operating costs.* Significant changes in operating costs of internal services or products should be reported.

- *Process variables.* There may be other, process-specific variables that should trigger events if they vary beyond defined thresholds.

- *Profit margin.* Profit margin is certainly a dependent variable. With an SOA, it should be possible to monitor profit more closely. Events might be generated when profits fall below an acceptable margin or when there is significant variance. Note that for some products or services, the configuration of a particular delivery may have a significant impact on profit for that delivery. For example, a product sales mix may have a significant impact on automobiles that have a high profit margin for a fully loaded model and minimal margin on a base model. Exceptional (high or low) profit on individual deliveries may be worthy of consideration.

- *Employee turnover.* Employee turnover could put the reliable operation of the enterprise at risk. Changes in the rate of turnover should be monitored. This may require consideration of a variety of categories such as enterprise total separations, those for particular job or skill categories, and those for particular organizations or service units. The loss of a key employee should merit special attention.

Innovation Events

Innovation within the enterprise can create significant opportunities to improve profit or gain competitive advantage, but there is no benefit if the innovations are not given appropriate attention.

Filing a patent should be a clear indication of innovation that could benefit the enterprise. Likewise, though innovations that are incorporated in products may not go unnoticed, some product innovation opportunities do not get sufficient attention to make them into products.

Many innovations may occur within operating activities such as new methods or tools. If the benefit can only be realized by the particular operating activity, there may be no need for further attention. However, there could be side effects or external markets for some innovations, and these events should be escalated for attention with a broader perspective.

Enterprise Change Events

Improvements to services can be made within a service unit or in collaboration with related service units. This could result in suboptimal solutions if they do not receive tactical or strategic planning attention. Consequently, the initiation of efforts to develop changes may be significant events. Action on these events may be triggered by requests to authorize funding for such efforts. Similarly, investments in new tooling, training, or software may be events that should trigger consideration at a tactical or strategic level. Many enterprise change events can be identified in automated business processes, but there may be many others that should be posted by people as they recognize the emergence of problems or opportunities in current enterprise operations. Posting should formally capture the event information along with attributes that support appropriate distribution of notices.

IDENTIFICATION OF EVENTS OF INTEREST

Obviously, the enterprise is not interested in every event happening anywhere—this would be overwhelming. It is essential that we determine what notifications are needed and how they can be captured.

Some event notices are duplications produced by different observers. Some represent different events resulting from the same root cause. Some event notices are simply ignored if the frequency becomes overwhelming. Consequently, we need to analyze what events are really needed and which event notices should be shared for different purposes. For example, an increase in the price of crude oil increases costs of materials and transportation and may result in a reduction in demand for certain consumer products or services. These consequences may be relevant to a number of different enterprise activities.

Relevant Events

There are two complementary approaches to analysis of event notice requirements: anticipated events and broken assumptions. Each service manager, LOB manager, and business executive should consider both approaches in the context of their scope of responsibility and planning horizon. The nature of all events and their potential areas of impact on the enterprise should be captured in a repository:

- *Anticipated events.* Here the focus is on specific, identifiable events that require attention. Either these events are expected to occur and require attention, or they are unlikely to occur but the consequences are such that if they occur they require immediate attention.

- *Broken assumptions.* The second approach is to identify business assumptions that are the basis for current operations but could become invalid. This might include assumptions like "there will be timely delivery of inventory replenishment," "our operations can accommodate vacations and absences," or "our operations will not be affected by a tornado." The next step is to identify the events that could break these assumptions.

Some assumptions are shared by many managers and some are unique. Managers should have access to each others' assumptions so they don't duplicate effort. At the same time, they can each contribute their own perspectives to a body of business assumptions.

The events repository should include specification of the entities and the associated attributes and relationships that could change if the assumption were broken.

Risk Threshold

Though there are many events that could affect the success of the enterprise, it may still not be practical to capture and process all such events. Figure 8.4 depicts a process for assessment of the level of interest. Both the potential business impact and the cost of monitoring an event must be considered. Essentially, the cost of capture and analysis must be balanced against the risk to the business.

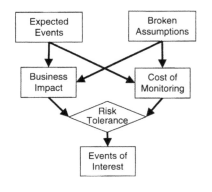

■ **FIGURE 8.4** Level of Interest Assessment.

The determination of tolerance for risk weighs the business impact against the cost of responding quickly to the event. In most cases, the potential loss to be considered is in the additional time it takes to become aware of the event and respond if there is no active monitoring. In either case, if the event occurs, there will be some unavoidable consequences. If the probability of occurrence of the event is high and the consequences of delay are significant, this may justify early detection and response.

The event specification repository should include, for future reference, the assessment of impact and the estimated cost of monitoring. Note that it may still be appropriate to define a response to the event, even though it may be recognized through less formal means.

SOURCES OF EVENT NOTICES

The agile enterprise needs to tap into many sources of event notices, both internal and external. Linking to event sources is an ongoing activity since sources of events change and new events will emerge as the ecosystem changes.

External Events

For external events, it may be very difficult to get event notices directly from the source. For example, competitors are not going to provide event notices that enable the enterprise to monitor their activities, or if they did, the events might not be a true representation of what is happening. So we need to look for *consequential events*—events that occur as a result of the root-cause event. For competitor events, we might look at product announcements or patent applications, which are much less likely to be misrepresented and more likely to be accessible.

There is a wealth of information on the Internet, but the holders of the information may not be prepared to generate event notices. Some might be willing to do so for a fee. Some data, such as stock trading prices, may be available as continuous updates, but it could be necessary to periodically poll various sources of data and watch for changes of state or significant trends.

Internal Events

Internal events are easier because the enterprise potentially has control over the sources. Some events can be generated by a business process, such as a patent application, a project approval, a budget overrun, an inventory shortage, or delayed orders. Other events require monitoring variables over time to identify trends. With internal systems, the sources are more reliable, but the mechanism for recognition of trends may be much the same as for monitoring trends on the Internet.

Some capabilities are already available in software products. Business activity monitoring (BAM) captures data from business processes for monitoring and analysis of exceptions and trends. Data warehouse systems and analytical processes are designed to support recognition of trends and correlation of events. Event notices might be automatically generated from some changes, but less obvious events require humans to realize insights and post event notices.

Business rules can be an important source of events, particularly exceptions. Violation of a business rule or the need to get extra approvals could be important for monitoring regulatory compliance as well as the need to modify business processes to resolve the exception in a more appropriate way.

Some event notices require employee initiative to identify a threat or opportunity and post an appropriate event. The enterprise must establish appropriate incentives.

Complex Event Processing

Complex event processing (CEP) is a technology for inferring events from other events and the surrounding circumstances. A CEP service is both a subscriber and publisher of events. For example, the National Association of Securities Dealers (NASD) monitors news feeds to analyze the relationship of company news events to stock trades, to identify potential insider trading and fraud.

Inference of an event relies on timely and accurate information on related events and circumstances. If the conclusion is to be based on the occurrence of two independent sources of event notices, there must be allowance for different delays in the delivery of the event notices. If the inference depends on related circumstances, there must be accurate and up-to-date information about those circumstances. The inferencing mechanism and event specifications must take these timeliness and accuracy factors into consideration. It is likely that the result of the inference can only be a probability that a particular event has occurred. It may be appropriate to publish an event notice only when the probability exceeds a particular threshold.

CEP technology is still evolving. An approach is to capture and retain a sequence of events for a period of time or a number of events for each event source or stream. Thus the sequences of events can be viewed as relational tables. An SQL-like query can join entries from multiple tables to find combinations of events that would suggest the occurrence of an underlying event of interest. This allows corresponding event notices to be considered together, even though they may have been received at different times. These queries can potentially include information about related circumstances. With special tools, queries can be implemented such that they are applied continuously as event notices are received.

At this point it would appear that CEP is primarily applicable to specific areas of concern such as fraud detection or security threats where there is a fairly focused domain of expertise and relevant events and the value derived from the inferred events is high. It essentially performs as a real-time expert system.

Internal systems are more controlled, and it may be effective to infer underlying events more directly, possibly adjusting for differences in timing. For example, warranty claims might be correlated with production events if the event notices are aligned based on the production date of the product. In this case, the receipt of warranty claims might trigger efforts to prevent or mitigate the consequences of similar production events. This, of course, requires a long history of production events.

Look-Back

Events may be captured and stored in a data warehouse; many enterprises already have such data warehouses for certain categories of events. Data mining is applied to data warehouse records to discover patterns and relationships that occur over time. The analysis is not in real time, so a data warehouse would not be considered an event publisher. Analysts could still submit discovery of certain trends or inferred events to a notification system, to be distributed to event resolution processes.

Emerging trends in CEP go beyond the inference of an event by the occurrence of a combination of related events. First, a broader spectrum of events can be captured and retained for future reference. When an event of concern occurs or is inferred, engaging in *look-back* at preceding events helps put the event of concern into context, to both understand the full nature of the event and discover potential causation.

By analogy, suppose a person is discovered murdered, but there is no source of information about events preceding the murder—no information about how the victim got where he is, no telephone calls, no witnesses, no information on where his acquaintances were at the time of the killing. In this situation it is very difficult to identify the perpetrator. These events are key to discovering the context of the murder and, so, the murderer.

Beyond the potential to look back, the precursor event patterns can be studied to discover patterns that might enable another unfortunate incident to be anticipated and prevented. The focus of attention can then shift to analysis of risk patterns to react earlier, to either prevent or respond more quickly to mitigate the effects of the undesirable event.

Verification and Consolidation of Event Notices

Besides inferring underlying events, there is a need to correlate events from multiple sources to either confirm the occurrence of an event or eliminate redundant reporting of an event.

Event notices from some sources may be unreliable. For example, event notices derived from news feeds may be the result of misinterpretation. There is often a need to confirm the event from another source. The speed of reporting may vary significantly, from minutes to days or longer. It may be appropriate to separately report such event notices, with an indication of the tentative nature of the notice (that is, having business metadata that reflect the quality of the event notice). The recipients of these notices would need to act accordingly.

Some events have many observers. These people may observe the event in different ways, characterize it differently, and publish event notices through different channels. It would not be desirable or appropriate to initiate an independent event resolution process for every redundant event notice. It may be necessary to leave the resolution of these redundancies to the subscribers. In some cases, the subscription criteria may limit reporting to certain event notices, reducing the number of redundant notices received. However, there is a risk that some events are not reported through all the possible channels, and when we ignore some notices, some events may be overlooked. Another approach is to notify event observers when resolution is identified (that is, a resolution event) so that they need not give further attention to the event notices they have received.

CEP systems may provide mechanisms for resolving these issues; however, the resolution may differ depending on the action to be initiated. The subscribers to such events should provide appropriate criteria for analysis and filtering of events.

EVENT NOTIFICATION INFRASTRUCTURE

The event notification infrastructure provides automated support for recognition, filtering, publication, and distribution of event notices. The Enterprise Intelligence service unit (see Chapter 9) is responsible for identifying the business requirements for capture of events and initiation of specific business processes, whereas the Information Technology organization is responsible for the technical infrastructure for event processing.

Surrogate Publishers

As noted earlier, many sources of events do not publish event notices. Instead, *surrogate publishers* are needed to determine when events have occurred and to publish notices. Three kinds of surrogates are described Here:

- *Polling.* It is necessary to periodically poll these sources to monitor their state.

- *Data stream analysis.* This form of surrogate publisher analyzes a data stream. Threshold values or patterns may be reported in different notices so that subscribers can selectively monitor different events in the same stream.

- *News analysis.* News feeds can be analyzed to identify relevant events. The NASD news feed analysis, discussed earlier, identifies securities trades and related news events.

For each of these mechanisms, the nature of the change must be considered:

- If an event is a simple state change, the publisher must keep track of the current state and send a notice whenever the state changes.

- If an event is defined as a variance outside a specified limit, the publisher must compare the state variable to the threshold and send a notice when the threshold is exceeded. The publisher must still retain the new value of the variable so that it does not continue to send event notices because the threshold remains exceeded.

- If an event is defined as crossing a rate-of-change threshold, the publisher must retain the state over a period of time and determine whether the threshold rate of change has been exceeded. Here, as in the case of variance outside a specified limit, event notices should be repeated only if a specified period of time has passed since the last notice was published.

The publication of event notices is further constrained by subscription specifications.

Publish-and-Subscribe Facility

The core of an event notification infrastructure is a publish-and-subscribe facility. This facility filters and delivers event notices. Typically, as depicted in Figure 8.5 an event broker receives event notices from *publishers* and forwards the notices to *subscribers* who have expressed interest in certain types of events. Publishers send event notices to the event broker. Events may be associated with *topics* and have attributes to describe the nature and context of the events. Subscribers may specify constraints on the event notices they want to receive. This may take the form of a topic designation and rules that filter events based on event notice attributes.

Note that a subscriber may subscribe to multiple categories of events, a publisher may publish events of interest on multiple topics, and each event notice may be forwarded to multiple subscribers.

Publishers may publish event notices even though there are no subscribers, and subscriber constraints may filter out many of the event notices. There is a possibility that many event notices are generated for which there is no interest, resulting in unnecessary network activity.

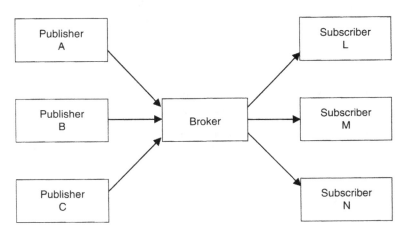

■ **FIGURE 8.5** Brokered Notification.

There are a number of products that implement this event broker capability. Some of them implement the Java Messaging Service (JMS) specification from Java Community Process (JCP) that includes the publish-and-subscribe capability.

More recently, the Organization for Advancement of Structured Information Systems (OASIS) has adopted the WS-Notification family of specifications. Under WS-Notification, a subscriber can request notices directly from a publisher. WS-Notification does not preclude the use of a broker.

Figure 8.6 depicts a nonbrokered notification topology. An event directory identifies sources of events. Publishers need to register with the directory, and a subscriber then uses the directory to identify sources of events of interest and subscribes directly to those sources. A subscriber can define restrictions on the events of interest through specification of a constraint that operates on the attributes of the event notice.

This removes the event notification broker as a potential bottleneck. Before the general availability of Internet technology, a broker was necessary to eliminate a multitude of point-to-point connections; now with point-to-point connectivity and standard exchange protocols, a broker no longer simplifies the network. Note that Publisher C sends notices to Subscriber L and N, directly, whereas in the brokered notification, Publisher C would send a single notice and the broker would forward notices to Subscribers L and N. Subscription requests should be recoverable so that if the publisher fails or is shut down, notices will resume when the publisher returns to operation.

WS-Notification can enable publishers to avoid generating unwanted event notices—no subscribers, no notices. The burden is that each publisher must be able to turn the notification mechanism on or off.

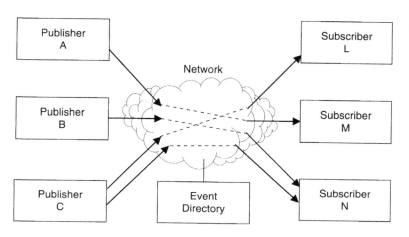

■ **FIGURE 8.6** Networked Notification.

The absence of a notification broker makes management of event notification totally decentralized. It may be preferable to at least use a notification broker between internal subscribers and external providers to monitor the activity and contractual compliance for purchased services. A broker also provides a central point of control for directing notices to subscribers so that publishers can be replaced when necessary without searching out all subscribers. As an alternative, the event directory could function as a broker of offers and requests, whereas the publishers each send event notices directly to subscribers.

EVENT RESOLUTION PROCESSES

A service-oriented architecture enables analysis of events to be decentralized, leveraging the local knowledge of service unit personnel, knowledge specific to lines of business or chief executive knowledge of the enterprise. Every manager receives events that could affect the service unit, line of business, or the executive staff activity he or she manages. Each service unit should have defined processes for responding to disruptive events.

Event resolution specifications should be reviewed from an enterprise perspective to ensure that they are directed to appropriate service unit(s). This analysis of events is different from an analysis of services or application requirements. The issue is, "when this event happens, what should be the result of the enterprise response?" The result should be appropriate for the enterprise, whereas if the event is only routed to a service unit that is directly affected, the result may be suboptimal for the enterprise. This analysis must be the basis for routing events for resolution.

A straightforward event resolution process receives an event and initiate activities to address the concerns. From a process-modeling perspective, an event notice can be viewed as a "request" for a process. We can take two alternative views. First, we define a continuously running process that is waiting to receive event notices. When an event occurs, the process determines what action to take and may invoke other processes to take that action. Alternatively, we can define a particular event as the start of a process. Different events may start the same process, or specialized processes can be initiated for different categories of events.

The processes that are initiated could be manual or automated. In general, we would expect that automated processes should be initiated even if the analysis, planning, decision-making, and response activities are manual. An automated process can at least provide assurance that the event notice does not fall through a crack.

These processes should be designed to deal with the various ambiguities, redundancies, and credibility of the event notices they receive. Generally speaking, the recipient of an event notice should perform some form of correlation and filtering of events to avoid unjustified or duplicated resolution activities.

It may be appropriate, given a certain magnitude of consequences and business risk, to initiate a resolution process immediately, even with an event notice of questionable credibility. However, such a process should be designed to take into consideration later event notices or the absence of supporting event notices at certain points in the subsequent activities. These considerations cannot be programmed into a CEP but must be part of the business logic of the resolution process.

Though each service unit and management chain has responsibility for resolving events that are relevant to their capabilities, there must be enterprise coordination to ensure that relevant events are recognized and responsibility for every event notice is defined. This is an appropriate responsibility for an Enterprise Intelligence.

In the next chapter we will examine the role of Enterprise Intelligence in the broader context of enterprise governance, and we will see how responses to disruptive events fit into the overall governance of the enterprise, to achieve agility and promote competitive advantage.

Agile Governance

The agile enterprise is described as the highest level of the SOA Maturity Model introduced in Chapter 1. Many factors must converge to achieve the agile enterprise level. SOA provides the basic architectural pattern for defining, integrating, and managing the capabilities of the enterprise—the service units. Other factors support integration, optimization, security, accountability, and adaptation of those service units. Governance is what pulls it all together and directs the efforts to achieve enterprise agility and stockholder value.

Enterprise governance is defined as:

> The set of responsibilities and practices exercised by the board and executive management with the goal of providing strategic direction, ensuring that objectives are achieved, ascertaining that risks are managed appropriately and verifying that the organization's resources are used responsibly. (Board Briefing on IT Governance, *second edition,* ©2003 ITGI; all rights reserved.)

This definition has also been adopted by the International Federation of Accountants (IFA) as expressed in *Enterprise Governance—Getting the Balance Right,* 2004.

This definition applies to the agile enterprise. Agile enterprise governance is enterprise governance extended to exploit the consistency, visibility, accountability, and flexibility provided by the architecture and disciplines described in the previous chapters. This chapter describes a governance framework as a basis for governance of an agile enterprise. Alignment with the governance framework gives the board of directors and executive management improved oversight and control of the enterprise operation—and much greater assurance that the enterprise is doing the right thing and doing it well. It also empowers individual service units to optimize the value they contribute from an enterprise perspective while holding them accountable for meeting performance objectives and complying with enterprise directives and government regulations.

Governance of IT is a byproduct of agile enterprise governance. Enhancement of IT governance for SOA, as proposed by some vendors, by itself does not meet the needs of the agile enterprise. The IT organization must be driven by the business needs of the enterprise in the context of the business architecture, process optimization, integration and support of service unit capabilities, and delivery of customer value. In this chapter we include discussion of how the IT organization contributes to agile enterprise governance and supports optimization of enterprise operations.

BENEFITS

The following sections highlight the benefits of agile enterprise governance.

Adaptation to New Business Pursuits

Management of the enterprise as a composition of service units enables value chains to be quickly adapted or developed to address new business pursuits. This adaptation exploits existing capabilities while minimizing operational disruption and the need to develop new information systems.

Improved Response to Change

Distributed responsibilities are explicitly defined for front-line responses to disruptive events. For events of strategic significance, assessment of impact and risk as well as relevant strengths and weaknesses drive consideration of appropriate actions.

Continuous Strategic Planning

Strategic planning is integrated into monitoring the enterprise ecosystem and managing enterprise operations so that strategic planning is not a periodic exercise but part of the continuous evolution of the enterprise. The changing competitive landscape, new challenges and opportunities, and product plans should be considered in the strategic planning context to ensure that the course is right and the enterprise is on the right course.

Enterprise Intelligence

Responsibility is defined for ensuring accessibility of timely and consistent data, information, knowledge, and expertise for monitoring, analysis, planning, and decision making throughout the enterprise.

Empowerment

Specification of service unit interfaces as distinct from the details of service unit implementation enables service unit managers and employees to use their creativity and initiative to improve their operations within the limits defined by interface specifications, budgets, enterprise directives, and government regulations.

Accountability

Well-defined service unit capabilities and interfaces, along with cost-based billing for service units, consolidation of redundant capabilities, and defined contributions to value chains, provide clarity of responsibility for performance and accountability for deviations.

Regulatory Compliance

Service units provide a structure, focus, and accountability for the application of regulations and assessment of compliance.

Risk Management

The governance framework defines responsibility for risk assessment, including security, business continuity, and cost control concerns as well as accountability for elimination, mitigation, or acceptance of risks.

Economies of Scale

Consolidation of similar capabilities, along with incentives for continuous improvement, can achieve economies of scale, not only in terms of improved service unit efficiency but in the ability to develop and sustain higher levels of expertise.

Disciplined Enterprise Design

Centralized design of service unit requirements and the resulting organization structure reflect consideration of enterprise objectives through a disciplined analysis, design, configuration, and optimization of the enterprise value chains and management structure.

Orderly, Incremental Transformation

Transformation planning and management reflect consideration of the full impact of changes to the business architecture, and the architecture enables a measured and orderly transformation with steps that provide incremental business value.

Optimization of Performance

Service units and their management chains have responsibility for optimizing their operations, whereas enterprise governance addresses performance from a value-chain perspective and ensures optimization at an enterprise level.

Optimization of Information Technology

The IT organization, like other service groups, is responsible for optimization of its operations. In addition, at an enterprise level, standards and technology preferences minimize the diversity of information technology and enable optimization of application development and data-processing operations.

AGILE GOVERNANCE FRAMEWORK

We now turn to consideration of the way governance of the enterprise should change to implement, continuously evolve, and exploit an agile enterprise architecture. Figure 9.1 depicts an agile governance framework. An actual organization structure may have additional activities and variations in structure, depending on the industry and characteristics of the specific enterprise. The point of this diagram is to identify the governance functions required and affected by transformation to an agile enterprise.

It is important to note that agile governance is not intended to be something separate from governance of the enterprise nor governance of IT; rather, it becomes a new approach to governance that adapts and extends traditional governance to align with a new business paradigm. That paradigm structures the enterprise as a composition of service units, exploits information technology, and optimizes business processes and the utilization of enterprise resources and capabilities.

In a fully mature agile enterprise, the entire enterprise is composed of service units and supports a consistent design and governance discipline. The primary organizational change for governance is the addition of service units at the executive staff level. Though a strategic

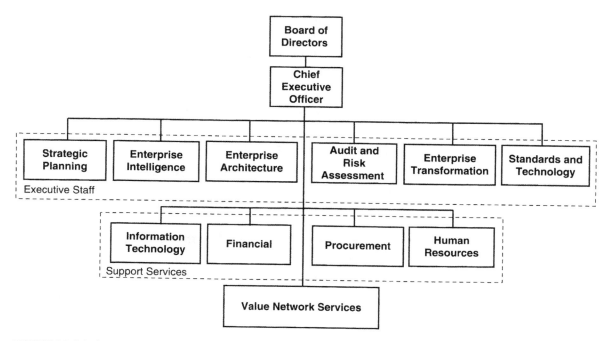

■ **FIGURE 9.1** Agile Governance Framework.

planning activity is typical of current enterprises, strategic planning is extended for the agile enterprise. The other five executive staff service units shown in Figure 9.1 are, for the most part, new, or at least clarified. Information technology services are peer to other support service units such as finance and accounting, purchasing, and human resources. Each of these contributes in some way to agile governance. Finally, the product value chains represent the business operations that deliver customer value and are primary targets for business change.

Enterprises should not expect to achieve agility in a single transformation. The capability must be developed in steps, and those steps should each be designed to realize business value. The SOA Maturity Model discussed in Chapter 1 provides guidance on the improvements needed to advance to each level of maturity. An industry framework such as eTOM, discussed in Chapter 2, provides guidance on the identification and relationships of service units in a particular industry. Business objectives guide the selection of service units to be developed.

Many incremental steps achieve the goal, probably as quickly as would a major transformation, and the cost and risk of the incremental approach are much lower. As the enterprise matures, executive management can grow the executive staff service units that are needed to guide and manage the transformation and improve enterprise governance.

The following sections discuss each of the elements of this governance framework, focusing on the changes introduced by SOA and required for an agile enterprise.

STRATEGIC PLANNING

Strategic planning is a conventional executive management activity, but it is extended for the agile enterprise to achieve a clear linkage to the operation and future design of the enterprise.

Conventional Strategic Planning

Figure 9.2 depicts a high-level view of the Business Motivation Model (BMM), a standard strategic planning model adopted by the Object Management Group. This is a foundation for strategic planning for an agile enterprise. The concepts are typical of common strategic planning practices.

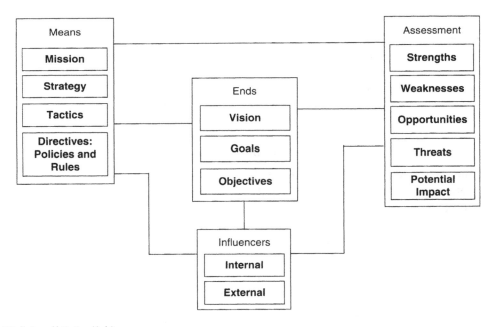

■ **FIGURE 9.2** Business Motivation Model.

Strategic planning is primarily the responsibility of the CEO with the participation of his or her direct reports. At the same time, there is a need for a support staff to gather information, support the analysis, develop the work products of the strategic planning effort, and coordinate with related activities. The leader of the strategic planning service unit typically reports to the CEO. The following points briefly describe each of the elements in Figure 9.2:

- *Ends.* Ends describe the ideal future state of the enterprise; they include Vision, Goals, and Objectives.

  - **Vision.** A Vision is a future, possibly unattainable state of the enterprise. It may be a characterization of the way the enterprise should be viewed by others, for example, as leader in a particular industry, preferred employer, innovator, etc.

  - **Goals.** Goals are more specific aspirations for the enterprise, but they tend to be ongoing rather than having a point of completion. Goals support the Vision.

  - **Objectives.** Objectives are achievable, measurable results that support goals with a defined time of completion.

- *Means.* Means are the mechanisms by which ends are pursued. The components of Means are Mission, Strategy, Tactics, and Directives.

  - **Mission.** The Mission is a general statement of the ongoing purpose of the enterprise—a generalization of the value to be produced.

  - **Strategy.** Strategy is a plan or approach to supporting the Mission and achieving Ends, particularly with a focus on Goals.

  - **Tactics.** Tactics are specific, near-term actions in support of a Strategy. Tactics typically focus on achieving Objectives.

  - **Directives.** Directives define restrictions or requirements on how business is conducted. They include Policies and Rules. Policies are high-level statements of intent. Rules are specific constraints on business operations.

- *Influencers.* Influencers are sources of effects that must be considered in assessment and planning. Influencers can affect the conduct of business, positive or negative, but do not have direct action or control. The Influencers segment is not a normative part of the BMM specification but is widely used. There are Internal and External Influencers.

- **Internal Influencers.** Internal Influencers are things within the enterprise, such as culture, attitudes, thought leaders, infrastructure, beliefs, and capabilities, that influence how business is approached or conducted. These are sources of internal disruptive events, as discussed in Chapter 8.

- **External Influencers.** External Influencers come in a wide variety, such as competitors, customers, the economy, governments, and technology. Changes in these Influencers may have a significant impact on business opportunities or the viability of the enterprise or its undertakings. These are sources of external, disruptive events, as discussed in Chapter 8.

- *Assessment.* Assessment deals with the evaluation of the impact of specific current and changing factors that should be considered in planning future pursuits or direction. Together these are often referred to as SWOT, short for Strengths, Weaknesses, Opportunities, and Threats. Strengths and Weaknesses are internal. Opportunities and Threats typically come from the environment. Influencers, along with strategies, tactics, and transformation plans, are inputs to assessments. An assessment effort will determine potential impact.

  - **Strengths.** Strengths are those factors that make the enterprise competitive or give it competitive advantage. Strengths are important in considering new undertakings.

  - **Weaknesses.** Weaknesses are those factors that could put the enterprise at a disadvantage with respect to competitors or the capability to undertake a new pursuit.

  - **Opportunities.** Opportunities represent potential growth or improvement of value and include such things as new endeavors, new markets, and advanced technology that may create a new market or provide competitive advantage.

  - **Threats.** Threats are circumstances that could put the enterprise at risk. These may include actions by competitors, economic, political or social events, natural disasters, supplier failure, shortage of resources, or lawsuits. They may include missed opportunities that could impact market share.

  - **Potential Impact.** Potential Impact captures the results of assessments—potential gain or loss. Typically, the affects of these impacts are relative to current or future business endeavors.

Adaptations for the Agile Enterprise

Figure 9.3 depicts the BMM structure modified to support strategic planning for an agile enterprise.

We have made five changes: (1) changed Influencers to Enterprise Intelligence, (2) added Business Architecture, (3) replaced Potential Impact with Risks within Assessment, (4) added Transformation to Means, and (5) added Standards and Technology to Means.

These five changes not only connect strategic planning to the operation of the enterprise; they provide the means for insight and participation in governance by the board of directors. Along with Strategic Planning, these changes align with the executive staff service units

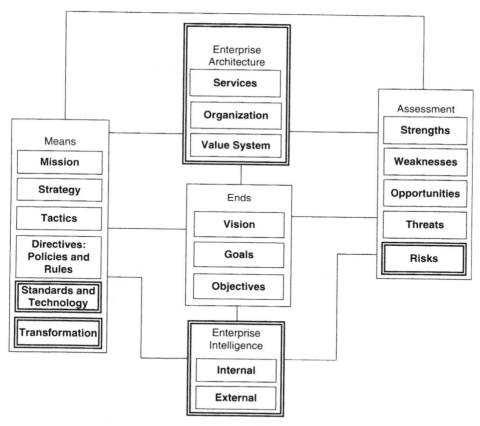

■ **FIGURE 9.3** Strategic Planning for an Agile Enterprise.

in the governance framework described in the previous section and in Figure 9.1. We discuss their roles in strategic planning activities in the following list, and their broader service unit capabilities and responsibilities in the sections that follow.

- *Business Architecture.* Adding this component makes the design of the business architecture a key part of strategic planning. It provides insight on both the current enterprise design and implications of potential designs of the future. Within the Strategic Planning activities, Business Architecture is a component supported by the Business Architecture service unit, discussed later. There are three key components that support the strategic planning process: Service Units, Organization, and the Value Chains.

- *Service Units.* The service units component is a model of the formal, sharable capabilities of the enterprise, which support the Means and are the basis of the Assessment. Resources for the service units are managed and leveraged by the organization. Service units are an addition to the standard model because they are the building blocks for implementation of Strategies and Tactics, and they are the focal point for assessing Strengths and Weaknesses as well as Risks. Specification, configuration, and implementation of service units become the realization of the strategic plan.

  Service units are also the targets of strategies and tactics. Strategies and tactics are developed for service units when we address threats and opportunities, possibly requiring some adaptation of existing service units and occasionally requiring the development of a new service unit. The investment required to implement strategies is lower and more predictable with service unit building blocks. For the most part, shared service units remain stable as the products or service units of the enterprise change. This means that they continue to operate effectively and potentially continue to improve.

- *Organization.* The organization structure defines responsibility for management of operations, resources, and facilities to fulfill service unit requirements. The business architecture must align organizational goals and incentives as well as other factors that achieve synergy, to promote optimal performance of service units. The organization structure is not the service unit integration network but instead represents the relationships between people that manage service units, perform the work, and adapt the enterprise to changing business needs. Organization design is discussed in Chapter 7. The organization structure also determines the responsibilities of managers for compliance with rules and regulations and mitigation of risks.

- *Value Chains.* The Enterprise Value Chain was introduced in Chapter 2 and is shown again in Figure 9.4. It defines the networks of service units that contribute to the value produced by the enterprise. The enterprise consists of a number of value chains. The primary value chains—the product value chains—produce customer value and generate revenue for profit-making enterprises. Other value chains produce value for internal customers and stockholders.

  Governance should, in general, seek to optimize the value delivered by the enterprise value chain, which is the composite of value chains that deliver internal and external value.

  In many cases, the focus for strategic planning is on value chains and the participating service units to deliver value, manage cost, and ensure compliance with rules and regulations. Analysis of a Production Value Chain reveals the contributions of cost, quality and timeliness of individual service units in the delivery of results to customers. This provides perspective on where to invest in improvements.

  In evaluating new products and assessing a line of business, the full life cycle of products and service units should be considered in the Product Value Chain. Analysis of a potential product value chain

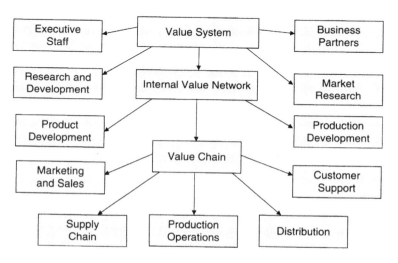

■ **FIGURE 9.4** Enterprise Value Chain Components.

can reveal both the ability or inability to deliver value as well as the direct impact on other operations and lines of business of the enterprise, including the utilization of strengths and the need to resolve weaknesses.

In the past, there has not been a direct linkage between the strategic objectives and the design of business operations to achieve those objectives. Generally, strategic planning has relied on the mental models of executive leadership to identify required changes and define initiatives for change. Initiatives can suffer from the lack of a detailed and balanced understanding of the effort required and the consequences to the rest of the enterprise.

In the agile enterprise, the Enterprise Value Chain makes it all real. It is the connection between change at a strategic, enterprise level and the operation of the business, both in terms of current operations and future plans. The Enterprise Value Chain and the service units it uses are the linkages that enable continuous strategic planning.

- *Enterprise Intelligence.* As a component of strategic planning, this provides visibility of the current state of the enterprise and provides insights on forces for change—those influences both from inside and outside the enterprise that affect the operation and future of the enterprise. As a supporting component, Enterprise Intelligence is the primary source of understanding of the enterprise ecosystem. It also provides input to the formulation of Ends and the assessment of Means. It gives an enterprise perspective on both the data collected and the presentation of information for planning and decision making. An Enterprise Intelligence service unit, discussed shortly, is responsible for the capabilities required to access and analyze data from across the enterprise as well as external sources.

- *Risks.* Risks are the potential effects of opportunities and threats on the success of the enterprise. Risks include latent risks in the design and management of the enterprise as well as risks associated with the pursuit of enterprise initiatives and noncompliance with regulations. This is the assessment aspect of risk management. An Audit and Risk Assessment service unit, discussed later, provides the capabilities needed to assess compliance and risks.

- *Transformation.* Strategic initiatives require more than statements of strategy, tactics, and directives. They require planning, coordination, and accountability. The transformation component addresses the broader scope of concerns associated with changing the enterprise to achieve strategic objectives. An Enterprise Transformation service unit provides the capability to address this strategic planning component and provide visibility into transformation plans and progress. The Enterprise Transformation service unit is discussed in more detail later in this chapter.

- *Standards and Technology.* This makes specification of standards and the selection of technology a key component of strategic initiatives. Standards and technology are important to both products of the enterprise and the internal operation of the enterprise. For organizational agility, standards are essential to interoperability of service units, the ability to combine and compare data from multiple sources, and the efficiency, reliability, and flexibility of information systems. A Standards and Technology service unit, discussed later, provides the capabilities needed to address this strategic planning component.

These additions to the strategic planning model are supported by corresponding executive staff service units depicted in the Agile Governance Framework illustrated in Figure 9.1. We will discuss each of these executive staff service units as well as the other units in the agile governance framework of Figure 9.1 in the sections that follow.

ENTERPRISE INTELLIGENCE

We define *enterprise intelligence* as "obtaining, interpreting, and presenting relevant information about the enterprise and its ecosystem." Here, the Enterprise Intelligence (EI) service unit addresses the need for consistent information across the enterprise and regarding the enterprise and its environment. EI is responsible for management of information resources that support enterprise governance as well as other activities related to analysis, planning, collaboration, and decision making from an enterprise perspective.

EI is not the only place in the enterprise where these capabilities should be considered or developed, but EI should ensure that they are addressed from an enterprise perspective and applied consistently throughout the enterprise. Much of the actual development and support of intelligence capabilities are provided by the IT service units.

EI should address intelligence as represented in the framework of Figure 9.5, sometimes called the DIKW hierarchy. The origin of the information-knowledge-wisdom hierarchy is attributed to a 1934 poem by T.S. Elliot. Addition of the data layer and association with information technology is attributed to Russell Ackoff in 1988.

■ **FIGURE 9.5** Intelligence Hierarchy.

In the long term, the agile enterprise must take this broad view of enterprise intelligence to optimize enterprise operation and agility and to make most effective use of its intellectual assets.

We briefly discuss each of the levels from an agile enterprise perspective in the following subsections.

Data

Data are the records stored in databases and files and communicated over networks. Data represent facts—attributes and relationships—about people, places, and things. Data have no meaning to humans until they are put into a context and presented in a form that associates the facts with the real-world entities they represent and describe.

Data are the foundation of the intelligence hierarchy. A critical challenge of SOA is to synthesize data from sources in many service units—to realize relevant information, knowledge, and wisdom for the success of the enterprise.

To ensure access to consistent and timely data about the enterprise and its environment, EI should have ownership responsibility for the following:

- Development and support of the enterprise logical data model
- Development and support of the Enterprise Information Integration (EII) schema and mapping to relevant databases based on the enterprise logical data model
- Identification, capture, and routing of disruptive event notices as discussed in Chapter 8 on event-driven agility
- Business intelligence systems [e.g., business activity monitoring (BAM), operational data stores (ODS), and data warehouses]
- The enterprise data management plan that defines the sources of master data and the mechanisms by which data sources are synchronized and replicas are maintained.

Information

Information is data in context that has meaning to humans. Humans require data to be presented in a way that reflects the meaning of the numbers and letters. Information is captured, communicated, and prepared by computers for interaction with humans. A human expresses information when writing an email message or submitting an order. The computer provides information when it produces a display or prints a report that presents the context and associated descriptions with the data elements being displayed. So, though the computer captures, stores, and communicates data, the systems are designed to capture and present the data to humans as information—meaningful information.

EI is responsible for ensuring that data are transformed and presented as meaningful information with consistent semantics (meaning) to support analysis, planning, and decision making. This may have a variety of forms. For example:

- Browser-based presentation of enterprise information
- Reports and displays, both textual and graphical
- Human interfaces to interactive, analytical tools
- Management dashboards that highlight key operating parameters and raise alarms

Knowledge

Knowledge is the expression of patterns, dependencies, and constraints occurring in the enterprise and the world in which it operates. Knowledge can be applied to understanding a situation or developing a plan. EI should support the management of enterprise knowledge, which may take a variety of forms:

- Business models
- Complex event-processing specifications
- Business rules
- Collaboration tools for sharing of knowledge
- Knowledge management and search capabilities for access to unstructured documents
- Expertise directory for finding experts within the enterprise

Knowledge can be codified and applied by computers but within narrow domains. Rule-based systems, often called *knowledge-based systems*, operate on human knowledge in the form of rules and apply the knowledge to specific problems.

Techniques such as case-based reasoning and neural networks enable computers to "learn" from experience and apply that learning to specific situations. So a neural network (an artificial intelligence model that simulates neurons receiving signals and adapting to feedback) can learn which credit card charges are "normal" and which are questionable, to reduce credit-card fraud. The underlying data structures of a neural network link characteristics of the transaction through various weighted relationships to determine whether there is a significant risk of fraud.

The knowledge and the applications for such solutions are narrowly focused and require specialized development skills. On the other hand, computers deal with massive amounts of knowledge on diverse topics. This knowledge is produced and applied by humans for humans but stored and communicated as computer data, most often in the form of messages and documents. Unlike the records described in the preceding "Data" section, these messages and documents are not defined or structured for use by computers, so they are often called *unstructured data*. They are typically the primary subject matter of knowledge management.

Wisdom

Wisdom reflects consideration of values with an understanding of complex causal relationships, behavior, and consequences. Wisdom yields optimal solutions for design, problem-solving, planning and decision making that goes beyond the application of computational algorithms. Wisdom is usually viewed as a human quality. People apply wisdom to problems and opportunities. Wisdom also implies the ability to consider solutions "outside the box." Computers don't apply wisdom; they only do what they are programmed to do, although computer scientists continue to work toward giving computers more human capabilities.

Wisdom is managed by engaging the right people in analysis, planning, and decision making and ensuring that they have appropriate access to available knowledge, information, and data. The expertise directory, created to support knowledge sharing, can also support engaging the right people for their wisdom.

Though EI may not be directly responsible for bringing wisdom to enterprise management, modeling tools help managers develop more effective mental models of the business so that they can be better prepared to exhibit wisdom in their plans and decisions. In particular models of organization structure, costs, business processes, value chains, and other enterprise design viewpoints will ensure consistency, support consensus building, and enable management of complexity.

Creation and refinement of the models are as important as the resulting representation. Design of the model requires the development of insights on the problem to produce a model that behaves in a way that is consistent with the real world. Simulation provides a validation of the model and can expose behavior that is not otherwise expected. Business analytics involves computational and mathematical techniques for discovery of correlations and behavioral characteristics in the enterprise ecosystem. These insights promote wisdom. Wisdom is essential in an agile enterprise if decisions and business changes are to be made quickly with appropriate results. Business models are discussed in greater detail in Chapter 10.

BUSINESS ARCHITECTURE

The Business Architecture (BA) service unit is the focal point for design of the enterprise. It is responsible for maintaining much of the Enterprise Business Model (EBM) that integrates models representing different viewpoints of the enterprise. The EBM is discussed in Chapter 10.

We have used the term *business architecture* rather than *enterprise architecture* because the latter has been taken by the IT industry to refer to the architecture of the information systems of an enterprise. *Business architecture* refers to the architecture of the enterprise from a business perspective—the way the components of the enterprise fit together to fulfill the business purpose and strategic plans.

BA develops and evolves the design of the organization structure, service units, and value chains as input to the strategic planning activity and receives direction from the strategic planning activity for further alignment with leadership objectives and insights.

BA should be a center of expertise for the design of the service-oriented architecture. At the same time, BA must be a center for collaboration with specialists from various segments of the business, to incorporate understanding of the effects of potential changes and achieve appropriate enterprise optimization.

Phased improvements should be defined for the business architecture, each of which realize business value and lead toward the desired strategic architecture. Each phase of architecture improvement is input to enterprise transformation.

BA is separate from the Strategic Planning service unit because the participants are different, the workload is substantial, and special skills are required. Development of the business architecture should reflect consideration of operating capacity, economies of scale, business continuity, security, outsourcing, compatibility of service units, optimization of performance, efficiency, and agility. At the same

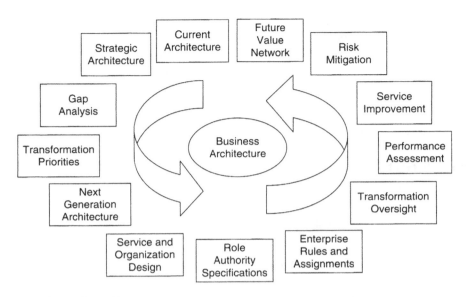

■ **FIGURE 9.6** Business Architecture Responsibilities.

time, BA should have liaisons with at least the major department heads of the enterprise to ensure that the business architecture and transformation roadmap are realistic and feasible. In addition, Information Technology service units provide key capabilities in support of the BA efforts.

Figure 9.6 illustrates the BA responsibilities that produce and manage the business architecture. The flow of these activities is generally counter-clockwise, but it is not a strict sequence. Rather, the evolution of the business architecture is driven by business needs and opportunities that are continually changing.

With support from IT, BA should leverage technology in development of the business architecture. We discuss each of the areas of responsibility of Figure 9.6 in the following sections.

Current Architecture

The current architecture is a depiction of the current state of the enterprise in a form that can be compared to the strategic architecture. For the conventional enterprise, this focuses on current business applications and processes. In the more agile enterprise, it reflects the service units, organization structure, and value chains. This defines the starting point for transformation.

Evolution of the architecture is influenced by current applications, the capabilities of current technology, and the skills of IT staff. Consequently, the IT organization has a significant role in these activities.

As part of this area of responsibility, BA is responsible for maintaining the current applications portfolio, service unit portfolio, and value chain models that provide insight into current enterprise operations.

Strategic Architecture

The strategic architecture is a potential future state, as currently envisioned. It is an ideal state under current business circumstances. Of course, business circumstances and thus the strategic architecture will likely change before the ideal state can be achieved, but the strategic architecture provides a valuable strategic perspective for implementation of plans and for consideration of operational and tactical changes.

Initially, the strategic architecture can be developed through a rigorous service-oriented analysis, as described in Chapter 2, but more likely it will be based on an industry best-practices framework that defines service units, a logical data model, and business processes. The fully developed agile architecture reflects the desired service units, organization structure, and enterprise value chain.

The purpose of the strategic architecture is to assist in the identification and development of sharable service units that will likely persist as the enterprise continues to evolve. It also provides insight on opportunities to improve cost or performance. In the long term, changes to the strategic architecture are driven in large measure by the service unit requirements and business objectives of value chains for multiple products.

Gap Analysis

The *gap analysis* is a comparison of the current architecture with the strategic architecture. The purpose of the gap analysis is to identify the variances and support analysis of changes that could yield incremental business value. The gap analysis should provide a general assessment of the costs, benefits, risks, and time required to transform current operations to conform to the requirements of service units defined in the strategic architecture. Emphasis should be placed on the transformations that have high potential business value.

A significant part of the gap analysis, particularly during the early stages of transformation to SOA, is the mapping of existing business applications to service units of the future architecture. Gap analysis helps identify both service units that are embedded in other activities and service units to be considered for consolidation. This information is an important factor in planning for incremental improvements.

Transformation Priorities

The gap analysis identifies potential transformations such as consolidation of capabilities that could provide direct business value through economies of scale, regulatory compliance, or improved product quality. These opportunities, along with current business priorities and the cost, risk, and delay of service unit implementation, must be weighed to determine an optimal course of action for the enterprise. Each transformation should be designed to yield business benefit. Transformations that are large and complex increase risks and may not have the anticipated business value by the time they are completed. If benefits are not realized on a regular basis, there is a risk that the commitment to SOA could be abandoned in favor of more immediate gains.

Next-Generation Architecture

The next-generation architecture is the next incremental improvement of the current architecture that realizes meaningful business benefit and is consistent with current business priorities. The planning horizon for such an architecture might be on the order of a year or two, so it represents significant change, but a target that is not likely to change significantly before it is reached. In particular, a next-generation architecture might reflect adaptations to support a new product or line of business. The next-generation architecture should not only include service units, it should define associated organizational changes and implement incremental infrastructure capabilities that support the development, integration, and management of future service units.

BA must maintain specifications for next and future generations of the business architecture. These align to a transformation roadmap that defines phases of transformation that provide incremental value and move the enterprise in the desired direction. Each phase of the roadmap must achieve a fully operational business architecture that realizes some level of return for the enterprise or supports a new business strategy. Essentially, BA is charting the course of the enterprise to transition from the current state to a strategic future state.

The transformation roadmap may include replacement or modernization of current applications to support adaptation of service units or to reduce operating costs. Information Technology should provide capabilities to support the planning and implementation of the technical transformation. The Transformation Management service unit has responsibility for management of the business transformation, ensuring a coordinated effort.

Service Unit and Organization Design

An approach to defining service units is outlined in Chapter 2, and an approach to organization design is outlined in Chapter 7. The service units and organization design activity is focused on the specification of requirements for service unit capabilities, interfaces, and associated service levels, along with placement of service units in the organization structure.

Since the incremental transformation is based in part on expected service unit implementation, BA must consider the alternatives of adaptation of legacy systems, the acquisition of commercial software, and service unit outsourcing to determine the cost, risk, duration, and business benefit of a service unit implementation and associated transformation.

Implementation of service units also requires consideration of the organizational context in which the service units are managed. A consolidated service unit must not favor one user over another as a result of organizational history or proximity. Users of a new service unit must be able to trust that their performance will not be jeopardized because they have delegated responsibility to an unresponsive shared service unit.

Role Authorization Specifications

Role-based access control (RBAC), discussed in Chapter 6, is an important aspect of effective management of access control. Individuals require role assignments for access to service units and information from across the enterprise. Managers cannot be expected to know or specify the technical details behind an authorization they grant. They must be able to grant authorization in terms of roles and responsibilities that are related to the purpose of the authorization. At the same time, there should be consistency in the semantics and authorization of the roles from an enterprise perspective.

Thus the specification of role semantics should be the responsibility of BA, whereas grants of authorization to individuals should be performed by their managers and details of the access authorization of elementary roles should be defined by the managers of service units responsible for protecting the resources. Changes to role definitions, assignments to participants, and authorization specifications must be controlled by appropriate specifications of grantor roles for authorization of role assignments, along with role assignment approval processes.

Enterprise Rules and Assignments

Enterprise rules express constraints on the operation of the enterprise based on enterprise policies and regulations (see Chapter 4). The business architecture provides a framework for the appropriate application of these rules. BA should manage the rule specifications and define the assignment of rules to service units, thus delegating responsibility for implementation of the rules to the specific service units. A rules repository must track the deployment of rules, to support verification of their application and rapid deployment of future changes.

Transformation Oversight

BA requires a different discipline and skills from those required for enterprise transformation. Consequently, the role of BA in transformation is one of specification of requirements and oversight of implementation to ensure adherence to the business architecture and make adjustments as necessary. BA should be represented as part of a transformation steering committee and should participate in progress reviews.

Performance Assessment

BA must support performance assessment of service units and lines of business and support evaluation of performance of the enterprise. The Enterprise Value Chain is key to this evaluation. Operational relationships and performance metrics requirements for the service units must be maintained by BA to support understanding and analysis of value chains. Whereas individual service units are charged with responsibility for continuous improvement of their internal operations, BA must address issues that go beyond the scope of individual service units. Access to much of the data for this analysis should be supported by the Enterprise Intelligence service unit.

Service Unit Improvements

Service unit improvements are changes to the interface, capabilities, and levels of service of service units to more effectively meet service unit users' needs. Some of this should be done by the individual service units, but there are barriers or trade-offs that require an enterprise perspective. For example, a potential improvement may require an investment. The investment would impact the cost of the service unit, and improvement might benefit some users and not others. The change in internal processes might improve timeliness but increase costs, and timeliness might not be a concern for all users of the service unit. BA should provide an enterprise perspective to resolve these issues and support investment where appropriate. BA should also review and approve all changes to service unit interfaces so that their impact on the architecture and other service units is fully evaluated and so that business architecture records are kept current.

Risk Mitigation

The Audit and Risk Assessment service unit, discussed later, is responsible for identification and evaluation of risks. BA is responsible for mitigation of risks from an architectural perspective.

Mitigation of risks resulting from practices within individual service units is primarily the responsibility of the managers of those service units. For example, in an application development service unit, developers might be allowed to informally accept new or modified requirements from service unit managers to maintain good relationships, but such practices increase the risk of cost and schedule overruns. This risk would be identified by the Audit and Risk Assessment service unit, but resolution would be the responsibility of the application development management.

On the other hand, reliance on application testing performed by the same application development team creates a risk that the test results may not be objective. BA should consider separation of an application-testing service unit from application development to eliminate this potential conflict of interest.

BA should also define requirements for event resolution services (i.e., process initiation) for each service unit that is identified as responsible for resolving disruptive events.

Future Value Network

When new products are being planned, an expected product value chain should be modeled. This future product value chain may be a change to the value chain of a current product or line of business or a significantly new product value chain. The product value chain should be composed of current and potentially new service units. Measurements for current service units should be obtained from Enterprise Intelligence services. New service units may be variations on the use of existing capabilities or capabilities that must be acquired. BA must support the line of business manager to configure the new product value chain and perform an appropriate evaluation of the potential cost, quality, and timeliness of the new product or service unit in collaboration with other affected service units.

In addition, the new product or service may require changes in existing service units such as increased capacity, alteration of service unit interfaces, or changes in level of service—possibly resulting in cost increases. These must be evaluated in support of strategic planning. Implications to other lines of business may require evaluation to anticipate the implications to the enterprise as a whole.

AUDIT AND RISK ASSESSMENT

Risk management is a topic of considerable concern given the increased risks associated with government regulations, potential liabilities associated with product defects, and breaches of security. SOA has the potential to increase risks through broader exposure of systems and the creation of consolidated service units that could be single points of failure. Understanding and either eliminating, mitigating, or deciding to tolerate risks is an important concern for executive management as well as the board of directors.

Audit is combined with Risk Assessment because both are concerned with identifying risks. Audits generally focus on compliance with policies, regulations, or standard practices. This group may not perform all levels of audit, such as security and recoverability of systems, but it should ensure that such audits are performed. Risk assessment goes beyond consideration of deviations from expressed requirements and considers circumstances, practices, events, trends, and enterprise design that create notable risks to the enterprise.

Audits and risk assessments are not intended to resolve risks. This separation of duties is important so that those assessing the risks do not become invested in the solutions. There are always risks. The purpose of this service unit is to ensure that executive management and the board of directors are aware of the risks and that they are at least mitigated to an acceptable level.

The following are examples of potential risks of interest:

- Overlooked threats and opportunities
- Single points of failure that could cripple the business
- Loss of enterprise assets
- Exposure of systems or confidential data
- Failure of programs or projects
- Regulations and legal liability
- Missed opportunities or loss of market share
- Risk to reputation
- Failure to meet or improve upon industry best practices

Each risk situation should be documented along with the level of risk. Resulting corrective action or mitigation efforts should be documented and followed by reassessment to ensure that an acceptable level of risk is achieved.

ENTERPRISE TRANSFORMATION

Enterprise Transformation (ET) is responsible for the implementation of change. ET does not focus on the development of a new product per se, but the ET responsibility includes coordination of enterprise changes that are needed to develop and deliver a new product or otherwise improve the operation of the enterprise.

Some changes occur within the scope of individual service units and remain the responsibility of managers of those service units. Some changes occur through the collaboration of service a unit with the users of the service unit—particularly changes that would affect the service unit interfaces, costs, or levels of service of the changing service unit. Changes that have a potentially significant impact on the enterprise, involve a number of service units, or have a risk of adverse impact on customers should be reviewed by EA and managed by ET.

Transformation to an agile enterprise is a major, enterprise-level endeavor that may take a number of years. This transformation must be managed by ET through a number of projects and phases. After the transformation, the agile enterprise should anticipate continuous change to adapt to new business requirements or advances in technology. In an agile enterprise, business operations no longer exist in silos but are interconnected through a network of services. There is a continuing need for enterprise-level management of transformation.

These transformations typically involve substantial investment as well as risk for the enterprise. Plans, progress, and associated risks should be recognized as important aspects of enterprise governance.

The ET service unit should have a permanent staff responsible for program and project management as well as expertise in organizational transformation. Though transformations to address new or changed products would require collaboration with the LOB management organization, with SOA, changes for one LOB will likely affect service units used by other LOBs. At the same time, most of the work of a transformation is performed by way of other activities, particularly those of the Information Technology organization. Planning and coordination require participation by representatives of all the affected organizations. This can take various forms, such as steering committees, task forces to address particular issues, communities to contribute input, and project teams to develop and deploy solutions.

For example, suppose there is an insurance enterprise initiative to consolidate four claims-processing activities into one shared service unit to achieve economies of scale. A new service unit will be formed and positioned in the management hierarchy to be relatively independent of the organizations currently managing claims processing. The requirements for the new service unit, organizational implications, the impact on the related service units and lines of business, and the expected investment and return on investment are developed by BA in collaboration with affected organizations. Each of the four organizations that have processed claims in the past are expected to use the shared service unit.

The IT organization is required to adapt, acquire, or develop the automated business processes and application software for the consolidated service unit. A steering committee chaired by ET might be formed with representatives of the affected organizations, including IT, ET, and BA. ET is responsible for a program plan that coordinates project plans, including an application development project and an organization transformation project. ET, along with the steering committee, is responsible for requirements change control. Each project has a project team.

ET must also address, directly or indirectly, issues of training, cultural change, alignment of goals and incentives, business process management, and standards compliance. A community of affected personnel might be formed to provide a forum for discussion and resolution of personnel issues and concerns.

STANDARDS AND TECHNOLOGY

The role of the Standards and Technology service unit is to develop consensus on adoption of enterprise technical standards and identify preferred purchased products for both products of the enterprise and its internal operations. This includes leadership of a standards and technology committee representing diverse enterprise interests, which approves standards and preferred technology and authorizes deviations when appropriate. The purpose is to achieve consistency, economies of scale, adaptability, extensibility, manageability, and compatibility of enterprise capabilities.

For information technology, the objective is to (1) ensure compatibility for exchange of information between service units, (2) ensure compatibility of data for cross-enterprise access and integration of information, and (3) promote economies of scale in information technology service units by avoiding unnecessary technology diversity.

Standards and Technology should have an enterprise perspective on the needs of the enterprise for standards and may be the focal point for participation of the enterprise in the development of industry standards. Standards and Technology should fund initiatives to evaluate and select preferred products, using the expertise of other service units, particularly the IT organization, to perform evaluations.

Standards and technology selections for information systems should include:

- Personal computer configurations and software
- Integration infrastructure
- Enterprise logical data model
- Business modeling and analysis tools
- Business process management systems
- Application development tools, languages, Web server, middleware, database manager, and operating system
- Security authentication, authorization, encryption, and signature mechanisms

Figure 9.7 depicts potential technical diversity in a service-oriented architecture. As long as the service units comply with the interface standards for the integration infrastructure and the data exchange is compatible with the enterprise logical data model or can be translated to be compatible, the service units can interoperate.

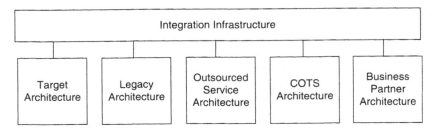

■ **FIGURE 9.7** SOA Technology Diversity.

However, diversity of technology within the service units increases costs and risks. Development and support of applications using diverse technologies require that a staff be maintained with skills in each of the technologies. The internal technologies of outsourced service providers and business partners are of minimal concern. The primary concerns are legacy systems and commercial off-the-shelf (COTS) software products that must be supported by the IT organization. Each of the technologies has its own problems and risks as well as different solutions to shared risks.

In the long term, the availability of skilled personnel for legacy systems diminishes, resulting in a limited ability to resolve problems and adapt to new requirements for those legacy systems. Transformation of the applications to shared technologies should be considered in enterprise transformation planning to reduce the costs and risks of diversity.

Product acquisition and application development processes must include review by the Standards and Technology service unit, and deviations from standards should be authorized only if there is a clear business case for the deviation. This consideration must reflect the likelihood that the loss of economies of scale experienced by the IT service units will persist many years into the future, whereas the benefits of using a noncompliant solution may be only temporary, since equivalent, compliant solutions may become available in the future.

The IT services organization has primary responsibility for recommending standards and preferred products. The Standards and Technology service unit is responsible for determining which standards and product preferences are appropriate from an enterprise perspective. Representatives from the various departments of the enterprise must be involved in these decisions as well as decisions regarding deviations from the standards and preferred products.

INFORMATION TECHNOLOGY SERVICE UNITS

Information Technology (IT) is responsible for management of the service units that support effective exploitation of information technology by the enterprise. We view the CIO as the top management leader of Information Technology services. The CIO is responsible for optimizing the use of information technology by the enterprise. IT services fulfill three primary roles:

- Executive staff support
- Service unit automation
- Infrastructure management

Executive Staff Support

IT brings technical expertise and insights to the executive staff. It provides development and support of modeling capabilities and may provide modeling expertise. At the same time it has different roles in support of each of the executive staff service units:

- *Strategic Planning.* The CIO should be a member of the strategic planning team, the same as other enterprise executives. The CIO brings a perspective on changes in technology and the application of technology to optimize the operation of the enterprise.

- *Business Architecture.* Business Architecture requires technical support for a number of its responsibilities. In particular, it requires support for service-oriented analysis, design and modeling, capture and management of business rules, gap analysis, and transformation planning. BA provides the enterprise perspective on transformation planning and optimization of service units, but IT personnel are needed to understand the details of the systems and processes involved and to develop and support the business models.

- *Enterprise Intelligence.* IT provides technical support for the planning and implementation of EI capabilities. In particular, IT provides the technical expertise associated with development of the enterprise logical data model, development of business activity monitoring (BAM), data warehouses, and Enterprise Information Integration (EII). IT also supports modeling tools, collaboration facilities, and knowledge management facilities.

- *Enterprise Transformation.* IT must provide the technical capability to develop and deploy detailed business processes and applications;

integrate service units, applications, and business rules; transform legacy applications; and implement appropriate security facilities.

- *Standards and Technology.* IT provides the primary input for defining information systems standards and technology selections driven by a need to minimize diversity and achieve economies of scale in IT service units. This must be balanced against potential business opportunities or improvements in other service units that would suggest the need for deviations. IT must request deviations or proposals for changes to standards where appropriate for adoption of new technologies or alignment with industry trends. Standards and Technology should also address standards for products driven by product development and standards for business practices in the various business disciplines such as accounting and human resource management.

Service Unit Automation

IT service units support automation of business service units. This includes development of automated business processes, development of supporting computer applications, implementation of commercial software, transformation of legacy systems, systems integration, problem resolution, and technical support. These are solutions owned and funded by the service units. Consequently, the basic requirements are determined by the service unit interface, the interfaces of other service units used, and capability requirements of the service unit.

Infrastructure Management

IT is responsible for management and operation of the technical infrastructure, including computers, communications, and data storage. The SOA infrastructure, described in Chapter 2, includes the following:

- Reliable messaging
- Event notification
- Security
- Message transformation
- Service unit registry
- Business process management system
- Service unit portals
- Service unit performance monitoring
- Billing for services

In addition to these capabilities, IT must provide shared facilities for human communication, collaboration, and knowledge management. This includes telephone, email, teleconferencing facilities, group/community servers, and other technical capabilities that support information sharing and collaboration. EI should be viewed as the business owner of these enterprise facilities.

FINANCE AND ACCOUNTING SERVICE UNITS

Within the Finance and Accounting services, SOA has a significant impact on cost accounting. The cost of every service unit must be determined both with and without the costs of services it uses. The total cost must be allocated to the units of service it provides for cost recovery in a way that achieves a reasonable representation of the actual cost of each unit of service.

Accurate cost accounting is essential for four purposes: pricing, performance evaluation, billing for services, and enterprise design. Cost determines the profit margin on products and services. Without accurate costing, it is difficult to determine an appropriate price or even whether a product or option should be continued.

Cost is an indicator of the efficiency of a service unit. Costs provide a basis for accountability of service unit managers, planning for process improvements, investment in new methods, service unit redesign, organizational changes, consolidations, outsourcing, and technology upgrades. Billing can influence users with respect to the utilization of a service, and it may influence the behavior of the service unit personnel in attempts to reduce costs.

Determination of the cost of a unit of service is not trivial, since there are both costs directly attributable to the particular service and costs that are shared. For example, the service unit incurs the cost of an employee even if the total work of providing all services does not require the employee 100% of the time. Since much of the work of a service unit may be automated, considerable employee time may be allocated to problem resolution and process improvement. From time to time, these employees may engage in projects funded by outside initiatives so that the service unit cost may go down, but then local projects may be delayed.

The costs of support services and facilities may not be associated with the delivery of specific services, but the costs are, nevertheless, a necessary part of providing the services. Consequently, the costs for each

Table 9.1 Assembly Service Unit Cost Model

Assembly Service	Operations						All Operations Total		Fixed Cost	Net Cost
Product 123	A		B		C					
Request Attribute	Volume	Cost	Volume	Cost	Volume	Cost	Volume	Variable Cost		
Base	400	4000	10	100	4	40	414	4140	$7,419.35	$11,559.35
V	200	40	3	30	1	10	204	80	$143.37	$223.37
W	150	45	2	40	2	2	154	87	$155.91	$242.91
X	130	26	5	5	1	1	136	32	$57.35	$89.35
Y	10	50	0	0	0	0	10	50	$89.61	$139.61
Z	25	75	0	0	0	0	25	75	$134.41	$209.41
Total	915	4236	20	175	8	53	928	4464	$8000	$12,464.00

unit of service are always approximations and vary as a result of the mix of services provided during a particular period of time.

Table 9.1 illustrates a hypothetical cost allocation for the Assembly Service applied to Product 123. This example illustrates the nature of cost accounting and some of the difficulty in defining reasonable cost for individual services. The example service provides three operations, A, B, and C. Operation A is the primary service. The rows represent variations in the request options where the first row, Base, represents the product without options. The Fixed Cost column is allocation of the total fixed cost of $8,000 based on the variable costs in the column to the left. Different ways of allocating fixed costs may be more appropriate for different types of service units; for example, the option cost variances may be only associated with the cost of purchased material and not the costs incurred in performing the operations in this service unit. It may also be important to divide costs between labor and material so that sources of costs of a service and total product cost can be better understood.

This cost model represents costs for a time period—for example, a week—and the product mix that occurred during that week is indicated in the Volume column. For some analyses, it may be sufficient to consider the average cost contribution of this service based on a typical product mix. For other types of analysis, such as pricing, it is important to understand the costs of the various options as well as the typical volumes, since marketing strategy should reflect profitability of different products and product options. A robust cost analysis model would support consideration of costs and pricing under simulated variations of product mix.

Note that the total cost of a particular product configuration in a time period (i.e., based on a specific mix) is computed here by adding the associated marginal costs of all the operations that contribute to that product. In the example, this would include the product base cost and the cost for any associated options. It must also include the cost of components produced by services that are not performed in direct response to a customer order, as where orders are filled from inventories. These may be included as cost of materials in the primary production process.

Consequently, billing rates for service units are approximations based on expected workload, product or service option mix, and use of support service units. If the workload goes down, the cost per unit goes up because there are fixed costs involved. Nevertheless, users of a service unit need to be able to plan for the costs they will incur as a basis for planning and decisions that may affect their operations as well as when and how this service unit is used.

PURCHASING SERVICE UNITS

Purchasing service units are affected by SOA in two ways: (1) purchasing services are part of the product value chain for acquisition of products and services that support product development and production capabilities and (2) purchasing must manage the acquisition of outsourced business services.

Purchasing is generally viewed as a support service, only indirectly involved in the delivery of customer value. In SOA, the impact of the cost, quality, and timeliness of purchasing service units has an impact on both product development and production operations. Delays in purchases can affect the timely introduction of new products and their success in the marketplace. The cost, quality, and timeliness of production components and services have a direct impact on production value chains. Purchasing is responsible for managing the performance of suppliers and therefore is responsible for supplier performance and its impact on customer value. Similarly, purchased products and services impact other value chains.

Requirements for outsourced business services should be developed by the Business Architecture service unit, but the purchasing service unit must obtain outsourcing bids, provide information to support the outsourcing and selection decisions, and establish a contract with appropriate service requirements and levels of service specifications. Purchasing has an ongoing responsibility for managing the contract relationship, but day-to-day monitoring and problem resolution may be managed by a branch of the organization equipped to assess performance, understand the context and technology of problems, and work with service users and providers both to resolve problems and respond to changing business needs.

In both cases, a supplier should have a single point of contact within the enterprise that assesses supplier performance and takes responsibility for its impact on associated enterprise value chains.

HUMAN RESOURCE MANAGEMENT SERVICE UNITS

The fundamental role of the Human Resources (HR) services does not change, but to support an agile, service-oriented enterprise, it should focus particular attention on the impact of service unit autonomy, the challenges of continuous change, and the need for appropriate incentives. This may involve the services of industrial psychologists, particularly during periods of substantial transition, but also where employee dissatisfaction or turnover are high.

Service Unit Autonomy

Service units expose interfaces but limit exposure of implementation. They serve multiple users, so they must not adapt to the unique requirements of particular users at the expense of others. These characteristics can isolate service unit employees from the rest of the enterprise. Where employees do have direct involvement with service unit users, they must limit their activities to the terms of the service unit agreement or they will inflate the time and cost to deliver services.

For example, an information systems application development service unit must provide a solution to a customer requirement, but as the solution unfolds, the customer realizes the need for additional features. The application developer must resist the temptation to continually improve the solution or the cost of the application will increase and the project cost and delivery schedule will not be met. Instead, the application developer must enforce a change control process that involves assessment of the impact of each new requirement and establishes an agreement regarding increased cost and delayed delivery. This can interfere with interpersonal relationships and may frustrate both the application developer and the customer until they accept the necessary user/provider relationship discipline.

HR must help employees adjust to these customer/supplier relationships. This is not a concern only for service units like application development; it affects the entire enterprise as it is transformed to an SOA.

Continuous Change

In addition to changing relationships, employees will experience significant organizational transformations and changes in job responsibilities as the enterprise implements a service-oriented architecture and as it develops a culture of continuous change as an agile enterprise. This may affect both employee motivation and skill requirements.

To become comfortable with continuous change, employees must see change as an opportunity rather than a threat. They must see changes in their jobs and the need for new skills as opportunities for growth. They need to see the enterprise as supporting growth so that people advance into new roles rather than being replaced.

HR should work with Enterprise Transformation to support employee transitions and ensure that employees have the necessary skills and understanding to perform in their changing roles.

Incentives

HR should work with Business Architecture to bring consideration of employee capabilities and attitudes into the design of the enterprise. HR should give particular attention to alignment of organizational goals and development of appropriate incentives to promote employee satisfaction and productivity.

For example, collaboration should be recognized as an opportunity for personal recognition along with career growth and greater self-esteem for the participants. However, unless there is clear benefit to the participating service unit, the manager may view this as competing for resources that are needed to maintain or improve the performance of the service unit he or she manages. At a minimum, the service unit should bill for the participant's services. This offsets the disincentive and also ensures that the cost of the collaboration activities is understood and properly authorized. Additional motivation for manager support should be considered.

HR must work with top management to define appropriate incentive programs. Some choices of incentives may be affected by government regulations. Incentives should address both the motivation of individuals and the motivation of managers and should recognize the difference between contributions that improve a service unit and those that achieve improvements on a broader scale. There may be a need for different types of incentives for employees of different service unit types, and some may be specific to individual service units.

In many cases, financial incentives cannot be based on measurable criteria but must be at the discretion of managers and project leaders. The funding for incentives should be based on identifiable improvements that directly or indirectly improve customer value or reduce identified risks to acceptable levels.

VALUE NETWORK SERVICES

In the Agile Governance Framework of Figure 9.1, Value Network Services represents the organization structure responsible for the service units that contribute to product value chains.

Product value chains are composed of the service units that contribute directly to value delivered to customers. Elements of the enterprise value chain were introduced in Chapter 2 and discussed earlier in this chapter. The product value chain segment is depicted again in Figure 9.8. A product value chain comprehends the full life cycle of a product, from concept through production and customer support. A production value chain identifies the value contributed to individual units of production for delivery to customers.

An enterprise can have multiple product value chains that may be managed in groups as lines of business based on the nature of the

■ **FIGURE 9.8** The Product Value Chain.

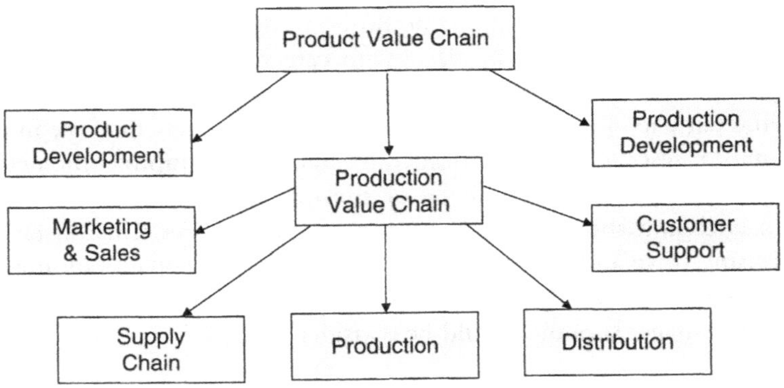

product and market. Product value chains and lines of business are the primary focus for strategic planning because they generally are primary sources of expenses and revenue aes ssssnd they have direct impact on customer satisfaction and enterprise profit.

Value chains are a primary basis for top management analysis, planning, improvement, and control of the operation of the enterprise. Value chain modeling is essential for understanding the contributions of service units and for understanding the sources and impact of service unit problems and potential changes. In the next chapter we will see how value chain models, along with other forms of models, represent different viewpoints of a more comprehensive model of the enterprise that supports more effective planning, decision making, and governance.

Model-Based Management

In the past, enterprise organizations remained relatively stable for decades. Changes, for the most part, shifted some responsibilities among managers, brought new products to market. or introduced a new technology, but the basic business model remained fundamentally the same. Occasionally, various forces caused a significant change to the organization structure to streamline or consolidate. These changes, if significant, had ripple effects for several years as unanticipated consequences emerged. But even with significant changes, executives could often focus on certain aspects of the enterprise and assume the rest of the enterprise would be relatively unaffected.

That time is gone. The world is a dynamic place, and enterprises must be able to make significant changes on a regular basis, doing it right the first time. Enterprises are finely tuned to remain competitive, requiring special skills and resulting in greater complexity. There is less margin for error and less tolerance for inefficiency. SOA supports specialization through consolidation of capabilities, but the granularity of service units and the interconnections resulting from sharing services increases complexity. Managers need computer-based business models to manage this complexity and make optimal plans and decisions. Toward that end, *model-based management* (MBM) positions business models as a critical means for management understanding and control of the enterprise.

Business is undergoing a paradigm shift similar to that experienced by the U.S. automobile industry in the 1970s. Prior to that time, automobiles were designed by development and refinements of physical prototypes. Design of a new model could take five years. In the 1970s the U.S. automobile industry moved to the use of computer-based models to develop and validate the automobile design. Today, a virtual automobile is developed as a set of computer-based models. The automobile is crash-tested by computer. Various other forms of testing such as stress testing, vibration testing, and heat-transfer testing are conducted with computer models. Interactions and potential interference between parts are evaluated by computer. The time to develop a new vehicle model has been drastically reduced, and the quality of today's automobiles could never be achieved with the old prototyping methods.

Business organizations are faced with fundamentally the same problems. Organizations must be able to change to keep up with advances in technology and changes in the marketplace. Those that are not agile will fall behind. The changes cannot be trial and error like the automobile prototypes; they must be well designed and analyzed, considering many dimensions of effects, and they must be highly refined to achieve the necessary efficiency and quality of performance. This can only be done with the support of computer-based models.

SOA and BPM provide the basis of a consistent business architecture to enable more robust models to be developed. Models are abstractions. To be valid abstractions, they must be able to make certain assumptions about the consistency of the problem space. Business models will build on the concepts developed in the preceding chapters to provide increasingly powerful models for managing, optimizing, and transforming the enterprise. Service units are persistent components of the business with consistent mechanisms for their interaction. An agile enterprise based on SOA and BPM preserves most of the operational units and their optimized capabilities as the business changes, even though the management hierarchy may change dramatically and new lines of business may require significantly new value chains.

The development and support of business models falls under the responsibility of the Enterprise Intelligence service unit discussed in the last chapter. Business models support knowledge management, collaboration, insight, and innovation by capturing knowledge about how the enterprise operates, integrating current business data, and enabling managers and specialists to understand interdependencies and explore plans and solutions. A comprehensive solution must support a number of viewpoints based on a consistent metamodel (specification of modeling elements) so that the various viewpoints have a common, underlying representation of the design of the enterprise.

In this chapter we examine requirements for business modeling, particularly those requirements related to business design and the agile enterprise. This is an emerging technology, so some of the capabilities are supported by modeling tools and some needs are just gaining recognition. We look at current modeling technology and examine some enhanced modeling capabilities that should be integrated into modeling tools in the future. Finally, we consider tactical approaches that use currently available tools and technology.

BUSINESS-MODELING VIEWPOINTS

Figure 10.1 depicts a number of business-modeling viewpoints that support the management of an agile enterprise, particularly the needs of executive management and the executive staff. Each viewpoint addresses an area of concern regarding the design of the enterprise. Managers also will deal with other models, such as financial models, product models, and distribution models, that are not included here. A human cannot consider all these factors together, and individuals with different areas of expertise need to be able to view different aspects of the business. In addressing a particular business concern, a team might collaborate, developing consensus around a solution while each views the solution from different viewpoints. The solution is consistent because the viewpoints are all related in various ways

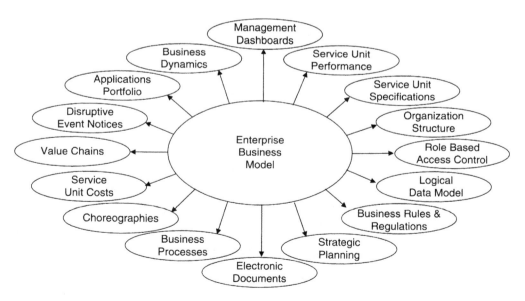

■ **FIGURE 10.1** Enterprise Business Model Viewpoints.

through a shared enterprise business model (EBM). Some models include data from business operations or records such as cost and performance data.

Each of these viewpoints could exist, independent of an EBM. The enterprise itself defines the current attributes and relationships of the concepts being modeled. These viewpoints could be supported by deriving supporting data from current enterprise systems. However, these viewpoints would only reflect the current state of the enterprise. The value of the EBM is to explore future states of the enterprise and ensure that the various viewpoints are consistent with a particular future state. This is how we rapidly design quality automobiles, and it is the way we must learn to design enterprises.

We briefly discuss each of the viewpoints, clockwise from the top of Figure 10.1, in the following subsections.

Management Dashboards

Management dashboards typically provide monitoring of key process variables derived from business activity monitoring (BAM) and may raise alerts for specific events of interest. These should be presented in the context of the enterprise organization, value chains, and service units so that the manager can go deeper, select events or variables to monitor, examine the relationships, and consider related information and implications.

Existing management dashboards require extensions to reflect the broader aspects of the EBM and to open the door to exercise of management control through the dashboard.

Service Unit Performance

Service unit performance is supported by BAM but should also include cost data as well as timeliness, quality, and user satisfaction. These should be considered in the context of the organization structure responsible for the service unit(s).

Though service unit performance can leverage BAM capabilities, extensions are required to appropriately track and present costs and performance of services against level of service specifications.

Service Unit Specifications

Service unit specification focus primarily on the business capability and interface specifications. Service units responsible for master data management should be identified and the scope of their responsibility defined. The specifications should provide access to other aspects such as business processes, costs, organization structure, and use of supporting services.

Elements of this viewpoint exist for tracing value chains and development of software to implement services, but integrated models are needed. Additional content is needed to depict the use of the services.

Organization Structure

The organization structure represents the people and their positions and relationships in the organization. This includes both the management hierarchy and other working relationships that may be more temporary, such as participation on committees, task forces, and project teams. The organization structure should identify service unit organizations and chains of command, for purposes of different types of approval. It should also provide a linkage to role assignments for role-based access control (RBAC).

Existing organization modeling tools require modification and extensions to address the needs of the agile enterprise. An Organization Structure Metamodel (OSM) specification to address this need is under development at OMG.

Role-Based Access Control

RBAC defines the access authorization associated with various roles and the assignment of roles to people. People are associated with the organization structure, and authorizations may be associated with positions in the organization and with the context of particular business activities that require references to business documents or services. RBAC is discussed in greater detail in Chapter 6.

Development of a standard metamodel (modeling language) for business modeling of RBAC has been initiated at OMG.

Enterprise Logical Data Model

The enterprise logical data model (ELDM) includes specifications for all concepts, attributes, and relationships of the EBM modeling elements as well as for all data exchanged between service units. Existing data modeling tools provide the basic capability, but the logical data model should be extended to support alternative vocabularies and semantics—representation of the meaning of concepts, attributes, and relationships.

Business Rules and Regulations

Business rules and regulations that define constraints on business operations must be captured in a formal syntax using terminology and semantics that are consistent with the ELDM. The rules and regulations are linked to the service units affected and should be linked to specific activities of business processes for traceability.

Tools that implement Semantics of Business Vocabulary and Rules (SBVR), the OMG standard, provide capture and presentation of enterprise rules in a business-friendly form.

Strategic Planning

The strategic planning model captures strategic plans and draws on a number of other models that define service units, the organization structure, value chains, and enterprise directives as well as other supporting information sources established by enterprise intelligence.

Tools are available that support the OMG Business Motivation Model (BMM) that is the basis of the strategic planning model presented in Chapter 9. The extensions discussed in Chapter 9 are needed for integration with the other viewpoints and full support of continuous strategic planning.

Electronic Documents

Electronic documents are specified with XML schemas. Electronic documents are exchanged between service units as well as with external entities such as customers and suppliers. Some of the same documents may be used by different services, so each document is associated with the service units, choreographies, and operations in which it is employed.

The ELDM modeling tool should be able to represent the content of electronic documents as views of the ELDM but not the actual structure of the XML documents. The Information Management Metamodel (IMM) specification under development at OMG will support specification of the XML structures as well as the transformation between the ELDM and the XML representations.

Business Processes

Business processes define how the capabilities of a service unit are applied to respond to service requests and deliver value. These business processes also define the use of other service units to fulfill the requests. Thus business processes are an essential link in the integration of services and analysis of value chains. The business processes should also identify the choreographies they support and the electronic documents they use in exchanges.

These models should include representations of both automated and manual processes as well as those processes embedded in legacy applications.

At the enterprise level, these process models may be expressed as abstract business processes that specify the linkage between service requests and the participation of people or other service units. An *abstract business process* does not include details of flow control and internal, service unit activity but includes uses of people and other service units in a particular situation—a use case. Typically this will appear as a network of services using other services and people to achieve the top-level objective.

There are many tools that support business process modeling; some support both the BPMN standard with the integration of choreography provided by BPDM (both from OMG). A BPMN 2.0 standard, currently under development. will combine BPMN and BPDM into a single language with a metamodel and graphics.

Choreographies

Choreographies specify the sequence, content, and constraints of exchanges between business processes of participating service units. A choreography becomes a requirements specification for new participants who want to participate in similar exchanges. Choreographies may be modeled with related business processes, but they are distinct components because the same choreography may be used in exchanges between different participating service units and business partners. So a choreography used between service units (or companies) A and B may also be used between A and C or between D and C. Different participants can design their processes to be compliant with the choreography and, consequently, will be able to interact with any participant that is compliant with the complementary role(s).

Standards for XML specification of choreography have been developed—ebBP by Organization for Advancement of Structured Information Standards (OASIS) and WS-CDL by World Wide Web Consortium (W3C), but these are not integrated with business process models. The BPDM specification provides this integration along with a modeling capability appropriate for businesspeople.

Service Unit Cost Models

The cost elements of operating a service unit must be defined and allocated to the services provided, to define billing rates for services. This includes the costs of services used, both direct (value chain) services and supporting services. Consequently costs are linked into service unit specifications and value chains.

Generally, costs depend on the parameters of the requests. For example, the cost of a particular automobile engine will depend on the configuration of the engine, such as different carburetion and support for air conditioning, power steering, or cruise control. Consequently, the cost of contribution to a value chain will depend on the product mix that is described for that value chain (in other words, the particular use cases). The cost model should support these cost computations.

Other than spreadsheet applications, there are no standard tools appropriate for modeling service unit costs as part of the EBM. Spreadsheets are an appropriate interim solution, but rule-based computations may be the most flexible and accurate solution.

Value Chains

Value chains define the services directly engaged to produce business value for an internal user or external customer. A production value chain begins with a customer order and involves each service that contributes to fulfillment of the customer order. Internal value chains begin with a requirement for support of a capability of another service unit. These indirectly impact value chains that produce value for customers. Value chains are derived from service and business process relationships, and analysis should include links to costs, quality, timeliness, and capacity data that impact the value chain.

In general, value chain models deal with an abstraction of business activities. The analysis of service unit relationships—and their value chain contributions of cost, quality, and timeliness—requires new modeling and analysis tools. Much of the supporting information for a value chain model is built on the service unit specifications and business process models.

Development of a modeling standard for value chains is currently under discussion at OMG.

Disruptive Event Notices

Disruptive events must be identified and associated with sources, filters, or complex event processing for recognition. Each event notice of interest must be directed to the attention of a responsible person in the organization or to a process that causes appropriate action to be taken.

There has been considerable industry discussion of event-driven architectures, but this discipline is still emerging. OMG is considering specification of event modeling as an extension to UML to include complex event processing. This does not address the business aspects of establishing event sources and responsibilities for resolution. Enhanced complex event processing should include capture of precursor events to support analysis of the context in which a disruptive event has occurred.

Applications Portfolio

The applications portfolio must be managed as a record of existing and future business applications, the responsible organizations, the associated service units, the costs, and the technologies involved. Business applications are components of service unit capabilities. The application information and association of applications to service units is important, both for management of the application portfolio and for planning business transformations or technology upgrades. Some applications have embedded business processes that should be represented as abstract business processes to identify the links between service requests and services used for value chain analysis.

Some tools exist for management of an applications portfolio from an IT perspective, but they are not designed to address the relationship of applications to service units and business processes.

Business Dynamics

Business dynamics modeling is a technique for modeling systems behavior and trends using the abstract concepts of *stocks, flows,* and *feedback*. It has been used for analysis of performance of major construction projects, automobile marketing strategy, effectiveness of strategies in the war on drugs, and production capacity planning.

For example, in his book *Business Dynamics*, John Sterman describes the application of business dynamics modeling by General Motors to analyze the impact of used-car superstores on the automobile marketplace. The concern was that the availability of relatively new used vehicles was increasing price competition in the new vehicle market. The analysis revealed that the short-term leases offered by automakers were the source of a large volume of relatively new used cars. The superstores were a symptom, not the underlying problem. Leasing brings relatively new vehicles back into the marketplace, drawing customers away from new vehicles. Further analysis established that longer lease terms, such as four years, reduce competition with new vehicles and also improve the resale value of returned lease vehicles, thus reducing losses at lease end.

The automobile market model represents *stocks* of new vehicle inventory, late model vehicles in service, late model used car inventory, and older cars on the road. Stocks are increased and depleted by *flows* of new vehicle production, trade-ins, sales, and aging or scrapping of cars. Various feedback factors affect the flow rates.

Business dynamics models should be used to better understand the dynamics of the business ecosystem. In this context, applications of business dynamics may draw on service unit performance and capacity data, data warehouse data on product trends and relationships, and other, external sources of economic and market data. Historical data will be important for validating a model. If these data can predict past trends, they are more likely to be able to predict future trends.

MODELING TECHNOLOGY STANDARDS

The OMG is the leading organization for development of modeling standards. OMG adopted the Unified Modeling Language (UML) for design of object-oriented programming applications in the late 1990s. Shortly thereafter OMG adopted Meta Object Facility (MOF) as the data model for storing and exchanging models. MOF with UML notation (graphics) has become the specification of a language for specification of modeling languages—in other words, a *meta-language*. MOF is essentially a subset of UML. It can model itself as well as UML.

Now all modeling languages developed by OMG are either UML profiles, i.e., extensions to UML or languages specified with MOF. A UML profile uses standard extension mechanisms of UML called *stereotypes* and *tagged values* to redefine standard elements of UML. This allows a user of a UML tool to apply a profile using an existing tool. A MOF model, on the other hand, represents the modeling concepts without the baggage of the existing UML specification. There are some things that a UML profile simply can't do because of UML restrictions—it's designed to model applications. In addition, a tool vendor that just wants to implement a specific OMG modeling language does not want to be required to implement UML first.

XML for Metadata Interchange (XMI) was developed for exchange of models between tools and repositories. XMI defines the way a MOF-based model is expressed in XML. Thus any modeling language that is MOF compatible automatically has a model exchange specification using XMI.

Around the turn of the 21stcentury, OMG recognized that the standards it had developed based on the Common Object Request Broker Architecture (CORBA) middleware standards were limited to that particular middleware technology. At the same time, UML was gaining momentum. Some earlier work had introduced the concept of generating application code from UML models to improve application development productivity and quality. Driven by these factors, the model-driven architecture (MDA) was developed.

Under MDA, OMG develops specifications in the form of models that are independent of specific implementation technologies. This enables standards for services and applications to be implemented in different technologies and survive market shifts in technology preferences. At the same time, with code generation, it enables users of computer technology to develop applications independent of current technology so that their investment can be preserved. When the technology changes, the application code can be regenerated. There were technical challenges to MDA, so it took some time before UML tools were able to demonstrate MDA capabilities, but this technology is well established today.

The foundation established by UML, MOF, and XMI was extended with Query, View, Transformation (QVT). QVT is a language for operating on MOF-based models. The primary importance of QVT is for transformation of models from one modeling language to another. In early MDA efforts, the focus of QVT was on transformation of platform-independent models (PIM) to platform-specific models (PSM), as depicted in Figure 10.2.

The PSM is more technology specific, and the associated language is expected to support the addition of features and tuning factors to tailor an application design to a particular technology. In some cases a PIM may be executed interpretively or translated directly to a computer programming language, but the transformation to a PSM provides the opportunity to optimize the executable design for the target technology.

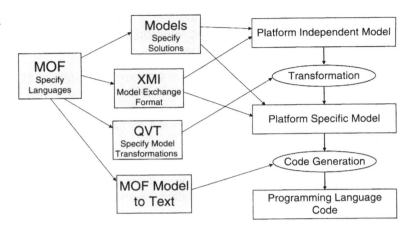

MOF Model to Text specifies the transformation of a model to program code or other textual form. This can be used to produce text for documenting a model.

QVT can also be used for transformations of other models that can be expressed as MOF models and exchanged as XMI. It could be applied, for example, to transformation of a business process model in a proprietary language to a business process definition metamodel (BPDM) process model, as described in Chapter 3. In that case the transformation would be from a platform-specific language to a platform-independent language (BPDM).

OMG, particularly the Business Modeling and Integration (BMI) task force, has developed modeling languages for business. Though some models ultimately may be used to generate programming language code, the emphasis of the BMI effort is on development of models to help managers and consultants manage complexity and adapt the enterprise.

Currently, OMG business-modeling languages tend to be focused on separate aspects of the enterprise. As they evolve and as new modeling capabilities are developed, they should complete an array of viewpoints as proposed earlier. The standard OMG modeling technology supports the consistent representation of concepts shared among the viewpoints and provides the foundation for development of integrated specifications for a shared EBM.

ENHANCED MODELING CAPABILITIES

Current modeling tools tend to focus on the use of diagrams to depict concepts and relationships. However, diagrams, with some supporting notes and attributes, are not enough to address some complex problems. Modeling tools that implement these standards should incorporate simulation, multiple vocabularies, and semantics.

Simulation

Most of our current modeling capabilities are static representations of a situation. For complex systems such as an enterprise, it can be very difficult to comprehend all the consequences and dynamic interactions of a change. It must be possible to explore the implications of change with models before betting the business on a new strategy.

Simulation requires the ability to perform some form of execution of a model. There are tools that provide "executable UML" that might be considered a form of simulation. However, simulation requires an environment in which the effects of changes in inputs, outputs, and variables can be explored. This is more than testing a solution; it requires functions to simulate business activity and additional displays or reports for analysis.

There are narrowly focused business simulation models today. Simulation of product distribution and production scheduling are well established. These tend to be mathematical models for optimization. There is a multitude of modeling technologies in product design. No manufacturer of airplanes or automobiles would consider going into production without first doing extensive modeling and simulation on all aspects of its products.

There are some products that provide support for simulation of business processes. This can be characterized as *discrete event simulation,* where simulated business transactions flow through the processes. This can be particularly valuable for recognition of potential bottlenecks. Business dynamics modeling tools (discussed earlier) provide another form of simulation.

In SOA, the relationships between business processes become more complex, so simulation is needed on a larger scale and the effects of exceptions and failures become more important because one process can adversely affect many other business functions. It should also be possible to simulate the effects of changes in business rules. This enterprise scope simulation requires that business processes be analyzed and the associated operating data be captured or imported into a single process simulation tool, thus reinforcing the importance of standards for the exchange of models as well as standards for exchange of performance data.

Multiple Vocabularies

The use of multiple vocabularies has been discussed briefly in earlier chapters and has been addressed in the OMG Semantics of Business Vocabulary and Rules (SBVR) specification. Alternative vocabularies can be defined for a model so that its concepts can be expressed in a particular vocabulary for one community and in another vocabulary for another community.

The fundamental idea is quite simple. The words (that is, the *vocabulary*) used to express concepts are represented separately from the representation of the concepts, so there can be words for different vocabularies associated with the same concept. Presentation of the model is associated with a particular vocabulary, so when the concepts are presented, the associated words come from the designated vocabulary.

This is a powerful concept, particularly for global enterprises and systems integrators. Much of the effort involved in development of a common logical data model is devoted to developing consensus on terminology. If different communities were allowed to use their own vocabularies for semantically identical concepts, some of this effort might be reduced. Furthermore, this could promote acceptance of an industrywide common data model. The concepts and the form of the data associated with those concepts could be common, whereas the terms used to reference and display the data elements might be in vocabularies tailored to each community of users.

OMG is exploring the application of this concept to other specifications. However, there is a risk that including this capability in a standard could deter acceptance of the standard because it places an additional burden on the modeling tool vendor that must implement the standard. The absence of a standard does not need to prevent vendors from implementing this capability, but, of course, a standards-based exchange of models would not include the alternative vocabularies.

Semantics

The meanings of modeling elements are generally defined in natural language text and implied in the names given to the elements. This is often not very precise, and it does not provide characteristics in a form that a computer can use for computations or validation.

For example, semantics has become a hot topic for Internet search because the user would like to be able to express search criteria in familiar terms and have the search engine look for items that incorporate the ideas of interest without being limited to the specific terms in the user's search request.

SBVR also provides support for capture of semantics. The semantics are expressed in terms of attributes, relationships, and rules that define concepts in terms of other concepts. Like multiple vocabularies, this is a desirable feature for other models, but it adds to the complexity of the modeling tools.

TACTICAL SOLUTIONS

Standards and tools for business modeling are still emerging in the marketplace. In spite of the limited tooling support, enterprise leadership should not wait for generally available solutions to pursue the benefits of an agile enterprise. An enterprise with appropriately skilled personnel could implement the essential models as database applications in lieu of commercially available tools. These models might later be transformed for input to commercial tools.

The full EBM capability discussed in this chapter is certainly not required to start development of the agile enterprise. The SOA Maturity Model provides insight on the capabilities that are needed as the enterprise advances. The following are fundamental viewpoints for beginning the transformation:

- Enterprise logical data model (ELDM)
- Business process models
- Business rules
- Service unit specifications
- Application portfolio

The ELDM can be captured and managed with existing data modeling tools. Business processes can be modeled with existing modeling tools. Tools are also available for business rules modeling. Integration of the ELDM, business process models, and business rules models with the EBM can come later; dependencies with other models can be managed manually in the short term. Management of service unit specifications and the application portfolio can be addressed as conventional database applications, or they can be implemented with generalized modeling tools that support the specification of custom modeling languages. Such tools are currently being used for modeling aspects of enterprise architectures.

The business modeling marketplace will develop over time, most likely with development of tools focused on particular viewpoints. If these tools implement MDA modeling technology, there will be technical compatibility. However, this alone will not achieve unification into an EBM. The viewpoints share concepts that must be represented in a consistent way for all the viewpoints in which they appear, even when the specifications for these models expand and change over time. As the scope of adoption of SOA and the level of maturity increase, reconciliation of the viewpoints will become more complex. Modeling tool customers should express their requirements for standards compliance and additional product features to their tool vendors.

At level 3 maturity, the enterprise should develop an initial EBM in a shared database to integrate the viewpoint models of interest at that point. This should add the following viewpoints:

- Organization structure model
- Strategic planning model
- Service unit costs model
- Role-based access control model

The EBM database may be a conventional database or it may be a MOF repository product that is designed for management of MOF-based models. A MOF repository would not require transformation of the models to a database schema (e.g., a relational structure).

The modeling applications may update the database directly, or views of the consolidated model can be exported for modeling a particular viewpoint and then imported to apply updates. The latter approach enables the modeler to explore alternatives without affecting other viewpoints until a final approach is defined. This also supports the acquisition and integration of modeling tool products that provide more robust modeling and analysis capabilities.

To maintain consistency in the EBM, there must be agreement on the segments of the model that each viewpoint can change as opposed to those elements that it can view (read only). As an analogy with enterprise master data records, only the human resources organization can create an employee record or change an employee's status, only the finance and accounting organization can create and update account records, and only the engineering organization can define and revise part specifications. Eventually the EBM must become a database of master data records that are coordinated with the business activity master data records to maintain a consistent representation of the state of the enterprise. Management of the EBM and support for the viewpoint models should be the responsibility of the Enterprise Intelligence service unit.

As the scope of modeling expands, development and maintenance of an integrated EBM become similar to the development and revisions of a complex product design involving multiple engineering disciplines. The agile enterprise has an EBM that represents the current design of the enterprise and one or more future versions that represent planned transformations.

Eventually, the EBM is a primary source of enterprise information, a context for planning, and a basis for performance evaluation, accountability, and control. Associated modeling tools enable top management to explore changes and simulate effects before committing to transformation initiatives. The models then support tracking of progress of the transformation, compliance with directives, and achievement of enterprise goals. That is the ultimate objective of MBM.

The agile enterprise is an enterprise in which managers are enterprise designers. They do not design, produce, sell, or deliver products themselves; they are responsible for creating and maintaining the enterprise system in which products are designed, produced, sold, and delivered. They must ensure that everyone knows their responsibilities and is accountable for results, and they must ensure that activities are coordinated and people have the tools they need to do their jobs.

In the past, managers could design the enterprise with paper and pencil, trial and error, based on experience and intuition. These tools are no longer good enough. Just as the automobile industry could not meet today's market demands without computer models, so managers cannot meet the competitive demands of today's emerging markets without computer-based models to design and adapt the enterprise.

Not all the needed tools are available today, but a general approach to design of an agile enterprise, as described in this book, provides a basis for development of more robust modeling capabilities. The tools are coming. At the same time, the limitations of current tools are no reason to delay the journey up the maturity model. The greatest challenge is not the current lack of tools, but the need to change the way people think about the design of the enterprise and the role of information technology. The time to start the transformation is now.

References

Books

Cummins, Fred A., *Enterprise Integration: An Architecture for Enterprise Application and Systems Integration*, John Wiley & Sons, New York, 2002.

Daft, Richard L., *Organization Theory and Design*, 9th ed., Thomson South-Western, 2007.

Drucker, Peter, *Managing in the Next Society*, Truman Talley Books, St. Martin's Griffin, New York, 2002.

Ferraiolo, David F., Kuhn, Richard, Chandramouli, Ramaswamy, *Role-Based Access Control*, Artech House, 2003.

Frankel, David S., *Model-Driven Architecture*, John Wiley & Sons, New York, 2003.

Harmon, Paul, *Business Process Change: A Guide for Business Managers and BPM and Six Sigma Professionals*, Morgan Kaufman, New York, 2007.

Inmon, William, O'Neil, Bonnie, Fryman, Lowell, *Business Metadata: Capturing Enterprise Knowledge*, Morgan Kaufmann, New York, 2008.

McComb, Dave, *Semantics in Business Systems*, Morgan Kaufmann, New York, 2004.

Michael, Porter, *Competitive Advantage: Creating and Sustaining Superior Performance*, The Free Press, New York, 1985.

Sterman, John D., *Business Dynamics: Systems Thinking and Modeling for a Complex World*, McGraw-Hill, 2000.

Thompson, J. D., *Organizations in Action*, McGraw-Hill, New York, 1967.

Standards

BMM. www.omg.org/technology/documents/br_pm_spec_catalog.htm#bmm.

BPMM. www.omg.org/technology/documents/br_pm_spec_catalog.htm#bpmm.

BPDM. www.omg.org/technology/documents/br_pm_spec_catalog.htm#bpdm.

BPMN. www.omg.org/technology/documents/br_pm_spec_catalog.htm#bpmn.

ebBP. www.oasis-open.org/specs/index.php#ebxmlbp2.0.4.

eTOM. www.tmforum.org/browse.aspx?catID=1648.

CWM. www.omg.org/technology/documents/modeling_spec_catalog.htm#CWM.

HTTP. www.w3.org/Protocols/.

HTML. www.w3.org/html/.

JMS. jcp.org/aboutJava/communityprocess/final/jsr914/index.html.

LDAP. www.ipa.go.jp/security/rfc/RFC3377EN.html.

MOF. www.omg.org/technology/documents/modeling_spec_catalog.htm#mof.

MOF Model to Text. www.omg.org/cgi-bin/doc?formal/2008-01-16.

QVT. www.omg.org/technology/documents/modeling_spec_catalog.htm#MOF_QVT.

SAML. www.oasis-open.org/specs/index.php#samlv2.0.

SBVR. www.omg.org/technology/documents/br_pm_spec_catalog.htm#sbvr.

SPEM. www.omg.org/technology/documents/modeling_spec_catalog.htm#SPEM.

UML. www.omg.org/technology/documents/modeling_spec_catalog.htm#UML.

WS-CDL. www.w3.org/2002/ws/chor/.

WS-Notification. www.oasis-open.org/specs/index.php#wsnv1.3.

WS-Security. www.oasis-open.org/specs/index.php#wssv1.1.

WS-Federation. http://xml.coverpages.org/ni2007-03-20-a.html.

WS-ReliableMessaging. www.oasis-open.org/specs/index.php#wsrx-rm1.1.

WS-Policy. www.w3.org/2002/ws/policy/.

X.509v3. www.ietf.org/rfc/rfc2459.txt?number=2459.

XACML. www.oasis-open.org/committees/tc_home.php?wg_abbrev=xacml.

XMI. www.omg.org/technology/documents/modeling_spec_catalog.htm#XMI.

XML. www.w3.org/XML/.

XML Schema. www.w3.org/XML/Schema.

XML Signature. www.w3.org/Signature/.

XPDL. www.wfmc.org/standards/docs.htm#XPDL_Spec_Final.

Other

SOA Consortium case studies. www.soa-consortium.org/case-study.htm.

The Origin of the "Data Information Knowledge Wisdom" Hierarchy by Nikhil Sharma, updated December 1, 2005, www-personal.si.umich.edu/~nsharma/dikw_origin.htm.

Board Briefing on IT Governance, 2nd ed., IT Governance Institute, 2003, www.isaca.org/ContentManagement/ContentDisplay.cfm?ContentID=39649.

Enterprise Governance—Getting the Balance Right, International Federation of Accountants, 2004, www.cimaglobal.com/cps/rde/xbcr/live/tech_execrep_enterprise_governance_getting_the_balance_right_feb_2004.pdf.

Eclipse Process Framework (EPF), www.eclipse.org/ept.

National Institute of Standards and Technology (NIST) Role-Based Access Control (RBAC) information Web page, http://csrc.nist.gov/groups/SNS/rbac/.

Stabell, C. B., Fjeldstad, O. D., "Configuring Value for Competitive Advantage: On Chains, Shops and Networks," Strategic Management Journal 19 (5):413–417, 1998; www.agbuscenter.ifas.ufl.edu/5188/miscellaneous/configuring_value.pdf.

Glossary

This glossary defines the meanings of terms as used in the context of this book.

Activity. A unit of work. In a business process model, a unit of work within a business process that may engage a human or other business process or service unit. In a value chain, the unit of work contributed by a service unit toward the delivery of value, or an abstraction that represents an aggregation of related activities.

Agile enterprise. An agile enterprise is capable of recognizing and adapting quickly to changing business threats and opportunities. In the SOA Maturity Model, it is the highest level of maturity reflecting adoption of SOA, BPM, MBM and related governance and operating practices.

Asserting party. The party in an interaction relationship that is asserting an identity or credentials.

Authentication. A process by which the identity of a subject (for example, person or system) is validated.

Authorization. A process by which a subject (for example, person or system) is given authority to perform an action or access a resource, or the process by which access authority is determined.

Backtracking. A mechanism in logic programming, or in the application of diagnostic rules, where the search for a solution has reached an unsuccessful result down one path and is able to back up and proceed down another branch of the search.

Backward chaining. A search strategy where a condition is evaluated by reference to supporting facts or conditions, so that success is achieved by finding a set of supporting facts or conditions that are true. The strategy is to assume the truth of a statement and attempt to substantiate it by finding supporting facts. This mode is typically applied to diagnostic or proof problems (for example, theorem proving).

BAM (Business Activity Monitoring). Information processing facilities that capture and report on business process events in real time for the purpose of monitoring performance and recognizing exceptions.

BI (Business Intelligence). Information processing facilities for capturing, analyzing storing and presenting data, typically through periodic extraction and integration of data from multiple production databases.

BMM (Business Motivation Model). An OMG standard that defines the modeling elements for business strategic planning.

BPDM (Business Process Definition Metamodel). An OMG standard that defines the modeling elements and relationships (that is, a metamodel) for modeling business processes including orchestration and choreography.

BPEL (Business Process Execution Language). An OASIS specification for an XML-based language to define automated business processes. Processes defined in BPEL reflect the nested element structure of XML. As of this writing, BPEL does not address the specification of choreography nor the participation of humans in business processes.

BPM (Business Process Management). A management discipline for defining, continuously improving and optimizing business processes.

BPMM (Business Process Maturity Model). An OMG specification of criteria for assessing the maturity of an enterprise with respect to business process management. The five maturity levels correspond to the five levels of the SOA Maturity Model, but with a business process management focus.

BPMN (Business Process Modeling Notation). An OMG specification of graphical elements for modeling business processes. BPMN 2.0 (Business Process Model and Notation) combines BPMN and BPDM as a single modeling specification.

Business dynamics. A technique for modeling dynamic, real-world systems using the abstract concepts of "stocks" and "flows." The model reflects behavior of the system over time based on accumulation or depletion of units in stocks as a result of flows in and out of the system and its stocks mediated by control functions and parameters.

Business metadata. Data about data that describes aspects of interest to business people such as the source, precision, timeliness and reliability of the data. Distinguished from technical metadata that describes the definitions, structure and relationships of data elements as in a database or exchange of records.

Business Process Management System (BPMS). An information system that automates the execution of business processes.

Business process. An orderly execution of activities to achieve a desired business result in response to a request or event. A process defines what work is to be done, who does the work, when the work is done in relation to others activities and events.

Business rule. A declarative expression of business intent. There are a variety of types of business rules. See also enterprise rule, production rule, diagnostic rule, event rule, qualification rule, and data integrity rule.

Business unit. An organizational element that has a designated leader and subordinates and may include subordinate business units (for example, department, division, group, team).

Capability. Service capability: an assemblage of people, processes, resources, facilities, skills, knowledge and motivation that can be applied to produce a desired result.

Case management. A process in which a number of relatively independent sub-processes are initiated and monitored as required to achieve a desired result for a particular instance (case) of the process.

CEP (Complex Event Processing). Processing of event notices that identifies relationships between separates events and infers the occurrence of other events.

Certification authority (CA). A trusted service that issues signed digital certificates that include the identity of the certificate owner and the owner's public key. The certificate provides the basis for authentication, encryption and non-repudiation. A CA maintains a Certificate Revocation List (CRL) for those certificates that have been compromised (for example, the corresponding private key has been exposed).

Choreography. A specification of the interactions between two or more participants to achieve mutual benefit. Choreography is not executed by a controlling entity, but describes the agreed-upon, collaborative behavior of the participants.

Class. For a logical data model, a computational representation of the attributes and relationships of similar entities. A specialized class may be defined by inheriting and extending the specification of an existing class.

Collaboration. An interaction between peers to achieve a result with mutual benefit.

Configuration Management Database (CMDB). A facility for management of hardware, software and application components and their relationships in a data processing center.

Consumer. A user of a service; the exchange participant that defines the context of the exchange, usually the participant that initiates the exchange.

COTS (Commercial Off The Shelf software). Refers to a commercially available software product in contrast to a custom application developed by or for an enterprise.

CWM (Common Warehouse Metamodel). An OMG specification for representation and transformation of data in different formats. Originally intended for specification of data transformations from various sources to feed a data warehouse. It has also been applied to Enterprise Information Integration (EII). It is expected to be superseded by IMM (Information Management Metamodel), a pending specification from OMG.

Data integrity rule. A rule that defines constraints on attribute values and relationships in a database in order to ensure that the database is consistent with the real-world concepts it is intended to represent.

Diagnostic rule. A rule used in the diagnosis of a problem, typically a logic programming rule or a rule executed by a backward-chaining inference engine.

Disruptive event. An event that indicates the occurrence of a change that has a disruptive effect on an enterprise or some unit of the enterprise and may require an adaptation in the way the enterprise operates or in the products and services it delivers.

ebBP (ebXML Business Process specification schema). A component of the ebXML (electronic business XML) family of specifications from OASIS that defines an XML-based language for specification of choreography.

ECA (Event Condition Action) rule. A rule that is activated by the occurrence of an event (that is, a change of state) and will perform a defined action if its conditional expression evaluates to true.

EDA (Event Driven Architecture). An information systems architectural perspective in which events (changes of state in the enterprise ecosystem) are monitored and trigger processes to perform consequential business functions or resolve concerns, threats or opportunities inferred from the events.

EIM (Enterprise Information Management). The information technology discipline for organizing and managing data in an enterprise. This involves data modeling and various techniques for the capture, communication, storage, retrieval and presentation of data in support of enterprise objectives.

Electronic signature. Data elements associated with an electronic record or document that establish that the signer has endorsed the content of the document and is accountable for it. See also XML Signature.

Embedded sub-process. A process contained in an activity of another process. An embedded sub-process is not shared.

Enterprise Application Integration (EAI). A discipline for adapting applications and exchanging and transforming asynchronous messages to achieve the integration of enterprise applications.

Enterprise architecture. The design characteristics of an enterprise. Depending on the context, the architecture may refer to the design and integration of information systems or the design of the enterprise including the people, processes, facilities, and organization.

Enterprise Business Model (EBM). A comprehensive, living model of the design of an enterprise that supports a number of different viewpoints or abstractions of the enterprise to enable Model Based Management (MBM).

Enterprise business rule. A business rule that expresses a management constraint on the operation of the enterprise. The enterprise business rule may apply to a number of contexts where an action could occur to violate the rule. In the event of a rule violation the action to be taken depends on the context and may be expressed as a production rule or an event-condition-action rule.

Enterprise Information Integration (EII). An information systems facility in which a database query is submitted with respect to a virtual database, the query is transformed as required to retrieve the desired data from one or more operational databases, and the responses are integrated to produce a response consistent with the virtual database and the original query.

Enterprise intelligence. A business discipline for the capture. storage and presentation of data, information and knowledge related to the enterprise ecosystem in support of enterprise analysis, planning and decision-making.

Enterprise logical data model (ELDM). A logical data model that encompasses the scope of the enterprise and defines consistent enterprise concepts, attributes and relationships as the basis for integrated views of the state of the enterprise and the exchange of data between business units, suppliers and customers.

Enterprise rule. See enterprise business rule.

Enterprise Services Bus (ESB). Middleware that implements web services integration standards to support a service oriented architecture.

Enterprise value chain. A composite value chain that incorporates all of the value chains that deliver enterprise value. It includes production value chains, product (lifecycle) value chains, supporting value chains, executive staff value chains, and other contributions to value that enable the enterprise to function and evolve.

ETL (Extract-Transform-Load). A capability in support of an operational data store (ODS) or data warehouse where data is collected from a number of sources, transformed and reconciled for consistency and loaded into the target storage facility for analysis and reporting.

eTOM. (extended Telecomm Operations Map). An industry framework developed by the TeleManagement Forum.

Event. A change of state of the enterprise or its environment. Usually restricted to changes of state that are of interest for various purposes. Information about an event may be communicated by an *event notice*. An event in BPMN is a graphic that represents the initiation, resumption or termination of a process flow as a result of the receipt of an event notice.

Event Notice. A message or record that communicates the occurrence of an event. In a publish-and-subscribe environment, an event notice is published by a system that observes or causes an event. The event notice is communicated by an event broker to subscribers who have submitted requests to receive events that meet certain qualifications as specified in their subscriptions.

Event rule. A rule that filters event notices for publication, distribution or processing.

Forward chaining. A rules execution mode where the condition expressions of rules are evaluated against a model of the problem domain, a rule is selected from among those that have true conditions, and the action of that rule is executed, typically causing the model of the problem domain to change. The change potentially changes the set of rules with true conditions, and another rule is selected from the set and executed. The execution chains forward as it drives the evaluation of selected rules. This mode is typically applied to configuration and planning problems.

Gateway. A diamond-shaped graphical symbol in BPMN that indicates a convergence or divergence of process flow. There are several icons that may appear in the gateway graphic that further define the action to be taken.

Governance. The set of responsibilities and practices exercised by the board of directors and executive management with the goal of providing strategic direction, ensuring that objectives are achieved, ascertaining that risks are managed appropriately and verifying that the organization's resources are used responsibility. (Information Systems Audit and Control Foundation, 2001).

HR-XML. A consortium for the development of standards for exchange of human resources-related data based on XML.

HTML (Hyper Text Markup Language). A character based language designed for specification of displays for Internet browsers, and for input and communication of data submitted through web page displays.

HTTP (Hyper Text Transfer Protocol). An internet protocol designed for the exchange of HTML in support of the World Wide Web.

HTTPS (Hyper Text Transfer Protocol Secure). An extension of HTTP designed for secure (encrypted) exchange of HTML data on the world wide web.

IETF (Internet Engineering Task Force). An international standards organization focused on the technical standards and protocols of the Internet.

IMM (Information Management Metamodel). A pending OMG specification for specification of data structures of various forms and the transformation of data between those different forms.

Industry framework. A best practices model that represents the business processes and potentially an information model and other aspects that are characteristic of enterprises in a particular industry. eTOM is an industry framework.

Inheritance. In information or object modeling, a relationship between classes by which one class may incorporate (inherit) the characteristics of another and extend the specification to address a more specialized category of entities represented by the inheriting class.

Interface specification. For a service unit, it is the specification of message types or requests that will be recognized, the restrictions on the interactions, and the levels of service that are to be expected when interacting with the service unit.

Interface. The interaction boundary of an organization, device, system, organism or service unit.

Job shop. An enterprise that specializes in the manufacture of custom products through performing processes (also known as routings) and operations specified to produce each particular product.

Lane. In BPMN, a segment of a pool. The pool represents a business entity performing a process. The lane defines a responsibility within the entity that is responsible for performing the activities drawn within the lane.

Line of business. A product or group of similar products produced by an enterprise generally associated with business activities engaged in developing, marketing, producing and supporting the product.

Logical data model (LDM). A data model expressed at a level of abstraction suitable for discussions that are independent of particular technologies or media used to store, communicate or process the data. See also Enterprise Logical Data Model (ELDM).

Loose coupling. A form of integration where the interdependence of participants is minimized to promote autonomy. Typically, this is accomplished by store-and-forward message exchanges with no shared resources and with minimal interactions that might require synchronization of their activities.

Master data management. Management of the data storage facilities that together represent the single version of the truth about the state of the enterprise. Master data is not limited to stable, reference data.

Maturity model. The SOA Maturity Model from EDS and Oracle describes criteria for assessment of the technical and business maturity of an enterprise with respect to adopting a service oriented architecture and related strategies and capabilities leading to an agile enterprise capability. Other business maturity models have similar levels of maturity but address different aspects of the organization. See also BPMM.

Message flow. In BPMN, a dashed arrow that specifies the transfer of a message from one business entity to another.

Metadata. Data that describes data. A database schema is metadata. A blank paper form with identified fields expresses metadata.

Metamodel. A specification of a modeling language. A MOF metamodel specifies the concepts and relationships for modeling a particular problem domain.

Model Based Management (MBM). An OMG strategy for the use of business models as viewpoints on the design and operation of the enterprise for management monitoring, analysis, planning and decision-making.

Model Driven Architecture (MDA). An OMG strategy for design of solutions using models supported by the ability to transform models and exchange them between different modeling environments.

MOF (Meta Object Facility). An OMG specification for the elements that represent the concepts of a modeling language for expression of models, storage of models and exchange of models. MOF is used for specification of modeling languages.

Non-repudiation. A principle regarding assertions or agreements that prevents a party from denying their assertion or agreement. For a record or electronic document the content can be reliably attributed to its submitter and cannot be repudiated. Potentially achieved through the use of an electronic signature.

OAGi (Open Applications Group, incorporated). An international standards organization focused on specification of records/documents exchanged between information systems.

OASIS (Organization for Advancement of Structured Information Systems). An international standards organization with primary contributions related to the application of XML.

OMG (Object Management Group). An international standards organization focused on information systems interoperability and modeling standards.

Orchestration. An executable business process; a business process that performs work as compared to a choreography that describes an exchange between participants engaged in a collaborative relationship.

Outsourcing. The practice of contracting for an external organization to own and operate a segment of the enterprise business. Outsourcing of information systems, accounting and human relations services are examples.

PIM (Platform Independent Model). In the OMG Model Driven Architecture (MDA) strategy, a model of a solution that is independent of particular implementation technology and thus is focused on modeling the solution rather than the implementation.

PKI (Public Key Infrastructure). The services and facilities associated with the use of public key encryption along with digital certificates for identification and authentication.

Policy. A statement of intent to influence or determine decisions, actions or other matters. For business, a policy is a statement of business practice intent which may be expressed more precisely as business rules. For XACML security access control, a policy is a set of access control rules. For WS-Policy, a policy is a service specification that expresses capabilities and requirements that are the basis for forming a collaborative relationship.

Pool. A stand-alone box that expresses the boundaries of a business entity around a business process model. Business processes are confined by the pool boundaries except that messages may be exchanged with other pools (that is, business entities).

Portal. A point of access to enterprise capabilities and services, usually designed to address the interests of a particular community such as employees, stockholders, customers or suppliers. Often associated with a collection of web pages but potentially extending to other services such as a call center.

Process context. The data and circumstances surrounding the execution of a process. The context is represented by data, such as an order record, associated with the execution.

Process instance. A single execution of a process specification. A process instance is often identified by the identifier of the request that initiated the execution, for example, a customer order number.

Process. See business process.

Product value chain. The chain (or network) of services that each contribute value to the lifecycle of a product including development, marketing, production and support.

Production line process mode. A type of process where the objects of production (for example, an automobile on a production line) move one at a time through a sequence of operations or stations where work is performed. All units go through the same stations, but the work at each station may vary depending on the requirements of the particular unit.

Production rule. A rule managed by a rules engine that performs forward chaining. The execution of the rules produces a result such as a product configuration or a travel plan. See also forward chaining.

Production value chain. The chain (or network) of services that each contribute value to individual units of production to achieve value for a customer.

Provider. A service unit in a role (or relationship) where it provides a service.

PSM (Platform Specific Model). In the OMG Model Driven Architecture (MDA) strategy, a model of a solution that is tailored for implementation in a particular technology. A PSM may be the result of a transformation of a PIM and be the basis for generating application code for execution.

Publish and subscribe. An integration approach where sources of event notices register with a broker and publish event notices to the broker as they occur. Entities interested in the events subscribe to event notices from the broker and the notices are forwarded by the broker as they occur. Rules can constrain which notices are published, forwarded or processed.

Publish. The act of issuing an event notice in a publish and subscribe environment.

Qualification rule. An expression that defines qualifications for fulfilling a process role, accessing a resource or being assigned to an organizational position.

QVT (Query View Transformation). An OMG specification for a language that specifies the transformation of models that are expressed in the Meta Object Facility (MOF) metamodeling language. It is designed, for example, for transformation of a PIM to a PSM.

RBAC (Role Based Access Control). An approach to access control specification where access authorization is specified for roles, and roles are assigned to people. This enables separation of responsibility between control of resources and authorization of people.

Registry. See service registry.

Relay process mode. A process structure where each process completes its work and passes responsibility to the next process, retaining no continuing responsibility for the completed transaction. A relay process mode is distinguished from a production line mode because here a transfer of responsibility may come from alternative sources and/or be passed to alternative destinations.

Reliable messaging. A message exchange protocol where message senders are assured that each message will be delivered once and only once.

Relying party. The party in an interactive relationship that relies on the identification or credentials of an asserting party.

Rete algorithm. An algorithm for processing production (forward chaining) rules where the rule conditions are linked to the model of the problem domain (working storage) through a network so that changes in the domain model propagate to the affected rules.

Role. The characteristics and/or behavior of an entity in a particular context. A person performs a role in an organization (a position or assignment) or a role in a process (as a participant/contributor) or a role that defines authorization to access resources. A business entity fills a role in a choreography that specifies exchanges in a business collaboration. A role generally has specifications that restrict selection from potential participants, and the role or its relationships may restrict the behavior of the participant in the role.

Rule driven process. A process where the activities are performed when enabled by an associated rule or rules. Activities do not occur in predefined sequences but occur based on the state of the process, its context and associated entities.

Rules engine. A software application/product that evaluates and executes rules according to a defined algorithm.

SAML (Security Attribute Markup Language). An OASIS specification for the exchange of participant credentials and authorizations for access control.

SBVR (Semantics of Business Vocabulary and Rules). An OMG specification for a language that combines a structured representation of rules, with a capture of semantics and the ability to express the concepts and rules in alternative vocabularies.

Semantic. A specification of meaning. In language, the meanings of words or expressions. In modeling, semantics are the meanings of the modeling elements.

Sequence flow. In BPMN, an arrow that specifies the order of execution or evaluation of flow elements such as gateways and activities.

Service. The application of a capability by a business entity to provide a business value that addresses the needs of a community of service users.

Service consumer. A business entity that uses a service—a service user. In a service oriented architecture, a service consumer defines the context for an exchange of value.

Service group. An organization that offers multiple services based on multiple business capabilities or a general capability that may or may not be implemented as multiple service units. An outsourcing provider that offers a number of related services without exposing the implementation of those services can be characterized as a service group.

Service oriented enterprise. An enterprise that has implemented a service oriented architecture as a business paradigm.

Service provider. A business entity that offers a service.

Service registry. A database or directory, accessible at runtime, that provides information on the current versions and locations of services. The registry supports selection of alternative services and provides support for management of IT functions of service units at runtime. Complements the Configuration Management Database (CMDB).

Service repository. A facility for storage of specifications for service units including versions in different stages of the lifecycle. Supports the design and integration of service units.

Service unit. A business organization unit that manages capabilities—processes, resources, facilities, intellectual property, personnel—to offer one or more services through a well-defined interface in order to address a business need of a community of potential users.

Shared Information Data (SID). An enterprise logical data model for the telecommunications industry developed by the TeleManagement Forum (TMF).

Single sign-on. An information technology industry infrastructure capability that enables a user to log on to a network environment once and subsequently access a number of different systems based on the single authentication. There are various strategies. For SOA, digital certificates and public-key encryption are recommended for single sign-on.

SOA (Service Oriented Architecture). An approach to design of an enterprise where distinct business capabilities are offered through well-defined mechanisms and media of exchange so that the capabilities can be used in multiple business endeavors both currently and in the future.

Subject. In security protocols or policies, a party being authenticated or authorized may be described as a subject that may be a person or system.

Sub-process. A process that is invoked by another process. An independent sub-process is accessible (may be invoked) from multiple processes and may be designed and deployed independently. An embedded sub-process must be deployed with and can only be invoked by one activity in one process. It is essentially an expansion of an activity with its own start and end.

Subscribe. The action of submitting a request to receive events. A publisher publishes events that are delivered to subscribers.

Task. An activity within a business process that is performed by a human. There is no further specification of the operation of a task.

UN/CEFACT (United Nations Center for Trade Facilitation and Electronic Business). A standards organization within the United Nations that deals with specifications for electronic commerce.

Unified Modeling Language (UML). The OMG (Object Management Group) specification for an object-oriented, application analysis and design language. The general nature of UML has resulted in its use for a number of system design applications outside object-oriented programming.

Value chain. The chain (or network) of services that contribute value to a result. A value chain may produce value for an external customer or internal business activities.

W3C (World Wide Web Consortium). An international standards organization that focuses on languages and protocols for communications over the Internet.

WfMC (Workflow Management Coalition). An international standards organization focused on the development of standards related to workflow management, which includes business process management technology.

Workflow. Business processes that move work through sequences of activities in predefined paths. Workflow often implies business processes that are focused on human activities where the performance of activities is driven by the movement of a business transaction or work order to various persons or work stations. Most BPMS (Business Process Management Systems) implement this process model with some variations.

WS-CDL (Web Services Choreography Definition Language). An XML-based language of the W3C for specification of the exchange of electronic documents between participants in a business exchange.

WS-Federation (Web Services Federation). A draft specification of OASIS for the federation of identification and authentication among independently managed security domains.

WS-Policy (Web Services Policy). An XML-based language of W3C for specification of the requirements and capabilities of a web services participant as a basis for establishing compatibility for an exchange.

WS-Security (Web Services Security). A specification from OASIS that defines message structure and elements for secure message exchanges.

XACML (XML Access Control Markup Language). An OASIS specification for expression of access control/authorization policies regarding access to a specified resource (for example, data or operation).

XBRL (XML Business Reporting Language). An XML-based language from XBRL International, for reporting of business and financial data.

XML (eXtensible Markup Language). A language defined by W3C. XML is a character-based data format that uses name tags to identify data elements that are variable in length and form a nested hierarchy. XML is, for the most part, technology independent so that senders and receivers may use different technologies, and the structure provides flexibility enabling recipients to ignore elements in which they have no interest. A number of related technologies have been built on XML including parsing techniques, electronic signatures, specification of XML documents using XML, and so on.

XML Schema. An XML-based language from W3C that is used to specify the structure of XML documents.

XML Signature. A W3C specification for electronic signatures in XML documents.

XPDL (XML Process Definition Language). An XML-based language from WfMC for exchange of BPMN process models.

Index

Edwards Brothers Malloy
Ann Arbor MI. USA
October 24, 2014